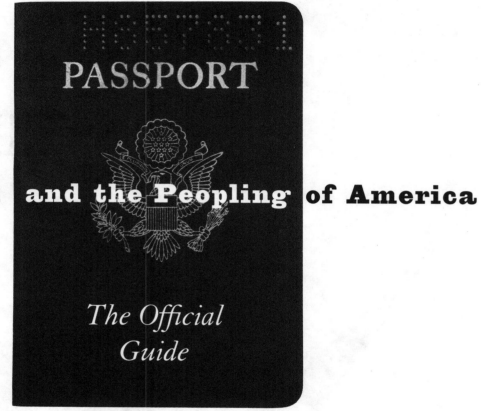

PASSPORT

Ellis Island and the Peopling of America

The Official Guide

Ellis Island

and the Peopling of America

The Official Guide

VIRGINIA YANS-MCLAUGHLIN AND

MARJORIE LIGHTMAN

with The Statue of Liberty-Ellis Island Foundation

designed by Hall Smyth / BAD

THE NEW PRESS NEW YORK

200770

published in the United States by **The New Press, New York**
distributed by **W.W. Norton & Company, Inc., New York**

THE NEW PRESS WAS ESTABLISHED IN 1990 AS A NOT-FOR-PROFIT ALTERNATIVE
TO THE LARGE, COMMERCIAL PUBLISHING HOUSES CURRENTLY DOMINATING
THE BOOK PUBLISHING INDUSTRY. THE NEW PRESS OPERATES IN THE PUBLIC INTEREST
RATHER THAN FOR PRIVATE GAIN, AND IS COMMITTED TO PUBLISHING,
IN INNOVATIVE WAYS, WORKS OF EDUCATIONAL, CULTURAL, AND COMMUNITY VALUE
THAT MIGHT NOT NORMALLY BE COMMERCIALLY VIABLE. THE NEW PRESS'S EDITORIAL
OFFICES ARE LOCATED AT THE CITY UNIVERSITY OF NEW YORK.

book design by **Hall Smyth/BAD**
production management by **Kim Waymer**
printed in the **United States of America**
9 8 7 6 5 4 3

Dedication

For our immigrant ancestors
and for all the immigrant men, women, and children
who will enter our country today and tomorrow.

Yes, Ellis Island is quietly immense.
It gives one a visible image of one aspect of this world-large process
of filling and growing and synthesis, which is America.

H.G. Wells, *The Future of America*, 1906

I still have a nostalgia for that great, great entry.
It, it was the gate to Heaven, if you will.

Morris Moe, Ukranian immigrant
Ellis Island Library Oral History Collection

Contents

Acknowledgments

Funding for this guide was provided by The Statue of Liberty-Ellis Island Foundation, Inc., which allocated generous contributions from the Ladies Auxiliary to the Veterans of Foreign Wars, the Geraldine R. Dodge Foundation, and the Christian A. Johnson Endeavor Foundation toward its production. The Statue of Liberty-Ellis Island Foundation, Inc., is a non-profit organization founded in 1982 to raise funds for the restoration and preservation of the Statue of Liberty and Ellis Island. With this extraordinary effort accomplished, The Foundation continues to sponsor the American Immigrant Wall of Honor ® located on Ellis Island and is planning the American Family Immigration History Center ™ there as well. We thank The Foundation and the more than two million American citizens who contributed to its goals for realizing the need for a historical and educational guide to accompany and supplement the Ellis Island Museum exhibits. The spirit behind each of these Foundation efforts is to create a truly inclusive national museum of the American people, one which honors all immigrants to America, not only those who came through Ellis Island.

This project has benefited from the extensive comments of many people. Several drafts were reviewed by scholars: Samuel Baily, Clarence Taylor, David Levering Lewis, Leon Litwack, Kevin Reilly, Carlos Rodriguez, and John Kuo Wei Tchen. At every stage of research and writing we have received important contributions from several secondary school faculty: William Fernekes, Margaret Houseman, Ernest Piro, and Edward Stehle. In addition, a draft of the guide was reviewed by Sheila Geist and her colleagues of the project Gender-Balancing the Secondary School Curriculum. Julie Leininger Pycior, Janice Brockley, Lisa Hirschberg and Serena Zabin provided research assistance. William Zeisel edited the final version. The authors also wish to thank André Schiffrin, Ellen Reeves, Hall Smyth, Davia Smith, Grace Farrell, and Noah Garfinkel at The New Press.

The writers would especially like to thank Hall Smyth for his understanding of how design and historical concept can inform and engage each other. If we, the writers, wrote the book, Hall Smyth saw the book and brought it to its unique design.

The staff of The Statue of Liberty-Ellis Island National Monument provided invaluable assistance. Diana Pardue, Chief, Museum Services Division provided help at every stage, sharing her knowledge and energy with both the writers and the designers of this book. Barry Moreno, Librarian and Historian at the Ellis Island Museum, reviewed the final draft, and assured accuracy. Jeffrey S. Dosik, Librarian and Historian assisted in research and identification of photographs; Kevin Daily, Staff Photographer, assisted in locating photographs; Janet Levine at the Ellis Island Library Oral History Collections identified appropriate interviews. The majority of the immigrant quotations used in this guide come from that collection.

Evelyn Jutte of the Immigration and Naturalization Service navigated us through the Service's computerized image archive. Richard Fahey of MetaForm, Inc., and Chermayeff and Geismar, Inc., identified photographs of the installations which the design firm created for the Ellis Island Museum. Unless otherwise noted, prints and photographs come from the collection of Virginia Yans-McLaughlin. Special thanks go to Gary Kelley, of The Statue of Liberty-Ellis Island Foundation, for his patience and willingness to address the needs of students, teachers, and visitors to Ellis Island. Sally Jones, also of The Statue of Liberty-Ellis Island Foundation, worked hard and skillfully to raise funds for the guide. The original concept of this guide resulted from a faculty seminar at Rutgers, the State University of New Jersey, funded by the New Jersey Department of Higher Education in 1984–1985. One of the authors, Virginia Yans-McLaughlin, an adviser to the National Park Service concerning the Ellis Island exhibits, learned of the need for this book through her interactions with the National Park Service and Statue of Liberty-Ellis Island Foundation staffs. We hope this book facilitates their work as they have facilitated ours.

Foreword

As Founding Chairman of The Statue of Liberty-Ellis Island Foundation, Inc., I have had the privilege of working for the past fifteen years with the American people to successfully restore our two great monuments to freedom and hope.

For the millions of immigrants who landed at Ellis Island, the place was their first American experience. It symbolized opportunity and the start of a new life. Today, the Ellis Island Immigration Museum has become a monument not only to the courage of those who passed through its doors, but also to the immigrant heritage of all Americans. Every one of us has a history that is rooted in an ancestor whose journey to the United States—whether it was three hundred years ago or yesterday—changed our family's destiny forever.

The museum at Ellis Island tells the rich and inspiring stories of these immigrants. It also speaks of the people who came long before there was an Ellis Island and of those who made the journey only recently. For both young and old alike, the museum provides an extraordinary and educational experience.

The Foundation is committed to fostering public knowledge of and interest in Ellis Island and the Statue of Liberty. In addition to a three-hundred–page book on the Statue, the Foundation has partially funded a centennial series of books on immigration-related topics. To further our goals, I am extremely pleased to present our new publication, *Ellis Island and the Peopling of America: The Official Guide*.

We think this book will be a valuable guide for parents and teachers who want to teach the younger generation about American and world history through an exploration of Ellis Island and the immigrant experience. It places Ellis Island within the context of the worldwide history and continuing social process of immigration. It can prepare one to visit the Ellis Island Immigration Museum, guide one in the process of doing a family genealogy, or direct one to many more sources for immigration study. We feel confident it will prove to be an important contribution for immigration scholarship.

—LEE IACOCCA

*Tabs (shown at left) are used throughout the guide and are helpful
for cross-references between chapters and corresponding documents in
Part 4. References to documents in the text are shown in bold to
indicate that there are additional materials available.*

0.1

How to Use This Guide

0.1 THIS IS A GUIDE BOOK IN SEVERAL SENSES OF THE WORD. It is meant to guide your thinking about immigration, a central theme in our nation's and perhaps your own family's history. Like any good travel guide, it is meant to prepare you for visits to a place, or to take you on an imaginary journey you cannot make. It is also intended as a guide for teachers and parents who seek to use Ellis Island and the immigrant experience to teach the younger generation about American and world history. For those who enjoy reading the original documents that historians use to write their histories of immigration, it is a guide for understanding how historians use such documents and the kinds of questions they ask of them. For those who want to read or see more, it is a guide to books, autobiographies, films, and videos about immigration.

This book was designed to fill a number of perceived needs. How could Ellis Island, the place where the majority of Europeans who came to the United States entered, be made relevant to people from other parts of the world, many of whom will visit the Museum today, many of whom are immigrants today? How could students, teachers, and families visiting the Museum be assisted in what museum experts call "informal learning" about immigration? And how could that learning be integrated formally into the classroom, or perhaps into a family history that a genealogist is writing, or an oral history of one's family? Finally, how could the visitor thirsty for more information about immigration be assisted in his or her quest for information?

This book was conceived with the goal of placing the Ellis Island Museum and site within the context of the worldwide, continuing history of immigration. It has, then, a point of view. Thinking of Ellis Island in this way allows readers to consider all Americans, not just those who walked through Ellis Island, as immigrants and descendants of immigrants—which is in fact the case. The guide also understands immigration as a continuing social process, one that brings people from one part of the world to another where they contribute the richness of their labor to their newly adopted home. It emphasizes those aspects of the immigration experience which immigrants shared in common. The creators of the Ellis Island exhibits soon discovered in their planning process that it would not be

The top portion of the guide features photographs, illustrations, quotes, dates, and additional information that are supplemental to the text shown below. These immigration artifacts originate from books listed in the appendices or from installation texts and photographs provided by the designers and curators of the exhibition.

Dates of interest are included to provide context to specific events or policies. Unlike the timeline on Pages 9-13, dates provided here highlight key events relevant to the text below.

Dates

possible to include the story of each of more than one hundred and twenty-two ethnic groups in the exhibits. Neither have we been able to do so here. While ethnic groups are represented in the guide's historical documents and in its bibliographies and filmographies, the guide focuses upon the shared experiences of immigrants to America rather than upon their uniqueness or their differences.

We begin the book in **Part 1** with a discussion of how experts and scholars describe the different ways in which immigration is organized and how it shaped American history. **Part 2** chronicles immigration to the United States, emphasizing Europe, Asia, Latin America, and Africa as places of origin from the Age of Exploration to the present. **Part 3** focuses upon immigration policy past and present and explains Ellis Island itself as an artifact of that policy. **Part 4**, which addresses the individual immigrant's experience, is a series of historical documents relating to or written by those who came to the United States. The maps and charts in this section contain some surprising information about the character, timing, and origins of immigration.

All of these documents are conveniently keyed to the preceding text; if you wish to approach the subject matter in this way, you may wander back and forth between text and documents. Also provided are a series of questions and activities for those who would like to explore the documents further. You may also browse through the guide's picture gallery. Scattered throughout are period photographs, images of the kind which you will find on Ellis Island if you visit it, as well as photos relating to contemporary immigration. **Part 5** describes how this guide may be used as a teaching resource and offers a special bibliography of resources for teachers and others who are concerned with immigration issues. **Part 6** contains annotated listings of related films, videos, and filmstrips.

Information about the Ellis Island Museum and the activities of The Statue of Liberty-Ellis Island Foundation follows this section.

Readers may begin their journey anywhere in the guide. Handy cross-references will suggest where to look next for more information. *Now, enjoy the trip.*

Introduction

Since the middle of the sixteenth century, more than one hundred million people have moved to new places. Some have crossed the Atlantic and Pacific Oceans to new destinations where they built multicultural societies like the United States, Canada, Australia, Brazil, and Argentina. Some chose to remain on their own continents, moving with thousands of fellow travelers from countryside to city. Others enlisted as contract laborers and found themselves thousands of miles from home, bound to work as servants, miners, or harvesters of crops. Still others were captured as slaves and brought to frontier areas or to parts of the world in need of human labor. Today, professionals and others seeking jobs in the service sector have joined this global procession.

Almost half of the migrants who left homelands between 1820 and 1930 ended up in the United States of America. The United States received more immigrants than the great immigrant nations, including Argentina, Australia, Brazil, and Canada combined. Between 1892 and the early 1920s, millions passed through Ellis Island and other U.S. immigrant-processing centers. The experience of walking through these gates to the New World lives in the family memories of many Americans. In 1970, 42 percent of Americans, most of them of European descent, claimed ancestors who migrated to this country between 1830 and 1930. Their stories are memorialized in the new museum at Ellis Island, in New York Harbor, which opened in 1990.

Today, the United States is again experiencing great waves of immigration, this time with people from Asian, Latin and Central American, and African nations predominating. Changes in immigration laws, entry procedures, and transportation technology mean that these sojourners are likely to enter through airports, not through processing stations such as Ellis Island once was. The museum at Ellis Island belongs to an earlier historic moment, but it is a monument to all of America's immigrants, reminding us that this great nation has a long history of accepting newcomers and renewing itself with their contributions.

U.S. Immigration Policy in Historical Context, 1788–1986

IMMIGRATION POLICY

Many laws have influenced the entry and exclusion of persons from the United States. The federal government did not begin to formulate a formal immigration policy until the late nineteenth century.

HISTORICAL CONTEXT

A broad range of circumstances including famine, depression, war, technological innovation, and industrialization influenced the course of immigration policy and immigration to the United States.

Timeline

Immigration policy

1788: U.S. Constitution, ratified by states, restricts presidency to native-born citizens and gives Congress authority to establish a uniform rule on naturalization.

1798: Alien Act, an attempt to control French radicals after the revolution, stipulates residency and deportation regulations is passed; repealed in 1801.

1808: U.S. forbids importation of slaves.

1819: Federal law establishes the obligation of ship's captains to supply a list of all passengers, indicating their age, sex, occupation, "the country to which they severally belonged," and the number who died en route.

Historical context

1790: First U.S. Census enumerates 3,227,000 residents, of whom about 64 percent are of British origin, 7 percent German, 18 percent enslaved black, and 2 percent free black.

1820–50: U.S. industrialization progresses rapidly with manufacturing techniques and inventions, as well as improvements in domestic transportation, including turnpikes, canals, steamboats, and railroads.

1840–60: More than four million immigrants arrive in the United States, mostly from western and northern European countries, with significant numbers of English, Irish, Germans, and Norwegians.

1846: The Great Potato Famine of 1845–50 prompts surge in emigration from Ireland.

1848: Suppression of the Revolution of 1848 brings German political refugees to U.S.

1849: California gold rush draws internal migrants from across the nation.

1855: New York State opens Castle Garden immigration station in lower Manhattan.

1858: Monetary crisis and famine in Sweden cause large-scale migration to U.S.

1875: Federal law restricts entry of prostitutes and convicts.

1876: U.S. Supreme Court declares state laws on immigration unconstitutional.

1882: Chinese Exclusion Act is the first federal law to restrict immigration by nationality. Congress also excludes convicts, lunatics, idiots, and persons likely to become public charges. Each immigrant is required to pay a head tax.

1885: Federal legislation prohibits the admission of contract laborers.

1891: Immigration is placed under federal control with the Secretary of the Treasury as overseer; new legislation also prohibits the admission of polygamists and persons suffering from contagious diseases.

1892: Ellis Island opens; federal immigration stations are established in other major ports, including San Francisco, Boston, and Philadelphia.

1903: The Secretary of Labor and Commerce assumes control over immigration until 1940. Congress excludes anarchists and persons who believe in or advocate the U.S. government's forcible overthrow.

1907: Federal law raises the head tax on immigrants and adds to the excluded list persons having physical or mental defects that may affect their ability to earn a living, those with tuberculosis, and children unaccompanied by adults.

1917: Congress requires that each immigrant older than sixteen be literate in a language; the requirement does not apply to persons fleeing religious persecution. Virtually all Asian immigration is banned.

1860–80: Immigration to U.S. numbers five million. More than 200,000 Chinese arrive in the U.S., while great numbers of French Canadians migrate to New England.

1861–65: Civil War causes major drop in immigration to U.S. Following the war, steam-powered ocean liners gradually replace sailing vessels in the immigrant trade.

1869: Central Pacific and Union Pacific Railroads span North America, built by Irish and Chinese laborers.

1880–1900: Nine million immigrants arrive in U.S. Immigrants from Italy, Austro-Hungary, and Russia start arriving in great numbers. Many are Jews fleeing persecution in Russia.

1900–20: Peak years of immigration see more than fourteen million people enter the U.S. A growing proportion come from southern and eastern Europe. First large wave of Mexican immigrants arrives in California to work on farms and railroads. In 1907, more than 1,285,000 people are admitted into U.S., a record for one year.

1914: Outbreak of World War I ends mass migration to the Americas. Labor needs of U.S. industry, a major supplier to warring nations in Europe, draw southern blacks to northern cities.

1921: Federal law establishes quotas limiting the number of immigrants of each nationality to 3 percent of the number of foreign-born persons of that nationality living in the United States in 1910. The law also limits European immigration to about 350,000 persons annually.

1924: National Origins Law (Johnson-Reed Act) sets temporary annual quotas at 2 percent of each nationality's U.S. population in the 1890 Census; also sets an upward limit of 150,000 in any one year from non-Western Hemisphere countries. The law reduces immigration and controls its ethnic character by excluding Asians and setting low quotas for countries in eastern and southern Europe. Immigrants are processed abroad, under direction of U.S. consulates.

1929: Quotas of 1924 are made permanent, apportioning immigration slots according to each nationality's proportion of the total U.S. population as enumerated in 1920 Census.

1939: Ignoring pleas from American families eager to sponsor admission of children from Germany, Congress defeats a refugee bill to rescue 20,000 children from the Nazis, on grounds that admission would exceed the annual German quota.
1940: As immigration is perceived more as a national security issue, oversight is transferred to the Attorney General in the Justice Department where it remains.

1942 Bilateral agreements with Mexico, British Honduras, Barbados, and Jamaica permit entry of temporary migrants to work in the United States under the so-called *bracero* or temporary day laborers' program.
1943: Chinese Exclusion laws are repealed.

1920–40: Immigration to U.S. totals 4.6 million, less than one-third the level of the previous decade. Nearly half a million immigrants arrive from Mexico during the 1920s, but during the next decade more than 400,000 Mexicans are deported.

1920: Anti-immigration sentiments become more widespread; "nativists" lobby vigorously for restriction.

1930s: Economic depression, combined with a rigorous enforcement of current immigration laws, further reduces immigration. For the first time, people leaving the U.S. outnumber those arriving.

1940: Alien Registration Act requires finger printing and annual registration of all resident aliens as a national security measure.
1940–60: Approximately 3.5 million people immigrate to U.S.

1941: U.S. goes to war with the Axis powers; industrial mobilization of civilian population draws many rural people to cities.

1946: War Brides Act allows GIs to bring foreign-born wives home.

1948: Displaced Persons Act passes, eventually allowing 400,000 refugees to enter the United States.

1950s: After the Korean War, about eight thousand Korean refugees, war brides, and orphans come to the United States. Refugee acts admit more than 250,000 East Europeans, including thirty-eight thousand Hungarians.

1950: Internal Security Act expands grounds for exclusion and deportation of "subversives"; also requires aliens to report their addresses annually.

1952: The Immigration and Nationality Act (McCarran-Walter Act): (1) reaffirms the national-origins system, giving each nation a quota equal to its proportion in the 1920 Census; (2) limits Eastern Hemisphere immigration to about 150,000 but leaves Western Hemisphere immigration unrestricted; (3) establishes preferences for skilled workers and relatives of U.S. citizens, and tightens security and screening standards and procedures; (4) prohibits admission of "subversives."

1957: Refugee Escape Act defines a refugee as any alien who has fled from a Communist country or the Middle East owing to persecution (or fear thereof) for reasons of race, religion, or political views.

· ·

1960: Congress establishes Cuban refugee program.

1964: U.S. ends *bracero* program.

1965: Immigration and Nationality Act amendments: (1) abolish the national-origins system; (2) establish an Eastern Hemisphere annual ceiling of 170,000, with a twenty thousand per-country limit, and distribute visas according to a seven-category preference system that favors close relatives of U.S. citizens and permanent resident aliens, those having vital occupational skills, and refugees; (3) establish a Western Hemisphere annual ceiling of 120,000, with no preferences or per-country limits.

1945: World War II ends; Cold War begins soon thereafter. Massive population shifts occur in Europe and Asia as result of the world conflict.

1956: Hungarian Revolt fails.

1959: Cuban Revolution succeeds.

· ·

1960–80: U.S. immigration tops 8 million; uncounted illegal immigrants add significantly to total. Immigration from Latin America and Asia steadily rises. By 1980, more than 41 percent of immigrants come from Latin America and 34 percent from Asia. More than 440,000 Cuban refugees immigrate to the United States.

1965–72: President L. B. Johnson and Fidel Castro sign a "memorandum of understanding" and 275,000 Cubans are airlifted to the U.S.

1975: Indochina Refugees Resettlement Program begins, admits approximately 130,000 refugees.

1976: Immigration and Nationality Act amendments: (1) extend the 20,000 per-country limit and seven category preferences to the Western Hemisphere; (2) maintain the Western Hemisphere annual ceiling of 170,000.

1978: Immigration and Nationality Act amendments combine ceilings for both hemispheres into a worldwide total of 290,000, with the same seven category preference system and 20,000 per-country limit uniformly applied. Congress passes a law excluding and deporting Nazi persecutors and their collaborators.

1980: Refugee Act establishes clear criteria and procedures for admission of refugees.

1986: Immigration Reform and Control Act establishes sanctions against employers who hire illegal immigrants and offers amnesty for illegal immigrants who request legal status. An agricultural guest worker program is established for alien laborers.

. . . .

Sources: Ellis Island Museum, *The Peopling of America* exhibit, and Thomas Kessner, *Today's Immigrants, Their Story*, New York: Oxford University Press, 1981.

1975: Fall of Saigon to Viet Cong. About 130,000 refugees from Vietnam, Laos, and Cambodia are admitted.

1

Migration and Examples from World History

Overview

1.1 **PART 1** introduces migration and immigration as commonly understood in everyday language, as personal experiences, and as analytical concepts. It provides examples of family histories as a means to understand migration and immigration.

Through examples from world history, it describes five categories that experts use when analyzing past and current migration.

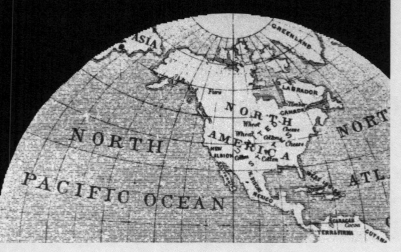

1.2 Definitions

1.2 PEOPLE HAVE ALWAYS MOVED. ALONE, IN SMALL groups and large, men and women have crossed mountains and valleys, deserts, rivers, and oceans. Since the earliest civilizations in the Tigris-Euphrates Valley, Egypt, the Indus Valley, and northern China, people have migrated. The history of ancient Greece and Rome is in part the story of migrations throughout the Mediterranean basin —by the earliest Greek tribes in the second millennium B.C.; by later Greek arrivals like the Dorians; by Germanic tribes that threatened the Roman Republic. The history of central and northern Europe is, likewise, a story of migrations and movements, including the Celts in the region of today's France, Spain, and the British Isles; and Germans in the regions now called Poland, Germany, and Scandinavia. Major shifts in Asia during the nineteenth and twentieth centuries, for example, include as many as forty-five million Indians leaving for Southeast Asia, East Africa, and the Caribbean, while millions of Chinese moved to Southeast Asia, Africa, and North and South America. Between four and five million Japanese moved to Southeast Asia, Brazil, and the United States. In Africa, historians estimate that over a period of three hundred years, from the sixteenth through the nineteenth centuries, almost ten million left as slaves for North and South America (**Documents 1, 13**).

Migration created the populations and settlements of the Americas, too. Humans arrived in the Western Hemisphere tens of thousands of years ago, probably from northern Asia. Moving southward from the region of Alaska, gradually settling North and South America, some established cultures based on agriculture and cities, while others kept to more nomadic ways, following seasonal harvests of game, fish, and plants. More recent newcomers to the Americas arrived during the past few hundred years, mainly from the east, sailing, at first, out of ports in Spain, Portugal, England, Holland, Italy, and other European countries; and then, from the west, too, out of ports in China, Japan, and the Philippines. In the more than twenty generations that have passed since the first Spanish explorer came ashore in the New World, tens of millions of people

First record of human migration into the Western Hemisphere across Bering Strait.

American Indians number 12,395,999 or 0.76% of U.S. population.

moved to the Americas in response to wars, famines, enslavement and persecution, or in search of work.

What are migration and immigration? Dictionaries treat the two words as virtually synonymous—the processes by which people change their residence from one locale to another. Common usage usually reserves *immigrant* to describe persons who move across national borders, but it applies *migrant* to individuals who move within national borders. Common usage also often distinguishes the immigrant as a person who settles permanently in the new locale, whereas the migrant is one who settles temporarily or without an evident intent to stay. We speak of Mexican workers as migrants when they enter the United States seasonally to harvest crops, but we call them immigrants when they enter with the intent of establishing permanent residence in Los Angeles, Chicago, or some other place in the United States.

These distinctions in definition can produce odd results if applied too literally. Strictly speaking, all people who inhabit the Western Hemisphere are the descendants of immigrants, since their ancestors were newcomers who settled a once unpopulated land. Even the Native Americans are descended from immigrants—Asian peoples who, 20,000 to 40,000 years ago, crossed the Bering Strait and began moving south into the New World. It seems odd to call Native Americans immigrants since they have been established here so long. It also seems odd to speak of the Puritans and other early European newcomers to the Americas as immigrants; rather, we usually call them colonists or settlers. Likewise, we do not commonly speak of African Americans as immigrants, since most of them are descended from people brought forcibly from Africa as slaves centuries ago. Instead, we generally reserve *immigrant* for those who moved to the United States voluntarily during the nineteenth century and later, such as newcomers from places like Germany, Ireland, China, or the Dominican Republic.

The terminology used in ordinary speech to describe newcomers to the United States and their descendants—immigrant, settler, slave, migrant—depends partly on the

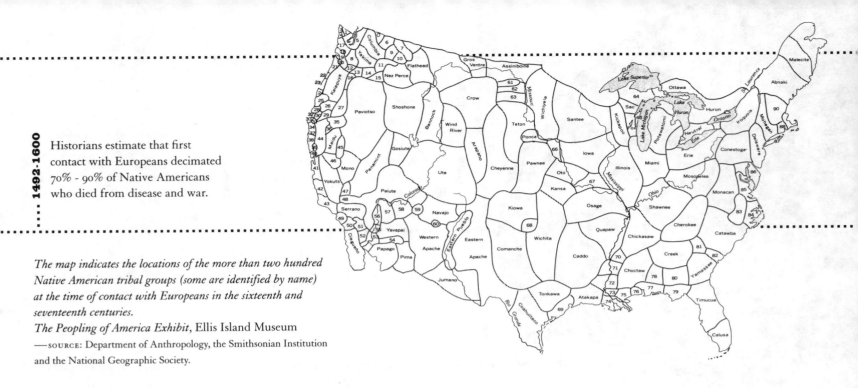

Historians estimate that first contact with Europeans decimated 70% - 90% of Native Americans who died from disease and war.

The map indicates the locations of the more than two hundred Native American tribal groups (some are identified by name) at the time of contact with Europeans in the sixteenth and seventeenth centuries.
The Peopling of America Exhibit, Ellis Island Museum
—SOURCE: Department of Anthropology, the Smithsonian Institution and the National Geographic Society.

perspective of the describer. From the point of view of people of European heritage, the first Europeans to arrive in North America were not immigrants or migrants to an established society but settlers and colonists of a seemingly unclaimed land about which they had little knowledge. After the Revolutionary War, these same colonists regarded themselves as Americans living in a nation-state with a federal government that had the authority to define citizenship. They could now exclude persons they deemed undesirable, and one day regulate the flow of new people into the country. They saw newcomers as outsiders and called them immigrants.

Recent scholarship approaches the study of migration and immigration as: (1) phenomena that can be understood through the experiences of the individuals who migrate and (2) a process resulting from social, economic, and political influences that motivate large numbers of people to move. Each of these approaches offers unique insights. The first recognizes that the private concerns of family, friends, and work have always shaped human events. Thus, when one of the immigrants who came through Ellis Island tells researchers, "I came to America because I wanted to be free"

or "I wanted a better chance for my children," we understand the meaning in a very personal way. When scholars use these statements and other testimonials to explain the migration process as an accumulation of thousands of individual decisions, the layperson easily comprehends.

The second type of analysis—social or structural—though more abstract and distant from everyday thinking about the world, is equally important to the study of immigration. The historian who writes that individuals came to the United States at the turn of the 20th century to be free and improve their economic standing might also point out that they were part of a massive exodus of free European laborers who left places undergoing major socioeconomic changes to seek their fortunes in America's expanding industrial economy. Whether they left the declining Russian Empire of the Czar or the poor tenant farms of the Italian south, European immigrants would soon become wage laborers in North America's rapidly expanding economy. From this historical perspective, scholars conclude that migrations occur as responses to demands in the world labor market.

Left: Exhibit at the Ellis Island Museum, A 6' diameter model of the earth identifies forty different historic migration routes which predominated from the 17th century to the present with fiber optics. *Right:* Exhibit at the Statue of Liberty Museum

METAFORM INC. AND CHERMAYEFF AND GEISMAR INC.

Both kinds of explanations—one emphasizing individual decisions and the other social, religious, political, or economic circumstances—describe the past. The history of immigration portrayed at the Ellis Island Museum and the history of immigration evident within the local community are powerful examples of this interplay. Gleaned from history textbooks, family histories, oral interviews, or the Ellis Island Museum itself, insights gained from the study of migration can help lead from one kind of analysis to the other and improve understanding of how social organization shapes and interacts with personal affairs, the history of the nation, and the history of the world. Thousands of personal decisions, seemingly unrelated, resulted in the movement of millions to the United States: people who responded to changes in the world around them as well as to the circumstances of their dearest relatives, and friends, and by their decisions changed the world.

Even though most people today are not accustomed to thinking of themselves, their families, and their identities as the result of historical forces, the analysis of migration and immigration suggests that contemporary differences — including ethnic, national, or religious distinctions—are rooted in great historical changes. The evidence for this and for each family's participation in great historical movements is apparent across the United States and can easily be seen in the histories of many American families.

Family Histories as Case Studies

1.3 CONSIDER AN IMAGINARY CLASSROOM THAT INCLUDES the following students: Patrick O'Malley, Jimmy Iannuzzi, Harriet Smith, Rachel Stein, Betty Lincoln, Julie Wong, and Carmen Blanco. If these students were asked to identify their immigrant heritage, they might reply, in order: Irish, Italian, English, Jewish, African American, Chinese, and Mexican. Some will know something about their family history; many will know nothing at all. Given an assignment to learn about their family histories, they might offer the following reports: Patrick O'Malley's great-great-grandfather left Ireland sometime during the Great Potato Famine that began in 1845.

1.3a *British Immigrants Leaving Gravesend Port, southeast England* —THE GRAPHIC, Feb. 27, 1875.

Immigrants Arriving at Los Angeles Airport *(Left and center)* Land port of entry, San Ysidro, California *(right)*—INS PHOTO ARCHIVE

Jimmy Iannuzzi's great-grandfather left Italy in 1905 to work on the B&O Railroad and sent money home to his small village in Calabria. Harriet Smith reports that her father has a genealogical chart that traces his ancestry back to 1760, when a young man named James Gray from Kent, England, arrived in Charleston, South Carolina, the state in which Betty's slave ancestors were emancipated. Harriet is surprised to hear her mother describe herself as the offspring of four different ethnic groups: Germans, who arrived in the United States during the early 1800s; Scotch-English, who intermarried with Native Americans in Florida; and New England Yankees of unknown origin. Rachel Stein knows that her grandmother left Nazi Germany in 1936, went to the Netherlands, and finally, came to the United States; also that she has cousins whose grandparents fled from Germany to Israel rather than to the Americas. Next to her is Betty Lincoln, five generations removed from slave ancestors, whose mother and father, now pharmacists, return every summer with the family to visit great-uncles and great-aunts in South Carolina. Julie Wong's mother came from Hong Kong at age four and later married a third-generation Chinese American whose ancestors came here during the California gold rush that began in 1848. Finally, Carmen Blanco's father moved north from Mexico in 1962 but went back and forth to Guadalajara several times before he decided to marry and settle down in the United States.

These imaginary family histories illustrate a vast canvas of historic circumstances taking shape over hundreds of years. They also reveal some common experiences that immigrant

ancestors had, as well as crucially different kinds of decisions they faced. Some of these histories can be retrieved through family memory; historians can conjecture about others. Jimmy Iannuzzi and Patrick O'Malley, for example, think of themselves as descendants of ancestors who freely chose to leave native lands to improve their economic circumstances in the United States. They know this because their parents (who spoke with their own parents) told them. But our young Italian American and Irish American would probably be surprised to learn that they, like Mexican American Carmen

1.3b *Chinese Immigrants Entering San Francisco before Angel Island Was Established as a Processing Center*—HARPER'S WEEKLY, Feb. 3, 1877

San Ysidro, California (left) Los Angeles Airport (right) INS PHOTO ARCHIVE

Blanco and African American Betty Lincoln, are also remote descendants of persons who lived under colonial domination. Now, Patrick, Jimmy, Carmen, and Betty may not be surprised to think of Mexican Americans and African Americans as former slaves—objects of European colonial expansion in Mexico and on the West African coast—but Jimmy Iannuzzi may be surprised to learn that his background contains Greek slaves transplanted to southern Italy by conquering Roman armies. Patrick O'Malley may not have thought of his great-great-grandfather as a colonial subject, yet historians have chronicled how England treated Ireland as a colony,

1.3c *Group of Japanese Arriving in the United States, ca. 1900s*

exploiting its land for grain and its people for their labor. The potato famine provided an immediate, urgent reason for Patrick's great-great-grandfather to leave Ireland. However the famine, which arose as the result of Irish dependence on a one-crop economy, and Mr. O'Malley's inability to survive on his small plot of land, was inextricably connected to exploitation of Irish land and peasants by English absentee landlords, the representatives of British colonial rule.

The first member of Julie Wong's family to travel to the United States came from Canton province in China in the nineteenth century. The family lived on a plot of land too small to divide among all the sons (daughters married into other families and inherited no part of the lands on which the family lived). As peasants, the Wongs shared with the O'Malleys a long history shaped by demanding landlords, subsistence agriculture, and vulnerability to nature's whims. For many peasants of Canton province, it was the floods, which destroyed the rice crops, rather than failure of the potato, that finally uprooted them from their land and forced them to seek their fortunes abroad.

Carmen Blanco's father, who moved back and forth between Mexico and the United States, seems to both Carmen and her classmates like many contemporary immigrants from Asia and Latin America, but different from the older immigrants who, the students think, rarely recrossed the ocean to their native lands; and certainly different from African American slaves, who had no choice about leaving Africa. Carmen is right about the African Americans who

1619 First African arrives in Virginia.

1620 Indentured servitude is introduced into the English colonies.

1628-1642 58,000 English people leave the British Isles for North America and the Caribbean Islands.

were forcibly detached from their people in Africa, and even about the famine-stricken Irish, who had nothing to return to at home. But other early twentieth-century immigrants, like Jimmy Iannuzzi's great-grandfather, did travel back and forth across the ocean in search of the highest wages.

1.4 World History and the Social Organization of Migration

1.4 FAMILY HISTORIES SUGGEST MANY PATTERNS OF migration and the multitude of decisions made by millions of people who migrated, as well as the different historical circumstances in which they made their decisions. Historically, most migrations have occurred as responses to global labor needs. Modern free market capitalism requires that workers sell their time and service for wages, and encourages them to migrate at their own expense from areas of low labor demand to areas where they expect to find employment. Since the nineteenth century, the great urban regions of the Americas, Europe, the Middle East, and Asia have been magnets to people in search of work. Scholars have identified some of the specific patterns underlying most migrations from the European Age of Exploration to the present, and they include: (1) forced migration, (2) voluntary migration, (3) circular migration, (4) chain migration, and (5) colonizing migration. Forced migration and its opposite, voluntary migration, refer to the degree of freedom or compulsion in the decision to move; in many historical periods,

one method of obtaining labor has been slavery or some other type of coercion, usually accompanied by forced movement to a new land. The third category, circular migration, refers to whether the migrant stayed in the new place permanently or temporarily. The last two categories address the social organization of migrations, that is, whether they are relatively spontaneous events consisting of chains of individual decision-makers or, rather, intentional and officially sponsored movements, as was the case with some colonial settlements.

FORCED MIGRATION

1.4.1 THE MOST IMPORTANT SINGLE DISTINCTION IS between voluntary and involuntary migration. Forced, or involuntary, migration describes the movement of people who have no choice or control over their movements. The difference between voluntary and involuntary migration appears most starkly in our imaginary family histories between the seventeenth-century Englishman James Gray, who could have chosen to stay home or gone to seek his fortune in London, Canada, or the New England colonies, and the ancestors of Betty Lincoln, who were slaves manacled in the holds of sailing ships. James Gray could choose whether or not to migrate and where he wanted to go. Africans, who had been enslaved even before they ever left Africa, had no choice.

Many historical eras and virtually all cultures have had slaves, convict laborers, indentured servants, and others, including women without the full rights of independent persons, who provided a large pool of cheap labor. Only in

Cheap Labor

Forced Migration: The Atlantic Slave Trade. Map illustrating waves of forced migration from West Africa to North, Central, and South America and the Caribbean from 1701–1810. —*The Peopling of America Exhibit*, The Ellis Island Museum adapted from Philip D. Curtin, *The Atlantic Slave Trade*, Madison: University of Wisconsin Press, 1975.

1654 The first Jews arrive in New Amsterdam.

1674 First shipment of slaves directly from Africa.

1695 England deports groups of gypsies to Virginia.

relatively recent times, with the advent of industrial capitalism (which organizes its work force using wage labor, whose value is regulated by supply and demand), has slave labor lost its appeal. During the seventeenth century, when European governments and ventures faced acute labor shortages as they staked their claims to new lands and sought to extract the wealth there, they obtained labor through use of slaves and indentured persons (persons who relinquished some personal autonomy for the term of their labor contract). The shortage of labor, combined with the drive for potential profits, explains the expansion of the slave trade. Slaves came primarily from

1.4.1a *Passsengers Aboard a 19th Century Slave Ship* —HARPER'S WEEKLY, *June 2, 1960.*

Africa; forced laborers, including prisoners and indentured servants, who were not free to move or change the conditions of their service, came from the overcrowded jails of England and from the ranks of those who did not have the money to pay for passage to the New World. The British reduced overcrowding in their prisons during the eighteenth century by sending prisoners to their colonies in Georgia and Australia. The first shipment of convicts to Australia, in 1787, including men, women, and children, was followed, in succeeding decades, by ships bearing 160,000 more (**Documents 1, 2**).

The English, Dutch, Spanish, and others who came to the New World seeking wealth turned to the importation of African slaves to work fields of sugarcane, tobacco, and later, cotton, after they discovered that white laborers were unable to tolerate the hot climate. Approximately 94 percent of enslaved Africans went to the Caribbean and Brazil to work harvesting cash crops, and the remainder were taken to North America. Until the 1840s, the number of Africans brought to North and South America as slaves exceeded the total number of all Europeans who migrated to the New World, and in some places, slaves far exceeded the number of European settlers. In North America, there is some evidence to suggest that during the early seventeenth century, Africans sold to Virginia planters may have served a limited term of bondage, as did white indentured servants. Within a few decades, however, statutes and court decisions established the principle of

Settlers and Servants: Immigration Before 1780. Pictograms to the left of center line represent white immigrants, more than half of whom were indentured servants. Pictograms to the right of center line represent black newcomers (slaves) — *The Peopling of America Exhibit*, The Ellis Island Museum.

—SOURCE: Professor Russell R. Men and University of Minnesota

1620-40	
1640-60	
1660-80	
1680-1700	
1700-20	
1720-40	
1740-60	
1760-80	

1700-1780

The importation of slaves at its height.

1718
England's Parliament passes a law providing for passage of convicts to America.

1808
Federal law mandates that no more slaves may be imported. The internal slave trade continues.

---

perpetual bondage and the right of masters to buy and sell Africans. *Negro* and *slave* became interchangeable terms. The U.S. Constitution distinguishes between *migration* and *importation*, the latter referring to slaves, who were considered *goods* not migrants. Although some owners treated their slaves more humanely than others, and sometimes a slave, especially one that worked in the house, might interact as a family member, these circumstances never altered the fact that the slave remained the legal property of the owner. The framers of the U.S. Constitution, as part of a compromise between pro- and antislavery factions, agreed that in 1808 it would become illegal to import slaves into the United States, though slavery and the interstate slave trade remained lawful.

Slavery and prisoner labor, however, were not the only kinds of servitude. Another kind, common among Europeans, was indentured servitude, a contract freely entered into, often for the purpose of relocating to a new place. During the colonial period, many people bound themselves legally to the service of another person for a stipulated period of time in return for a benefit, such as free passage abroad (**Documents 3, 4, 5**). Like slavery, indentured servitude (and apprenticeship, another form of contract) was a means to find and keep workers in the colonies. A British resident, for example, who wanted to migrate to North America in search of a better life but lacked passage money, could become the indentured servant of someone in the colonies who needed a helper or assistant on a farm, in a household, or in a business. Like any freely arranged contract, the indentureship combined elements of choice and com-

pulsion. The migrant freely chose to travel abroad, selected the destination, and decided whether or not to become the servant of another person. Once the contract was signed, however, the indentured servant was subjected to the commands and whims of another person. Nevertheless, unlike slaves, indentured servants never lost their legal rights and, even more important, could expect to become entirely free at the end of their term. Many indentured servants saw their period of service as a first step to the ownership of land—something unimaginable in the old country. As a practical matter, people who found themselves bound as servants to demanding masters and mistresses

1.4.1b *Refugee Children from the Famine-Stricken Volga District in Russia on Their Way to the United States, Berlin, 1923*

In 1916, the area where we came became a no-man's land.
The French were on one side and the Austrians
on the other. And they exterminated everything that we had.
The houses were burned down. Our livestock was lost.
So in April of 1917, we had to flee as refugees.
— Stephen Peters, Albania

1850 Hawaiian planters found the Royal Hawaiian Agricultural Society to import contract labor from China.

1870 Louisiana and Mississippi planters bring Chinese laborers in an attempt to constrict freed Black workers during Reconstruction.

1894-1896 Thousands of Armenians massacred in Turkey.

1956 First plane arrives in U.S. with Hungarian political refugees.

often simply ran away and found employment elsewhere which, in the labor-starved colonies, was generally not difficult for white male workers.

Indenture becomes uncommon by the 1840s, as masters began using forms of contract that did not obligate them to provide room and board for employees (**Document 6**). The newer form of contract differed from indentured servitude (and also slavery) in that it was based on a cash relationship, wherein the cost of passage was considered an advance against future wages, and the laborer often assumed responsibility for living expenses, including housing and food. Contract workers agreed to remain with an employer until they repaid the advance against wages. Labor agents from U.S. companies journeyed to China, India, and many parts of Europe to recruit laborers for building railroads, harvesting crops, or making steel.

By the second half of the nineteenth century, stories of virtual slavery and personal servitude under the guise of contract labor led to laws seeking to protect migrants from abuses by labor bosses or businesses and corporations. In addition, organized labor considered the labor contract a means for getting cheap foreign workers to undercut U.S. wages and diminish labor's bargaining power. In 1885, the combination of moral outrage and the political influence of unions led Congress to outlaw contract labor. The illegal use of contract labor with all its dangers of abuse, however, continues to thrive in the United States and abroad. Women have been sold by their families to agents, kidnapped to become "mail order brides," or forced to be prostitutes. Today the transport of women across national borders for sexual exploitation is a major part of illegal international trade, along with the traffic in drugs and arms. Korean women who fill Japanese brothels, and South Asian women working in New York City's massage parlors, are evidence of the traffic. Many of these women were lured with contracts promising work in entertainment, hotels, and other legitimate businesses but, upon arrival in the strange new country, had their passports confiscated and became virtual prisoners of international rings of pimps organized as transnational businesses. Ignorant of their rights, often unable to speak the local language, usually lacking any money of their own, and fearing expulsion if they complain to the authorities, these women have been invisible victims of a form of migrant labor exploitation with old historical roots.

A more ambiguous kind of involuntary migration occurs when people feel compelled to move to avoid violence and discrimination in which the state colludes. In such circumstances the threat of violence makes the decision to migrate feel like an imperative need. During the final decades of the nineteenth century, for example, Russian Jews came to the Americas fleeing local outbursts of persecution. Although anti-Semitism pervades Russian history, with numerous outbreaks of violence against Jews, the state was not then formally expelling all Jews nor was it trying to jail them, but

early 1880s Pogroms in Russia and Poland spur out-migration.

We had witnessed some terrible things.
As a child, I have witnessed two thousand or so Armemians burned alive in a church.
We even heard their cries from where we were.
And one woman tried to escape from that burning church. And of course,
there were Turkish soldiers outside who shot her.
Sometimes I hear their screaming and shouting even now.
— Vartan Hartunian, Armenia

1948 The U.N. adopts the Universal Declaration of Human Rights.

1956 800,000 flee Hungary as Russian troops quell revolt.

it was sanctioning violence against them. In Turkey, two major forced resettlements occurred during the early twentieth century. The first involved hundreds of thousands of Armenians, whom the Turkish government regarded as a potentially subversive minority. Local massacres of Armenians during 1894–96 preceded a major resettlement effort by the Turkish government, starting in 1909 and lasting through 1915, that impelled many Armenians to flee to other countries, including the United States. Then, after World War I, the Turkish government expelled its Greek population (which had lived there since antiquity) after a brief war with Greece, and the redistribution of population was acknowledged with the Treaty of Lausanne in 1923. Not far to the south of Turkey, other redistributions occurred some years later as the result of the creation of the state of Israel in 1948, when approximately 700,000 Palestinians fled to Muslim-inhabited areas, while about 300,000 Jews living in Muslim countries moved to the new state. North America provides many examples of forced migration when the indigenous peoples, facing relentless pressure from white settlers and miners throughout the nineteenth century, migrated west until they had nowhere else to go and became a conquered people settled on reservations. More recently, the United States has offered haven to refugees like the anti-Castro Cubans who fled during the 1960s.

These involuntary movements have greatly multiplied the number of refugees in today's world to the extent that they now constitute an important share of all migrants. They live on every continent and in almost every nation, often confined in camps near the boundaries of their home countries, caught in an odd kind of political and legal trap. Although the Universal Declaration of Human Rights, adopted by the United Nations in 1948, guarantees the right to leave one's homeland, it does not compel nations to receive migrants who may find themselves stateless, (**Document 7**),without a legal right to stay in the host country yet unable to return to their homeland. The United Nations has tried to address this problem by establishing camps run under its auspices, to provide food and housing until the refugees either return home or are resettled elsewhere.

1.4.3 *Dinnertime in Steerage on a Transatlantic Steamer, 1890.*
Cheap sea transport made circular migration possible.
—HARPER'S WEEKLY, Nov. 22, 1890.

VOLUNTARY MIGRATION

1.4.2 THE EXAMPLES OF SLAVERY, PRISON LABOR, indentured labor, and refugees suggest that a surprisingly large part of domestic and international migration has been involuntary; yet, when we think about immigrants and the movements of people, we usually focus on voluntary migration. Truly voluntary migration has historically been a response to economic, educational, or political aspirations. Usually it is not the poorest people who move nor the richest and most privileged, but those who have some means and are dissatisfied with economic conditions or some other aspect of their lives. Voluntary migration may be arranged formally, under the auspices of labor agents or government or corporations; it may be organized informally through personal ties of kinship, occupational bonds, or a common place of origin. Scholars have discerned several patterns to voluntary immigration and have labelled them *circular*, *chain*, and *colonizing* migration.

CIRCULAR MIGRATION

1.4.3 PEOPLE STAY IN THEIR NEW PLACES FOR DIFFERENT lengths of time: some remain only for a harvest season; others settle for the rest of their lives, though reserving the option to return to their birth land; still others move back and forth in a process called circular migration. Mexican and Puerto Rican agricultural workers, Chinese railroad laborers, and many of the Italian and Greek men who passed through Ellis Island

participated in circular migrations: they came to the United States to work and save money, and when they attained their goal, they returned home. The Chinese laborers who came to the United States before the Chinese Exclusion Act of 1882, and the Indians with Ph.D.s who came to the United States for career advancement during the 1980s, have all been part of a voluntary migration that is economic in motivation and often circular in form.

Circular migration can occur across national boundaries or within the boundaries of a single country. Most countries undergo a process of urbanization wherein large numbers of people move from the countryside to the city in pursuit of work. Puerto Rican sugarcane and tobacco workers who left the island during the 1920s and 1950s to work on the main-

Steamer trunks from the permanent exhibition at the Ellis Island Museum

land, and African Americans who left the South for jobs in northern cities during the world wars, exemplify the impetus and pattern of circular migration (**Document 8, 9**). Throughout Europe and North America, people set out to seek their fortunes in contiguous countries. Though millions of Poles who moved from rural villages during the nineteenth and early twentieth century went to the United States, many also moved to the growing industrial cities of Germany and Russia.

Sometimes migrants settled permanently in their new urban settings, often after having gone back and forth several times between their rural places of origin and their new city homes. Of the millions of Irish migrants to the United States, most of whom came from the countryside, only about 12 percent returned to live in Ireland because the home country could not provide inexpensive farmland or comparable economic opportunities. Armenians from Turkey and Jews from Eastern Europe, two largely rural groups who immigrated to flee persecution and were not welcome in their home country, had some of the lowest return rates—about 15 percent and 5 percent respectively. Italians were actually more likely to return than to stay: an estimated 60 percent of Italians who entered the United States during the heyday of Ellis Island returned to Italy.

Circular migration became more common with improvements in transportation after the middle of the nineteenth century. Before then, sea travel required weeks of time and

entailed risks that only the bold or desperate would willingly undergo more than once or twice in a lifetime. With the advent of scheduled service, first by large sailing vessels and later by steamships, ocean voyages became safer, more comfortable, and much quicker. During most of the nineteenth and twentieth centuries, the majority of migrants to the United States were responding to the demand for unskilled, often temporary, or seasonal labor. During the slow season, they would often return to the home country to visit family and friends.

Class and gender significantly influence voluntary migration patterns for women. At the height of the Ellis Island era, for example, when many Italian men and women came to the Americas looking for work, Italian women did not have nearly as good opportunities to find employment. They were generally less educated and skilled than men and, since their daily lives were circumscribed by family and community, they were less accustomed to dealing with the affairs of commerce, industry, and government. Though a small number of Italian women migrated alone and worked as domestics, most came as members of families or to marry men to whom they had been affianced. The most common pattern was for the wife and children, sometimes accompanied by other relatives, to follow the husband to the new country after he had become settled and accumulated some savings. Women, however, did come

to the United States alone, including young women from Ireland in the middle decades of the nineteenth century, to work as domestics. During the Ellis Island era, sisters, cousins, aunts, and nieces came from southern and eastern Europe and Russia. Women today continue to enter the United States under laws that permit them to immigrate in order to join their families.

Recently women have become circular migrants, in response to new demands for their labor, typically in lower-paying domestic and service occupations, and they often return to the homeland when their term of service expires or the work slackens. At the turn of the twentieth century, when the heavy-industry sectors of the economy were expanding, the greatest demands were for unskilled male laborers. Today, the participation of U.S. women in the paid labor force, the professions, and government has created a demand for domestic workers and child-care providers that draws unskilled women to the United

Steamer Trunks from the permanent exhibition at The Ellis Island Museum

States. Caribbean women, for example, may come to the United States as housekeepers and childcare providers and travel back and forth to visit their own children and families.

The demands of the labor market also open opportunities for semi-skilled and professional women as well as men, who are sometimes circular migrants. The gendered character of the labor market encourages either male or female migrants, depending on the job openings. In response to a shortage of nurses during the 1980s, many skilled Filipino women migrated to the United States where demands for their services gave them economic leverage and even the choice of settling permanently in the United States or preserving their original nationality through circular migration. There was no equivalent U.S. demand for large numbers of Filipino men. Yet, by the 1990s, demand for the nurses declined sharply as the rapid consolidation of hospitals— a result of market forces—began shrinking the size of staff.

The increasing globalization of business, the advent of cheap international travel, and the revolution in electronic communication have democratized circular migration. Male and female, skilled and unskilled, even young and older workers have been drawn into the flow. Japanese workers, often accompanied by their families, live for several years in the United States while employed by Japanese firms, and American personnel of U.S. firms live in Japan.

Circular migration remains an important choice for people of all classes and many nationalities: Mexicans who seek unskilled work in restaurants, farms, and industries; Irish

who leave impoverished areas of their homeland in search of greater opportunity; and U.S. entrepreneurs developing import businesses in mainland China. U.S.-based businesses that maintain foreign operations often send American-born staff to temporary assignments abroad, where they live as circular, voluntary migrants. Some professions have an increasingly international employment pattern. Civil engineers work on major infrastructure projects around the world that are funded by multinational corporations, national governments, or banks. U.S. workers staff projects supported directly by the federal government or work under contract with firms tied to the government. Many of these people migrate from contract to contract, country to country, following the work in a manner analogous to itinerant agricultural harvesters today, or Slovak steelworkers of the early 1900s. In higher education, which has long had an international aspect, U.S. professors frequently teach in Great Britain, Europe, South Asia, Latin America, China, and Russia. Foreign professors teach in the United States. Scholarships and international student exchange programs usually bypass immigration barriers such as quotas. In these cases the people on the move are not tourists, visitors, or vacationers, but are taking part in a special kind of circular migration that has them living part of their productive years outside their home country.

CHAIN MIGRATION

1.4.4 *Chain migration* DESCRIBES A PATTERN OF MIGRATING through networks of people who know one another. Kin, friends, fellow townspeople, and other acquaintances make up the strands of the network and transfer information to each other over long distances via personal report, mail, and today phone, fax, and email (**Document 9**). A Polish coal miner in Silesia, in 1900, would write his brother working in the steel mills in Gary, Indiana, asking about opportunities in the United States; or he might write his cousin working on the docks of Bremen in Germany. One way or the other, he would garner enough information to choose where to go. Then he would use his kinsman or friends abroad as contact persons when he arrived from Silesia. The steelworkers in Gary might get him a job as a laborer stoking blast furnaces; the dock worker in Bremen might find him a spot as a longshoreman and perhaps set him up in a rented room. The chain helped to support him until he got settled.

The *chain* in chain migration stretches from the original homeland across continents, rivers, even oceans. Young unmarried men are often the first members of a community to make the decision to leave for another place (**Document 10**). They usually have the best chances of finding work in the new place and the fewest needs for daily life. However, chain migration has always depended on women for the exchange of information among family, friends, and people from the same village or town, and also for taking care of the family and the

1830 The U.S. removes 90,000 Creeks, Chactaws, Cherokees, Chickasaws, and Seminoles from the southeast to Indian Territory. 20,000 die en route.

early 1880s Pogroms in Russia and Poland spur out-migration.

1920s Nearly half a million Mexicans arrive in the U.S.

1930s Over 400,000 Mexicans are deported during the Great Depression.

1.4.4a *A Practical Example of Chain Migration, 1884. Through Old Country connections this farmer found a wife at the Castle Garden immigration station.*
—FRANK LESLIE'S ILLUSTRATED NEWSPAPER, Sept. 13, 1884

children who remain with them while husbands go to the new city or country. The women often take over the farm work, arrange marriages, and maintain family stability. When the men become more settled, they usually begin thinking about bringing over their family or, if single, getting married. Typically, parents prefer to marry their sons to women from the hometown or village, and many of the men return home to find a bride or ask family members to send an appropriate one (**Document 11**). The new migrant and his wife become a permanent link in the chain, an aid to other migrants, a source of important information for potential migrants still living in the homeland.

Chain migration and circular migration are not mutually exclusive, and often they complement one another. People who move seasonally, like the Mexicans who enter the United States to harvest crops, move in a circular pattern that involves their return to Mexico after the harvest. At the same time, they base their movements partly on information garnered from friends and relatives already here, who form a *chain* of contacts. Chain migration is often associated with a circular pattern but does not require it, as in the case of the many immigrants who use the *chain* to make one trip to the United States and take up permanent residence there.

COLONIZING MIGRATION

1.4.5 COLONIZING MIGRATION establishes political, economic, or military dominion over a land through the presence of soldiers, settlers, and other state representatives. Europeans colonized much of the continental United States and Latin America by taking territory from the Native Americans (**Document 12**).

The use of migration to gain control over new territories has a long history. The Roman conquest of northern Europe provides an early example of a process that was repeated in Western history many times. The conquest began during the first century B.C., when Rome possessed an army that had defeated all immediate enemies and was looking for new places to conquer, partly out of the need for military glory, partly to satisfy the interests of traders, government functionaries, and others interested in exploiting new lands and acquiring slaves. By the middle of the first century A.D., Roman armies had reached the Rhine on the east, Scotland on the north, and the Atlantic shores of France, Spain, and Portugal. Everywhere in western Europe, the Romans developed towns, roads, forts, bridges, and markets and made Latin the language of government, town life, and the social and economic elite. Many veteran Roman soldiers who had

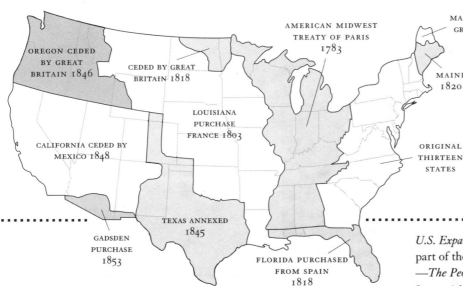

OREGON CEDED BY GREAT BRITAIN 1846

CEDED BY GREAT BRITAIN 1818

AMERICAN MIDWEST TREATY OF PARIS 1783

MAINE CEDED BY GREAT BRITAIN 1842

LOUISIANA PURCHASE FRANCE 1803

MAINE 1820

CALIFORNIA CEDED BY MEXICO 1848

ORIGINAL THIRTEEN STATES

TEXAS ANNEXED 1845

GADSDEN PURCHASE 1853

FLORIDA PURCHASED FROM SPAIN 1818

The Peopling of America Exhibit, the Ellis Island Museum (right)
METAFORM INC. AND CHERMAYEFF AND GEISMAR INC.

1820-1840
The federal government acquires land from European colonial powers and pushes most Native Americans west of the Mississippi. Almost 750,000 immigrants enter the United States.

U.S. Expansion Map of the U.S. divided by major territories that became part of the nation through purchase, annexation, and war.
—*The Peopling of America Exhibit*, the Ellis Island Museum
Source: Adapted from Rand McNally's *Atlas of World History*, Chicago, 1983

fought in northern Europe settled there when they retired from active service. Thousands of Roman citizens and other outsiders, including settlers, traders, and government officials, filled the towns and bought up much of the countryside. Many of today's cities were founded as Roman colonies. Cologne, in Germany, takes its German name, Köln, from the Latin *Colonia Agrippinensis*, the name that Emperor Claudius gave the settlement in A.D. 50 to honor his wife Agrippina. The cities helped transform Germanic culture to Roman.

Another colonizing migration occurred when the British seized control of the Indian subcontinent, beginning in the early seventeenth century. During the first two centuries, the British exerted their control over the subcontinent through scattered garrisons that operated under the aegis of the East India Company, a private business entity that was chartered by the crown and was expected to provide considerable revenues to the British government. It became traditional among some British families for their members to spend a portion of their adult lives in India as soldiers, administrators, or traders. The length of stay in India varied by individual from a few years to nearly a whole lifetime, though the children typically remained in England for their education or, if born in India, were sent to England for schooling. The adults, if they spent most of their lives working in India, would usually retire in England, which they regarded as *home*. Although the number of native-born British citizens who settled permanently in

India was never large, especially in comparison with the Indian population, British presence determined the official language, the educational system, and the institutions that govern the independent nation of India today.

In the Western Hemisphere, the United States has exercised great influence over the affairs of Latin America since the nineteenth century, though its *colonies* have generally been small and consisted of military bases and businesses rather than large numbers of colonists in the traditional sense. Large-scale colonization occurred mainly in North America during the expansionist nineteenth century, when the federal government annexed present-day California and New Mexico, whose residents became U.S. residents (whether they wished it nor not) and were quickly augmented by a large influx of settlers from the east. The purchase of Alaska from Russia in 1867 likewise made the Native Americans automatically, and without their consent, part of the American empire, and soon soldiers and colonists began arriving from the continental United States. During the late nineteenth century, the acquisition of Hawaii, Puerto Rico, the Virgin Islands, and the Philippines involved the extension of U.S. control through arms and trade. Hawaii and Alaska, like California and New Mexico, formally obtained statehood, while Puerto Rico, the Virgin Islands, and the Philippines did not, but all experienced a period of colonizing migration which helped establish U.S. control.

The Family Histories Revisited

1.5 IT IS USEFUL TO RECALL THE IMAGINARY STUDENTS'
family histories in light of the discussion about the social
organization of migration. Patrick O'Malley's great-great-
grandfather, who migrated from Ireland during a famine,
came voluntarily, though under tremendous economic
pressure, and probably benefitted from a chain of information
from relatives in the United States who had already made
the move. He came to stay and put down roots, though he
maintained ties with family and friends in his Irish
home village.

Jimmy Iannuzzi's great-grandfather, who came from
southern Italy in 1905, planned to save money in the United
States and return home to buy farmland, only to decide that
life in the United States offered more than he expected. At
some point in his stay as a resident alien, he ceased sending his
savings to the homeland and, instead, invested the money in
establishing his own household.

Harriet Smith's migrating ancestors represent several
categories that we have discussed. Those who went to South
Carolina were colonists who came with the intention of
staying and creating a new society. Those who migrated later,
the Germans and Scotch-Irish, arrived when the United
States existed as a nation; we, therefore, speak of them as
immigrants, not colonists. Most Germans and Scotch-Irish
who migrated to the United States planned to settle down;
the height of their influx came before 1860, before the major
improvements in transportation that made circular migration
so much safer and cheaper.

Rachel Stein's migrant ancestors took full advantage of
improved sea transport when they sailed to the United States
in 1936 to flee the Nazis. Their movement was nominally voluntary but could also be called forced, especially in light of the
terrible fate of so many Jews who remained in Germany.
They came to their new home with no intention of returning.

Betty Lincoln's early ancestors came unwillingly as slaves
from Africa, but later generations, children of the first freed

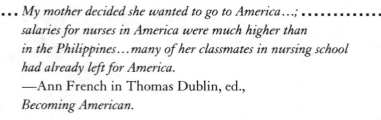

slaves, moved north voluntarily looking for better opportunities. They followed a chain of friends and kin to their new homes, where they settled permanently except for visits to the South, and raised families.

Julie Wong's first Chinese ancestor migrated to the United States under a labor contract. The first of his family to come, during the gold rush days, he may have arrived without any personal contacts in the United States, but he had heard about the United States and about how one could make a lot of money in a short time. Maybe he agreed to come when a steamship or railroad agent came through his village looking for contract workers. Maybe he ran away from home. Just as likely, the whole family discussed his trip and expected to benefit from the money he would earn. He planned to return to China, but events turned out otherwise. Later family arrivals probably relied on a chain of friends and relatives already living in the United States. Racial barriers in the United States encouraged Chinese immigrants to stay among kin and friends in an alien world.

Carmen Blanco's father, the first of the family to spend much time in the United States, began as a migrant moving across the border for the harvest season then returning to his family in Mexico. Finally he decided he wanted to live permanently in the United States. He was able to move to the United States with a legal residence permit, known commonly as a Green Card, although the permits are no longer green or even cards. As a legal U.S. resident Carmen's father could bring his family to the United States.

THROUGHOUT HISTORY MIGRATION AND IMMIGRATION have involved complex sets of choices and circumstances. Migration and immigration have led to shifts in population from one place to another, the settlement of uninhabited lands, and a change in the ethnic, religious, or racial character of populations. You can examine your own family background to see how they illustrate the various kinds of migration that have existed throughout history: forced and voluntary, circular, chain, and colonizing, as well as internal and external migration.

2

Migration and the New World

Overview

2.1

Many Americans think of migration as a simple, linear process wherein a family pulls up roots and moves, in one step, to another place, usually the United States, where they are welcomed without reservation. In fact, since the European Age of Exploration the migration process has involved a complex interaction of global economics, transportation, and technology that underlies many other historical transformations.

PART 2 shows how conditions in sending and receiving nations influence the immigration process as well as the reception that newcomers meet.

Crossing the Ocean: A Guide ....

TIMELINE .....

1870 Steamships replace sailing vessels in transoceanic migrations.

INS PHOTO ARCHIVE

2.2 Sending and Receiving Regions

2.2 IN A DISCUSSION OF IMMIGRATION IT IS WORTH pausing to remember that most people do not leave their homelands: only a minority of people in any one country move to another. In some fashion, a person's decision to migrate usually rests on a calculation that opportunities will be better in a new place. In other words, the decision rests on a comparison of conditions in one place—the sending region, country, town, or village—with anticipated conditions in another place. Although economic criteria may be critical, even in voluntary migrations, they alone do not always determine the destination. The existence, for example, of a chain migration pattern between one region in a sending country and another region in a receiving country may guide migrants to a particular locale even though another place might have provided a better choice from purely economic considerations.

Changing circumstances abroad also contribute to the fluctuations in the number of people who migrate (**Documents 13, 14, 15, 23, 40, 42, 46**). Causes for migration from Europe and Asia to parts of the Western Hemisphere have included natural disasters such as famines and floods, religious or political persecution, population pressure on family land-holdings, political revolutions, and government efforts to settle colonized areas. A country may provide many migrants at one time in its history and few or none at other times. Spain, whose royal government sought to colonize the Americas, sent thousands of conquistadors, monks, clerics, and traders, during the sixteenth and seventeenth centuries, but not later. Russia provided thousands of immigrants to the United States in the days of the czars, but fewer during the later period, when the Soviets usually denied exit visas.

At the same time, conditions in the receiving countries may change in ways that encourage or discourage immigration. Economic fluctuations alter the demands for labor, as well as popular opinion about immigrants and national policy toward immigration. Consider the case of immigrations from Mexico. Early in the twentieth century, the U.S. government encouraged the seasonal migration of Mexicans to harvest perishable crops in the West and Southwest, but as the economy stag-

A week or more across the Atlantic. You leave one world for another. We were seasick. And when you're seasick, you wish you were dead…And we were third class. Down at the bottom… they would always tell us to go up on the deck…and sometimes after a while you would feel a little better and then at night you'd go back into your dungeon cabin again and the cabin was two by four.
—Regina Sass Teppin, Polish Immigrant

1521 The seige of Tenochititlán begins in May and lasts until August 13, 1521. Cortez and his Spanish conquistadores emerge victorious against the Aztecs.

1598 First permanent Spanish settlement in New Mexico.

1716 First Spanish missions established in Texas.

1769 First Spanish missions established in California.

Colonization of the New World

2.3

gered in the Great Depression, the government began expelling Mexican migrants in order to keep the harvesting jobs for U.S. residents. Then the government reversed its policy during World War II, when labor was scarce and farmers and fruit growers desperately needed laborers, no matter where they came from. After World War II, the U.S. government changed its policy toward imported immigrant labor under pressure from organized labor and other groups who argued that Mexican migration was taking jobs from Americans. The United States is not unique in changing its policies to suit it own purposes. Turkish migrants found a welcome in Germany during the postwar decades when labor was in short supply, but began encountering less hospitable private and public environments during the economic slump that followed German reunification in 1990.

2.3 BEGINNING IN THE FIFTEENTH CENTURY, EUROPEAN states and trading companies began sending out seafaring expeditions of exploration and conquest all over the world. The first states to prosper from exploration, Spain and Portugal, became models for others, like England and Holland, that wanted to assert control over the world's riches. In only a few generations Spain conquered most of Central and South America, seized the great treasures of the Aztecs and other indigenous peoples, and subjected the inhabitants to near slavery in the gold and silver mines. Other European kingdoms were disappointed in their hope of finding treasures like those seized by the Spanish, nor did they ever find the fabled Northwest Passage, the open stretch of water that was supposed to provide direct access to China, Japan, and the other empires of the East. Instead, the explorers mapped vast lands rich in forests, water, animals, and minerals, and already inhabited by both settled and nomadic peoples.

With the passage of time and a growing knowledge of the conditions and possibilities of North America, it became apparent that the region's true wealth would never materialize

The waves of immigration to the United States have long been the focus of public attention, but the outgoing tide has been largely ignored. During the twentieth century, while an estimated 30 million immigrants entered the United States, about 10 million people left the country. Many of those who left were "birds of passage," workers seeking decent wages who shuttled back and forth between the old country and the United States many times. In recent years this pattern has been followed by Mexican migrant workers.

3.0	1900-19
2.2	1910-19
1.7	1920-19
0.6	1930-19
0.3	1940-19
0.4	1950-19
0.9	1960-19
1.2	1970-19

without a great influx of people to clear and farm the land, saw the timber, fish the rivers and lakes, and mine the rich mineral deposits. Finding enough human hands to create a *settled* country required a new approach —overseas colonization, which differed from trading voyages and wars of conquest in its methods, risks, and outcomes.

Colonization required a different kind of person than the explorer—someone willing to leave the familiar homeland yet prepared to invest a lifetime in creating a new place rather than looking for a pot of gold. Colonists did not expect to be paid in cash but hoped to recoup their investment through cheap land and their own labor, while the patrons who provided the initial funding for a colony expected much quicker returns on their investments and often complained about the slow pace of migration and economic development.

Of the various European nations that tried to colonize North America, the British had the most success, and their colonies began growing at a faster pace than the settlements of the French, Dutch, and others. British success came from a confluence of circumstances in the homeland (discussed below), including a large rise in the population and a consolidation of farm lands (the enclosure movement) that drove up the price of

land and decreased the amount of labor required per unit of land. Peasants driven from the land fell into poverty and drifted to the growing cities and towns. Many went to Channel ports such as Plymouth and Bristol where they signed contracts as indentured servants and boarded ship for the Americas; others traveled as the free servants of affluent countrymen (**Documents 3, 4, 5**).

Another cause of migration from Great Britain was religious tension between the Anglican church and various nonconforming groups like the Puritans and Quakers. The first Puritans to leave for the New World sailed for Virginia and landed in Massachusetts, where they decided to stay because it seemed as good a place as any to establish a religious commonwealth free of restrictions from the Anglican church and other state-sanctioned religious authorities. Their aim was not to maximize return on investment but to secure freedom of conscience, something that transcended financial and economic considerations (**Documents 16, 17**). William Penn's Quakers flocked to North America for basically the same quest of freedom; English Catholics emigrated to Maryland. In the process the British rid themselves of many religious dissenters, prisoners, and poor people who were perceived as potential troublemakers.

The Peopling of America Exhibit, the Ellis Island Museum source: Robert Warren and Ellen Percy Kraly, "The Elusive Exodus," Population Reference Bureau, 1985.

Period	Value
00-1910	8.2
10-1920	6.3
20-1930	4.3
30-1940	0.7
40-1950	0.9
50-1960	2.5
60-1970	3.2
70-1980	4.3

1624 Thirty Dutch and Walloon (Belgian) families arrive in New Amsterdam.

1638 First Swedes arrive in Delaware.

1686 First Germans arrive in Pennslyvania.

2.4

The Industrial Revolution

2.4 MORE THAN ANY OTHER CIRCUMSTANCE, THE Industrial Revolution set in motion the mass migrations to the Americas and other lands that mark world history since the middle of the nineteenth century. The Industrial Revolution began in Britain during the eighteenth century and spread to Europe and then to the Americas. New methods of production, which saw factories and large-scale agriculture replace artisans and small farms, along with major improvements in transportation and the organization of capital, expanded the desire and ability of people to move within countries and between them.

TRANSPORTATION AND MIGRATION

2.4.1 THE AMOUNT AND SAFETY OF TRANS-ATLANTIC travel improved only slightly until the early 1820s, when the advent of sailing packets operating on regular schedules marked a significant improvement in convenience and predictability. Major improvements in transatlantic travel were achieved by the 1870s when larger ships entered the trade and steam-powered vessels, which were the safest and fastest, far outnumbered sailing vessels. Within the United States, too, transportation was also undergoing major improvements, as the nation began a rapid demographic expansion west of the Appalachians, along rivers and lakes and on trails and tracks that served an ever-increasing level of traffic. Early in the nineteenth century, canals and the first toll roads helped large numbers of settlers move into areas that offered inexpensive farmland and abundant natural resources, while the success of Fulton's steamboat in 1807 speeded up water travel. Since mechanical power had only begun to enter the construction industry, the building of roads and canals required huge amounts of human and animal labor, providing thousands of jobs to immigrants and native-born alike.

The Sweatshop, Factory, and Shovel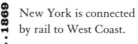

I went to work when I was about fourteen years old and at that time in this country there was a law that not until sixteen or seventeen, whatever the age was, you couldn't come into the shop.

So, when the inspector used to come in, the boss used to come and grab me by the neck and throw me into a bathroom and lock the door so he would never catch me.—Clara Larsen, Russia

1869 New York is connected by rail to West Coast.

1870 Kilometers of railroad track in service: Argentina 732, Brazil 745, Canada 4,211, U.S. 85,170.

Soon railroads revolutionized travel, especially for emigrants, who commonly reached their ports of embarkation in Europe by train and, once they arrived in the United States, took other trains to their final destinations. By the 1850s, New York City, the nation's largest port and its major immigrant entry point, had a rail link with New England via Albany; by 1869, it had rail connections with the West Coast. By the 1880s, federal land grants and private capital, along with the intelligence and labor of tens of thousands of immigrants from all over the world, from China to Norway, created the world's largest rail system. More than just a means of transport, railroads were also avenues of settlement and, like expressways today, became the axes around which people lived and worked. The construction of a railroad in a thinly inhabited region usually produced an influx of people and the creation of towns.

In 1942, the U.S. initiated the bracero *program importing Mexican contract laborers needed during World War II in agriculture. In 1954, Attorney General Herberty Brownell launched operation "wetback." Mass roundups and deportations of undocumented Mexicans occurred.*

AGRICULTURE AND MIGRATION

2.4.2 RELIABLE AND INEXPENSIVE TRAVEL CAME AT THE same time as a stream of surplus labor began flowing from Europe in the nineteenth century. This was no coincidence, for the technological sophistication that led to the invention and commercial use of steam-powered ships and then to railroads also transformed many other aspects of life, often in ways that encouraged people to migrate. The Industrial Revolution was an economic and social transformation that

And the coal mines are one of the worse places to work.
You say a prayer while your husband or your son goes to work
in the morning. You say another when he comes home at night.
—Elizabeth Nimmo, England

1870-1910

Population increases:
Austria-Hungary 46%
Denmark, Norway,
Sweden 38%

France 8%
Germany 59%
Ireland -20%
Portugal, Spain 27%

Russia 89%
U.K. (England), Wales
and Scotland 58%
U.S. 130%

Canada 75%
Argentina 300%
Brazil 210%

These photos from the INS Archives document Mexicans leaving their country, crossing U.S.-Mexico borders, and interacting with immigration officials.

INS PHOTO ARCHIVE

affected how people earned their livelihood, where they lived, and where they moved.

Historically in western Europe, most farms produced for local needs. By the early sixteenth century, however, the development of regular agricultural surpluses available for export, combined with improved transportation, produced a major change in the nature of farming. During the next three centuries, farm owners began regarding agriculture as a means of obtaining cash for the purchase of goods that were not necessarily made or grown locally. Since the new farming methods often worked best on a large scale, landowners began buying out small farmers, grew crops that were in high demand in cities and other markets, and cut labor costs by replacing human hands with machines. This combination of developments helped displace many peasants and farm workers from the land.

The growing number of displaced rural workers came at a time when the population of Great Britain and western Europe was increasing owing to a rising birth rate and a rapidly declining death rate. Great Britain experienced a quadrupling of population between 1801 and 1911. The populations of Russia and Austria-Hungary more than doubled between 1810 and 1900. Even countries that were not undergoing massive industrialization, like Ireland and Sweden, saw large population increases. Ireland's population doubled between 1780 and 1840, from four million to more than eight million inhabitants. The increasing population was absorbed by internal migration to cities, where industrialization was

creating new jobs, but by the early nineteenth century emigration began to other parts of the world (**Documents 18, 19**). Between 1814 and 1844, before the Great Potato Famine, about one million Irish migrated to the United States

INDUSTRIALIZATION AND SETTLEMENT PATTERNS

2.4.3 INDUSTRIAL JOBS AND WEALTH BROKE THE AGE-OLD bond between the laborer and land. Around the time of the Civil War, most Americans worked in agriculture; on the eve of World War I, only fifty years later, two-thirds of Americans worked in factories and other business settings. The first factories, which appeared early in the nineteenth century, were water-powered textile mills that drew many migrants and immigrants. In the United States the Northeast, a leader in fisheries and commerce during the colonial era, led the industrialization process. The first cotton mill was built early in the nineteenth century outside of Providence, Rhode Island; Massachusetts and New Hampshire quickly became centers for factories. The factory system created an industrial working class that labored in twelve- to fourteen-hour shifts, lived in cramped housing near the mills, and was likely to be laid off during periodic economic slowdowns. Sometimes the owners provided housing for workers, either to control their personal habits (such as excessive drinking) or, as in the case of factory operators in Waltham, Massachussetts, to attract young single women as mill workers (**Documents 20, 21**). Factory jobs for wages had a special significance for women,

Immigrants from the Iberian Penninsula populate the American West.

Joe Ubillas (bottom photo), a Basque sheepherder from the Basque region of Spain watching a Wyoming herd. Basque farmers were in the United States for three-year work periods to answer the Rocky Mountain Wyoming sheep farmers' demand for labor.

INS PHOTO ARCHIVE

Post-war immigrants travel to the U.S.

An INS watercraft on patrol.

INS PHOTO ARCHIVE

1860 Populations born abroad:
Boston 1/3, New York City 1/2, Chicago 1/2, St. Louis 1/2.

especially young and single women, who no longer had to depend on support from their fathers, brothers, or husbands. Historians have speculated that despite difficult working conditions or uncertain job tenure, women preferred the independence of factory wage labor to the supervision that came with domestic service. Changed family patterns also allowed a greater degree of female autonomy, expressed through the opportunity to choose a husband, greater authority over household income, more frequent practice of birth control, and increased education (**Document 22**).

From New England and the Middle Atlantic states, industrialization spread to the Midwest, which developed rapidly with the construction of canals and railroads. Midwestern industrialization emphasized heavy industry such as steel manufacture and industries related to commercial agriculture such as grain processing. The same combination of industry and agriculture appeared also on the West Coast a few decades later. Mass immigration from abroad provided many of the workers. Cities attracted thousands of unskilled immigrant laborers who soon formed ethnic neighborhoods, the destination points of chains of migrating laborers. New York City, Chicago, and San Francisco, for example, developed large Italian communities by the turn of the twentieth century; Chinatowns appeared first in San Francisco and, later, in Chicago and New York City. Immigrants usually traveled along routes picked for them by friends, relatives, labor agents, or other persons or organizations that had an interest in their arrival in the new land. The process of chain migration, for

Ethnic Groups in America 1990

"Where We Are": in 1990 the U.S. Census Bureau reported how Americans identify themselves ethnically. The four largest groups were English (50 million), German (49 million), Irish (40 million), and Afro-American (21 million). *The Peopling of America Exhibit*, the Ellis Island Museum.

At right are totals by state of people identified as American Indian.

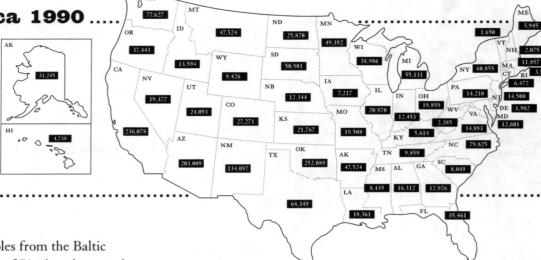

example, helped move thousands of Poles from the Baltic town of Gdansk to the Polish Hill area of Pittsburgh to work in the steel mills. Labor agents brought Greeks and other migrants to work on western railways and in the metals industry. Coal mines in Pennsylvania brought Hungarian miners over through labor contracts, which were legal until outlawed in 1885.

Railroads and real estate developers provided another kind of impetus to immigration, since untenanted land had little value to investors. Whole groups of Germans and Scandinavians were settled en masse in the Midwest by speculators who had bought vast tracts of prairie and forest. The railroad companies encouraged settlement of land around their tracks to increase the volume of economic activity, which improved the revenue of the company and the value of its landholdings. Many U.S. railroads advertised and recruited people in Europe for settlement along their tracks, another way in which business directly stimulated immigration.

Many parts of the United States still show the effects of the varying patterns of migration that marked the different regions of the country during the nineteenth century. From the colonial era through the early nineteenth century, the East Coast has been home to Europeans from the British Isles and northern and western Europe. The great turn-of-the-century migrations from eastern and southern Europe were also drawn to the East Coast and to the rapidly growing industrial areas of the Midwest, while Chinese and Japanese immigrants, entering through Pacific ports, heavily settled the

West Coast. Early in the twentieth century, Mexicans began to settle the Southwest; and today, as a result of recent migrations from Central and South America and the Caribbean, the Miami area contains more Spanish than English speakers. Many parts of the South maintain a predominantly Anglo-Saxon, Celtic, and African American mix, while the Great Plains, where there are few large towns and life revolves around agriculture and ranching, maintains a heavily native-born American population with ancestral roots in Great Britain and northern and western Europe. These historic patterns explain regional variations in the ethnic *flavor* of different parts of the United States (**Document 23**).

WORLDWIDE EFFECTS

2.4.4 POWERFUL EFFECTS OF INDUSTRIALIZATION reached even into lands that had little industry. Through the efforts of colonial powers, subjects found their business and economic opportunities controlled by others. Those industrializing nations that possessed overseas colonies often used government policy and financial controls to prevent or guide industrialization in the colonies, so as to avoid competition with firms in the home country. France ruled and developed its African colonies in such a way as to make them providers of raw materials and markets for French goods but not

Left and center: SOURCES OF IMMIGRATION, A three-dimensional chart, visible from all four sides, that shows the patterns of arrival of immigrants from seven major geographical areas since 1820 organized in 20-year increments. —*The Peopling of America Exhibit*, the Ellis Island Museum
METAFORM INC. AND CHERMAYEFF AND GEISMAR INC.

Right: IMMIGRATION SINCE 1820, chart shows year by year flow of immigration to the U.S. Photos above and text below describe important events directly and indirectly related to immigration during the time span depicted.

competitors with France. The Dutch did the same with their colonies in Indonesia, which at first supplied spices, tea, and coffee and, later, were sources of petroleum. Such limitations on local economies encouraged people to migrate abroad, especially to the center of the empire: Algerians to France, Javanese to the Netherlands, Nigerians to England. Even when industrial nations interacted with less industrialized regions outside of a colonial framework, the industrial nation could exert enormous influence through demands for materials and labor, as in the case of the United States during the nineteenth century, which attracted cheap labor through immigration. The United States still has great attraction for immigrants seeking work, but recently, a major shift has occurred, owing to the capabilities of modern communications and transportation technology. Increasingly today, instead of importing workers, major industrial nations are simply moving production to countries with the cheapest labor. In the Pacific basin since World War II, for example, Japan, then later Korea, and still later Southeast Asia became production centers for U.S. firms. (**Documents 24, 25**).

Immigrants from several countries awaiting inspection at Ellis Island.
ELLIS ISLAND LIBRARY ARCHIVES

Reactions to Mass Migration

2.5 RAPID GROWTH IN THE RATE OF IMMIGRATION BY the mid-nineteenth century raised concern among many native-born Americans that their interests might suffer from an excess number of newcomers (**Document 26**). In the mid-nineteenth century the arrival of hundreds of thousands of Irish dramatically announced the beginning of a new age of immigration and stirred up deep anxieties that were fueled by stereotypes of the newcomers as uneducated, lazy, inferior, and uncivilized. Some feared for the nation's Protestant heritage, which they saw threatened by a wave of Irish Catholic immigrants. Others worried that the influx of cheap labor would depress wages and pauperize American workers. Still others fretted over the presence of so many outsiders in a culture that had seemed reassuringly Anglo-Saxon in character. These attitudes toward immigration—many still with us today—warrant examination.

2.5

To me, it was like the House of Babel. Because there were so many languages and so many people and everybody huddled together. And it was so full of fear. It was pathetic.—Barbara Barondess, Russia, describing Ellis Island

1834 Burning of an Ursuline Convent in Charlestown, Mass. begins a series of violent anti-Irish incidents.

1863 New York Irish participate in draft riots, but the Northern Irish are overwhelmingly committed to the Union during the Civil War.

1873 "Honest John Kelly," New York's first Irish-born political boss, arrives on the scene.

2.5a *Cartoon Parody of Immigrants at Castle Garden, ca. 1889. The cartoon expresses American fears that the Irish and other newcomers would be politically subversive*—PUCK

1846-1854 The Irish potato famine causes thousands to migrate; the Irish contribute more than 1/4 of all immigrants to the U.S.

1855 The anti-Irish Know Nothing Party scores an electoral victory across New England.

THE IRISH INFLUX

2.5.1 LARGE-SCALE IRISH MIGRATION BEGAN AS THE RESULT of a famine in 1845 that left hundreds of thousands of people impoverished, undernourished, and susceptible to disease. The famine arose after decades of rule by British absentee landlords, military officers, and parliamentarians, who tried to strengthen their hold by eradicating Irish cultural identity and keeping the indigenous population uneducated and poor. Irish peasant families worked land they did not own and lived as subsistence farmers with little left over for rent and taxes. They relied on the potato, a crop cheap and easy to grow, as their main food. When the staple food crop was devastated by blight during the 1840s, famine ensued.

The Irish who migrated abroad during and after the potato famines had little money, few skills, and except for their ability to speak English, a background ill-suited to urban life. Nevertheless, those who came to the United States usually congregated in cities like Boston and New York, where they could find enough manual labor to support themselves and even establish households. Some of the men worked building railroads and lived in labor barracks; others became laborers on construction jobs, longshoremen, or laborers in stables and slaughterhouses. The women usually sought domestic work or worked on their own as laundresses or washerwomen; some became prostitutes. A small portion of the immigrants established themselves as entrepreneurs—shopkeepers, saloon owners, peddlers—catering mainly to their fellow immigrants. In many U.S. towns, the Irish used their voting clout to enter local government and city services such as the police. The political machine of New York's infamous mayor William Tweed rested in part on the political patronage of Irish Americans who, by the 1860s, were an important part of the city's population. As recently as the 1970s, Chicago's Democratic Party organization drew heavily on Irish Americans.

The Irish newcomers, whether self-employed, poorly employed, or unemployed, shared in the stigma of inferiority attached to them by most native-born Americans during the middle decades of the century. Newspapers and magazines portrayed them as primitive, apelike creatures, members of an immoral, rum-swilling race beyond the reach of civilization. Heavily Irish New York neighborhoods like Hell's Kitchen came to stand for the worst in American urban life. Newspaper stories sensationalized the ugliest aspects of daily life in the Irish slums. Murders that occurred frequently at certain notorious hangouts intensified public fears about the growing community of newcomers.

Religious differences increased the animosity against the Irish who were accused of placing their allegiance to the Pope before the ideals of American citizenship. Most native-born Americans, including those of northern Irish descent, were of Protestant stock; the new Irish immigrants were Catholic. In the nineteenth century, many Protestants thought of the Pope as a worldly prince who ruled vast landholdings in Italy, and his followers as subjects of an alien government.

1871-1914

Italy's population increases from 28 to 35 million. 14 million leave Italy:
44% to other European countries
30% to North America (U.S. 29%, Canada, 1%)
24% to South America (Argentina 13%, Brazil 9%).

1870-1914

Argentina's population rises from 1.7 million to 7.9 million.

EXAMPLE: COMPARISON WITH THE ITALIAN MIGRATION – THE U.S.A. COMPARED TO ARGENTINA

2.5.2 RELIGIOUS ANIMOSITY AND RACIAL STEREOTYPING also affected the Italians. In the case of Italians, however, we can more easily isolate the role of prejudice because we have a *control* group in the large Italian migration to Argentina, which began in the 1870s, somewhat earlier than the flow to the United States, and remained strong until about 1900 (**Document 27**). To put the matter simply, if the migrant Italians were, in fact, as undesirable as some native-born Americans thought, we would expect them to have fared poorly in both Argentina and the United States.

The great wave of Italian migration to the United States began during the 1880s, only a few years after the nation of Italy was created out of the welter of cities, principalities, and small states of the Italian peninsula and Sicily. Unification dissolved ancient borders and enabled many residents of Italy's poor, agricultural south to find work in the cities and factories of Italy's north. But internal migration provided for only a portion of the rural southerners who sought better opportunities. Large numbers of young Italians from the south and even from the industrial north began emigrating to other countries, especially the United States and Argentina. They settled primarily in the major port cities, New York and Buenos Aires. Three hundred and seventy thousand Italian immigrants lived in New York City and 312,000 in Buenos Aires by 1914.

The newcomers fared differently in New York and in Buenos Aires partly because the cities differed in their economic development and culture and partly because of cultural differences between immigrants to the two places. In the United States, which possessed a full array of highly developed industries and businesses, the main demand was for unskilled and casual labor, especially factory workers and construction workers. Italians in New York often worked as masons and stonecutters, grocers and peddlers, and in heavy construction or on the docks. Some took jobs in railroad construction, which brought them into the small towns of the Hudson River valley and the central portion of New York State.

Sharp differences in dialect, culture, educational level, and economic background marked the peoples of Italy, but such nuances were lost on most North Americans, whose views were based on contact with southern Italians and Sicilians. Although southern Italians were a numerical majority of the immigrants to both the United States and Argentina—80 percent of those in the United States and 55 percent of those in Argentina—the greater proportion of southern Italians in the New York migration meant a slightly lower level of overall education, since the Italian south was the poorer, less developed region. Since many Italian immigrants arrived with little education and a tradition that each family should

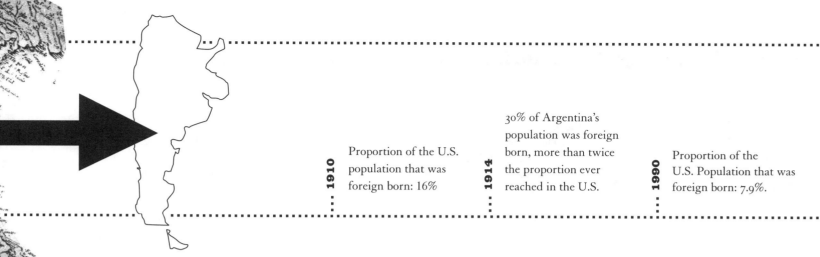

1910 Proportion of the U.S. population that was foreign born: 16%

1914 30% of Argentina's population was foreign born, more than twice the proportion ever reached in the U.S.

1990 Proportion of the U.S. Population that was foreign born: 7.9%.

take care of its own members without intervention by the legal and judicial systems, they often appeared to native-born Americans and other ethnic migrants as uncouth, unruly, and even dangerous. Like the Irish, the Italians were subjected to stereotyping as, for example, when members were accused of being members of criminal gangs like the Mafia. More of the Italians in New York were single men, who would return to Italy to marry and settle down, compared with Argentina, where a larger proportion of immigrants consisted of families who saw their new homes as permanent. For their part, immigrants found comfort and a sense of security by settling in enclaves, which served the same social, economic, and psychological functions as the enclaves of other ethnic groups, such as the Chinese and the Jews. A shared culture and language reinforced the belief that only through mutual support could immigrants protect themselves against a hostile society.

The Italians in Buenos Aires were far more successful in obtaining good jobs and housing and in achieving social mobility, owing mainly to the more receptive local economy and culture. The process of industrializing began somewhat later in Argentina than in the United States, which enabled the newcomers to find more of the unskilled jobs that they could perform without additional education or training. Moreover, in contrast to the situation in New York City, during the years of peak Italian immigration Argentina's small middle class was in the process of formation and open to newcomers, including immigrant Italians. Italian migrants to Argentina enjoyed a linguistic and cultural affinity with the receiving country, since many elite Argentines considered Italian immigrants bearers of European culture, fellow Latins in the "campaign" to "civilize" the interior with its Native American and *gaucho* (cowboy) population. Italians and Argentines shared a Catholic religious heritage, and therefore, religious discrimination was not an issue as it was in the largely Protestant United States. Moreover, the Argentinean Italians also benefited from the large size of their influx, since they were one of only two large immigrant groups (the other being the Spanish) to Argentina during the forty years before World War I, whereas in the United States they were only one group among many.

From this sketch of the Italians in New York City and Buenos Aires, based upon publications of Professor Sam Baily of Rutgers University, we can see that conditions in the receiving country were at least as important as the characteristics of the immigrants in determining socioeconomic success.

1720 Massachusetts colony passes a law to discourage Irish immigration.

1850 Australians known as the "Sydney Ducks," who came to the U.S. for the gold rush are blamed for introducing organized crime into the U.S.

1850 The first Polish language newspaper, *Echo Zpolski* (the Polish Echo), is founded.

1886 An attempt to drive Chinese out of Seattle results in a riot and the declaration of Martial Law.

2.6

The Italian immigrants tended to fare best in the country that was most friendly to their religion and culture and that valued their skills in agriculture. Though we in the United States rightly claim that Italian immigrants have done well here, our nation was not necessarily the best choice facing a young Italian man or woman at the turn of the century, at least not in the social and economic conditions that prevailed at that time.

A Range of Views about Immigration

2.6 THE HOSTILITY THAT OFTEN greeted newcomers to the United States, including not just the Italians and Irish but even many Germans and eastern Europeans, grew out of rising anxiety about large-scale immigration, which began to influence U.S. politics by the middle of the nineteenth century. The first strong nativist response was the appearance of the Know-Nothing movement, begun in the 1850s as a reaction to the mounting influx of Irish. The Know-Nothing party took its name from the oaths of secrecy sworn by members of nativist lodges. During its few years of prominence, when it rivaled the Democratic party, the Know-Nothing

2.5 *Cartoon Parody of U.S. Exclusion of Chinese Immigrants, 1882. This drawing from a popular magazine lampoons anti-Chinese attitudes by showing that they are the product of a double standard of admission criteria.*
—FRANK LESLIE'S ILLUSTRATED NEWSPAPER
APRIL 1, 1882

party won a few major political victories by making Catholic immigrants scapegoats for many issues of general concern, including the rapid growth of cities and their perceived social disorder, labor discontent, antislavery reform, and concerns about personal indulgence and immorality. By placing the onus on newcomers, the Know-Nothings removed some of the responsibility from native-born Americans for the problems they saw around them. The Know-Nothings helped crystallize the perception that the nation consisted of both insiders and outsiders, two groups that had somewhat different interests.

The insiders saw themselves increasingly as custodians of a brilliant, independent, largely Protestant culture that was being threatened by the influx of thousands of Catholic and foreign-tongued immigrants. Immigrants generally were unable to mount an effective defense in the public eye, since their foreignness isolated them from the media and public figures, the shapers of public opinion.

The Know-Nothing party was too much a one-issue movement to last very long, even if the Civil War had not preempted its audience. Nevertheless, the immigrant issue survived the war and flourished during the closing decades of the nineteenth century. Anti-immigrant

No Irish Need Apply

—a sign often seen in nineteenth-century America
outside businesses and workplaces.

1892 The first Arabic language newspaper is founded in New York.

1894 *Atlantis*, one of the first Greek language newspapers, is founded in New York.

1907 An anti-Hindu riot occurs in Bellingham, Washington.

1934 The first mosque in the U.S. is constructed in Cedar Rapids, Iowa

feeling waxed and waned thereafter, as Americans of succeeding generations came to grips with the continual arrival of new peoples from every part of the world (**Document 28**). A virulent anti-immigrant crusade led to the federal Chinese Exclusion Act of 1882 and culminated with the National Origins Act of 1924, which tried to preserve the nation's white Protestant profile by favoring the entry of northern and western Europeans.

While the Know-Nothings and their spiritual and political heirs deplored the tide of immigrants, the owners and managers of the nation's businesses welcomed immigration as a source of inexpensive labor. Some plant operators used recent immigrant workers as informal recruiting agents who could persuade friends and relatives in the sending country to migrate and come to work in their shops. Whether initiated by factory operators or spontaneous, this kind of chain migration appeared wherever immigrant workers found good wages and steady work. The constant influx of cheap labor that so pleased many businessmen worried many native-born working men, who feared that the huge supply of low-wage newcomers would depress everyone's earnings and create unemployment (**Document 29**). The labor movement of the late nineteenth century was especially torn by the immigrant issue because, depending on how the situation was viewed, unionists could regard migrant workers as either a threat or a pool of potential union members. The emergence of well-organized labor unions late in the nineteenth century brought the immigration issue into sharper focus by providing a

national leadership that could enunciate policy and attempt to carry it out. Some unions, such as the Knights of Labor and the American Federation of Labor, formally opposed large-scale immigration as a threat to good wages and full employment. A united stand by organized labor was impossible, however, because of ethnic and racial differences among workers. Many immigrants of long residence, who had become skilled workers and craftsmen, shared the union's hostility toward more recent immigrants.

Feelings against immigration ran strongest when reinforced by racial differences, as, for example, in the case of immigrants from China and Japan during the late nineteenth century (**Document 30**). At a time when Americans regarded the dominant, Christian religion as synonymous with civilization, most Chinese, Japanese, and other Asians were non-Christian and therefore "uncivilized." The Chinese also labored under the burden of coming from a nation that was experiencing a long period of governmental weakness in both internal and foreign affairs. During the first half of the nineteenth century British, and European traders and merchants, supported by diplomatic and military muscle, began gaining control of important aspects of China's commercial life and gradually carved out zones of influence where the Emperor in Peking had little say. The inability of the Chinese to stop this European penetration, which accelerated during the second half of the century, caused most Westerners to have a very low opinion of China as a nation and a culture. Paradoxically, however, many native-born Americans also attributed to

1840s Cincinnati, Cleveland, Boston, and Indianapolis develop bilingual German American public education.

1893 Congress authorizes withholding federal support from American Indian families who refuse to send their children to special schools for Indians.

1930 Enraged by an engagement between a Filipino and a white, 400 white men attack a Filipino dance hall in Watsonville, California and four days of rioting ensue.

1942 Alien Italians in the U.S. no longer designated with enemy-alien status; only 228 alien Italians are interned. 500,000 Italian Americans will serve in the armed forces.

Asians mysterious powers that derived from their exotic philosophies and religions, and they even demonized Asia through the image of the Yellow Peril, the wave of people that might swamp the West if not contained (**Document 31**). Beneath the ominous images lay some simpler realities, such as the fact that Asians were racially different from the dominant U.S. culture, and that many workers feared the competition of cheap labor. Congress banned the immigration of Chinese laborers with passage of the Exclusion Act of 1882, which made Chinese aliens ineligible for citizenship (**Documents 32, 33**). It forbade the entry of Chinese laborers—but not others—for ten years, a ban renewed in laws of 1892 and 1902 and made permanent in 1904. A series of exclusion acts prohibited Chinese entry until 1943, at the height of World War II when Nationalist China was an ally of the United States.

Despite the legally sanctioned discrimination, many Americans were willing to accept Chinese immigrants if they seemed to measure up to American standards. A good example of this attitude was published by a newspaper in the medium-sized town of Albany, N.Y., in 1903, in an editorial criticizing a perceived misapplication of the federal laws against the importation of contract labor:

A few days ago the immigration authorities in New York refused to admit to this country an educated Greek, the representative of a prominent business house in his country, holding that, as he was under salary, he came under the provision of a law that prohibits the admission of aliens who are under contract to give their services when they arrive on these shores.

Now San Francisco presents an analogous case. At that port the wife of an educated Chinaman has been detained, virtually as a prisoner, because under a technical interpretation of a clause of the Chinese Exclusion Act she has been held ineligible to admission to the United States on the ground that she is the wife of a laborer. Her husband is Loo Lin Ben, a progressive, educated, and cultured Chinaman, thoroughly Americanized in most respects, a convert to Christianity, and the senior member of a firm that deals in general merchandise. But he also has an interest in a restaurant, and, for a reason that is not at all clear, the owner of the restaurant is classified as a laborer. Therefore, Loo Lin Ben is a laborer, and as under the law, the wife

1905-07 Japanese resist a San Francisco School Board requirement that Asian children attend separate schools.

1910 More than 25% of foreign-born Americans over the age of ten can speak no English.

1922 Harvard University institutes new admissions criteria including photos to deal with increasing Jewish enrollment.

of a Chinese laborer may not enter the country, Mrs. Loo Lin Ben is detained at San Francisco and prevented from joining her husband.

Her husband says she is well educated and progressive, has been a teacher in Canton and has edited a newspaper devoted to the interests of Chinese women. Moreover, arrangements have been made to have her give instruction to some of the children of New York's Chinatown who do not understand the English language. But all these facts are naught against the legal status of her husband.

Loo Lin Ben has appealed to President Roosevelt and is hopeful that the red tape which is keeping his wife from him will be cut.

Again, it is in order to remark, as it was in regard to the case of the Greek who was barred out, that the framers of the immigration laws never intended that any but undesirable persons be excluded. And it is the intent of the law that is to be considered.

SOURCE: *"More Immigration Red Tape," Albany Evening Journal,* May 26, 1903, p. 4.

The editorial writer found that the Greek man and the Chinese couple met the major criteria expected of respectable people in the United States: education, Christianity, and personal ambition. Instead of treating Loo Lin Ben as an "Oriental," that is, as a racial stereotype, he made him into a real person by describing his merits: "a progressive, educated and cultured Chinaman, thoroughly Americanized in most respects," even "a convert to Christianity." Furthermore, Loo Lin Ben was a successful entrepreneur, able to compete in the world of business. The writer described Loo Lin Ben's wife in terms nearly as favorable: "well educated and progressive," "devoted to the interests of Chinese women," and skilled in English, America's language. Through this process of personalizing Loo Lin Ben and his wife, the writer transformed them from stereotypes into unique individuals of great accomplishment and merit. They were worthy of admission to this great nation, this promised land, because they had the qualities that Americans most admired. Those who did not measure up, in the minds of many Progressive-Era Americans, should not be admitted; and those already living in the United States who did not measure up, including many African Americans, Native Americans, and white ethnics, needed to be brought up to the higher standard before they could contribute properly to the national culture. Until they attained that higher level, they were regarded as fair game for exclusion or economic exploitation.

Today, as a century ago, immigration remains a contentious issue, as Americans again debate the merits and values

1947 A U.S. Court of Appeals declared that the segregation of Spanish-speaking children violated California law.

1954 *Brown v. Board of Education of Topeka*—the Supreme Court rules that the doctrine of "separate but equal" has no place "in the field of public education."

1968 The Bilingual Education Act calls for "forward-looking" instruction for "the special educational needs" of children without English-speaking ability.

1978 *Bakke v. University of California*—resentful whites complain of "reverse discrimination"; the Supreme Court outlaws quotas but upholds the principle of affirmative action.

of admitting large numbers of newcomers. Many argue, as people did a century ago, that newcomers deprive longtime residents of jobs and challenge the preeminence of Anglo-Saxon traditions of language, law, family, hard work, and rugged individualism. This new anti-immigrant feeling also attacks state welfare support of illegal aliens and it questions the use of tax money to support education and health care for illegal aliens and even for legal ones. Other Americans argue that immigrants, both legal and illegal, are only one cause for declining wages and job opportunities. Foreign competition, felt through the importation of goods and the exporting of jobs, they maintain, significantly affect wages and the number of jobs in the United States. Other observers point out that many of the immigrants now entering the country are likely to help the nation return to its traditional emphasis on family values, hard work, and individual responsibility.

3

Ellis Island and After

Overview

3.1 **PART 3** describes the Ellis Island processing experience during the station's busiest years, within the context of U.S. immigration policy and the values that shape it. As an orientation for visitors to the Ellis Island museum, Part 3 focuses on the island's busiest years, from the 1890s to the early 1920s, and then describes how the subsequent period reflected major changes in U.S. immigration policy. The conclusion discusses the island's diminishing importance as a processing facility and describes some important aspects of migration and immigration today.

This portion of the book leads the reader on a walking tour through the spaces and rooms of the museum; the authors inform us how these spaces were used and what a prospective immigrant would have encountered upon arriving at the Island

TIMELINE

1790 A 1790 law provides that only "white" persons could become citizens.

1820 Number of legal immigrants admitted, 8,385.

3.2 Immigration Law

3.2 THE UNITED STATES HAD NO FEDERAL laws about immigration, with one exception, until the 1870s. The exception was the Alien Act of 1798, one of several laws that Congress passed mainly out of a short-lived anxiety that political radicals from the French Revolution might stir up trouble in the new United States. The act dealt with requirements for residency and deportation, not specifically with immigration, and was allowed to expire after one of its major opponents, Thomas Jefferson, became president in 1801.

During the next 80 years, the states, not the federal government, supervised immigration—when they bothered to do so at all. As a general matter no one really cared how many newcomers came to the United States, since there was plenty of land and work for everyone, and only states or towns that received the greatest share of the flow attempted any oversight. Some European immigrants landed in Boston, Baltimore, or Philadelphia; others passed through ports on the Gulf of Mexico. Most Asian newcomers entered on the West Coast, especially Los Angeles, San Francisco, and Seattle, while migrants from Canada and Mexico generally traveled by land.

Two-thirds of migrants to the United States from 1786 until the opening of Ellis Island in 1892 came through New York City.

New York City, as the nation's largest city and greatest port, was the main entry point for Europeans, who constituted the majority of immigrants to the United States until early in the twentieth century. The city made the nation's first attempt to systematize the arrival of immigrants in 1824, when the legislature in Albany passed a law, upheld by the U.S. Supreme Court in 1837, that required ship's masters to provide state agents with manifests that listed each passenger's name, birthdate, occupation, and physical condition. State law (later declared unconstitutional by the U.S. Supreme Court) also required a head tax on every passenger ($1.50 for cabin, $1.00 for steerage), to finance a hospital that served travelers. To give the ship's operators an incentive for carrying only "desirable" kinds of immigrants, they were required to post a bond for immigrants whose character or financial condition suggested they might become criminals or wards of the state. Neither New York nor U.S. authorities required immigrants to have any other kind of entry documents — no passport or visa.

Stereocard of Castle Garden.—UNDERWOOD AND UNDERWOOD

Castle Garden and Liberty Statue, New York City. U. S. A.

New York City took the lead again in 1855, when it established a formal immigrant landing and processing station in lower Manhattan at Castle Clinton, originally a military installation and later a theater, located on the waterfront. Henceforth, all immigrants who entered the port had to pass through this state-operated station, renamed Castle Garden, where they received a brief medical examination, passed through customs, and finally had their name registered as having entered the country.

New York City also assumed responsibility for helping some newcomers find work and housing, an effort aimed at protecting new arrivals from falling into the clutches of thieves, con artists, and dock sharks who found them easy pickings. Men claiming to be agents of employers would promise a job and lodging for a cash deposit, and then disappear. Worse were the pimps, who found some of their prostitutes among the naive or desperately poor young women arrivals as they walked out of the dock area. Benevolent efforts by the state, which many citizens supported as a way of reducing immorality and inhumane treatment, also served the interests of local employers, boardinghouse operators, and other business people who had good connections at Castle Garden. Succeeding years showed that the intentions of the

reforms were difficult to carry out in the face of indifferent or venal state employees and a constantly rising number of immigrants. Similar local efforts to oversee immigration appeared at other ports that served significant numbers of immigrants, such as Boston, Baltimore, Galveston, and San Francisco, to name only the largest.

3.2a *Cartoon Parody of Castle Garden "Emigrant-Catchers," ca. 1870. Reformers hoped that the new processing center at Ellis Island, surrounded by water, would enable immigrants to avoid the kinds of scoundrels and con-artists found on Manhattan*— PUCK

The immigration officer sat on a podium like a judge. **Ellis Island: Promised Land**
And to a child looking up, you know, it looked like he was up in the sky.
—Alex Eckstein, Hungary

1907 Number of legal immigrants
admitted: 1,285,349.

The failure of the states to resolve the problems that continued to plague the entry of immigrants brought calls for change. In 1876, a ruling of the U. S. Supreme Court that declared unconstitutional all state laws on immigration led to federal control of immigration. The Supreme Court decision came after nearly two decades when the nation had undergone a major transformation in outlook, resulting both from the Civil War, which strengthened the authority of the central government, and from rapid industrialization and urbanization. A truly national economy, national culture, and national transportation system were emerging, just when the states had come to accept the need for an expanded central government. Immigration, as an issue of growing national discussion, inevitably felt the hand of the national government; it became a matter of national policy, controlled by federal law and enforced by federal officials.

Once the principle of federal jurisdiction was acknowledged, Congress passed laws during the 1880s and 1890s that systematized immigration according to current values and prejudices. When the labor movement complained about the practice of contract labor, which it saw as a threat to good wages, Congress responded in 1885 with legislation outlawing the practice. Again, during the 1890s, as the nation was becoming more sensitive to issues of public health and hygiene, laws excluded immigrants who had "loathsome or dangerous diseases." The Immigration Act of 1891 created the office of Superintendent of Immigration within the Department of the Treasury and required all entering aliens to answer questions about their place of origin, destination, and health. Those traveling in third class (steerage) had to report to federal immigration offices before landing in the United States. In San Francisco, the Immigration Service established the Angel Island (1904) receiving station and in New York City, the Ellis Island station (1892). At these and other federal immigrant processing stations in several American cities including Charlestown, Philadelphia, and Boston, the object would be to apply immigration laws to aliens entering the United States. Immigrants underwent medical examination by United States physicians to determine their mental and physical condition. Immigration Service inspectors determined if they were otherwise acceptable for admission under current immigration laws.

3.2b *Interior Rotunda, Castle Garden*
—FRANK LESLIE'S ILLUSTRATED NEWSPAPER, NOV. 28, 1878

or Promised Anguish? ....

1868 The Fourteenth Amendment is adopted and declares that "all persons born or naturalized in the U.S. and subject to the jurisdiction thereof" are citizens. American Indians are excluded.

INS PHOTO ARCHIVE

The Ellis Island Station

3.3 ABOUT THREE-FOURTHS OF THE MIGRANTS WHO entered the United States between 1892 and 1924 went through the Ellis Island immigration station, which was built on a small island in New York Harbor that had once been the site of a powder magazine. Originally, federal immigration authorities thought of siting the facility on Bedloe's (now Liberty) Island, where the Statue of Liberty had just been erected, but many native-born Americans thought the symbol of liberty might be tainted by the daily passage of thousands of Europe's unwashed masses, and public opposition, led by the New York *World* newspaper (which had helped lead the campaign to erect the statue) caused the government to look elsewhere. Ellis Island's processing buildings opened on January 1, 1892, but after a major fire in 1897, were replaced with the brick structures we see today.

The experience of passing through Ellis Island frequently left a deep impression that did not fade with time. The twelve million who went through processing there produced tens of millions of children and grandchildren who heard stories about the trip from the Old Country and the anxious hours spent during the inspection on Ellis Island. These stories and recollections, some incorporated into the exhibits of the Ellis Island Museum, have preserved the island as a part of the American memory. Certain images are especially moving. Many immigrants recall the moment when their ship entered New York Harbor and they sighted the Statue of Liberty with its arm extended as if in welcome. The connection between the statue and Ellis Island is preserved today in their joint administrative status in the National Park Service as the Statue of Liberty/Ellis Island National Monument. Other immigrants have more ominous memories—of the island as a place of trial and judgment, where government officials decided who would enter the promised land and who would be turned away. Although only about 2 percent of Ellis Island migrants failed to gain entry to the United States, stories about families having to split up when one member was turned back add to the dark recollections of the island's past. But what did the immigration authorities themselves see as the true purpose and nature of the facility during its peak years?

3.3a *Ellis Island, Main Building, (above) (left) Statue of Liberty* INS PHOTO ARCHIVE

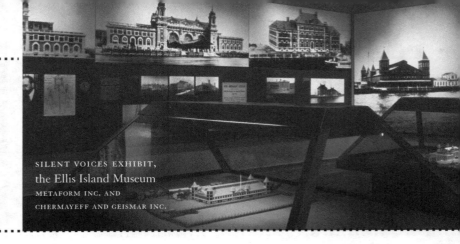

You put an end, forget about your childhood and became a man here, all of a sudden and start life new, amongst people whose language I didn't understand. Different life, everything was different. But I never despaired. I was optimistic.
—Lazarus Salamon, Hungary

1906 The Bureau of Immigration and Naturalization is established.

1907 Expatriation Act states that any woman who marries an alien looses her citizenship.

SILENT VOICES EXHIBIT,
the Ellis Island Museum
METAFORM INC. AND
CHERMAYEFF AND GEISMAR INC.

3.4 Progressive Ideals and Attitudes

3.4 THE IMMIGRATION POLICIES PRACTICES AT ELLIS island grew out of the progressive ideas of the time, which saw government as having important, legitimate interests in protecting society against certain evils and abuses. The Progressive Era, conventionally placed in the 1890s through the 1920s—precisely the period of Ellis Island's heyday—saw the creation of state, federal, and local legislation and administrative bodies to regulate a wide variety of human activities, including public hygiene, the length of the workday, the purity of foods, the creation of public parks and forests and, of course, immigration, to name only a few. Progressive reformers redefined philanthropy by

shifting the emphasis from private and church-based charity intended to ameliorate suffering to government-based or government-sponsored action intended to improve society. Reformers like Jane Addams, of Chicago's Hull House settlement, and Lillian Wald, who developed a visiting nurse program in New York City, augmented traditional charity with a network of voluntary social service agencies that addressed the growing problems of city and industrial life, problems that touched many immigrants. The Progressive ideals of administrative efficiency and concern for the public good began to color all aspects of government, including those relating to the immigration question, such as concerns about child labor, which led to passage of a federal law in 1907 that forbade entry of children under age sixteen unaccompanied by a parent.

Ellis Island, Main Building, ca. 1910

I grew up around Hull House, one of the oldest sections of the city.
In those early days I wore blinders. I wasn't hurt by anything very much.
When you become involved, you begin to feel the hurt, the anger.
You begin to think of people like Jane Addams and Jessie Binford and you realize
why they were able to live on. They understood how weak we really are
and how we could strive for something better if we understood the way.
—Florence Scala

1913 California law prohibits ownership of land by aliens ineligible for citizenship. The majority of Asians will be excluded from ownership.

The Immigration Service at Ellis Island expressed the Progressive idea of using institutions to address social issues. The facility's federal sponsorship, its bureaucratic methods, including the use of public medicine and the presence of social work aides, and its efforts to correct abuses like the prostitution trade and contract labor—all these embodied the noblest sentiments of the time. Reformers regarded its location in New York Harbor, inaccessible to labor recruiters, pimps, con artists, and others, as a protection for newcomers. But it was also a protection for the nation, and every day, as the facility processed its average of five to ten thousand immigrants, it refused entry to some whom Progressive standards considered undesirable (**Document 34**). In 1903, William Williams, the Ellis Island commisioner, who brought about many reforms to protect the immigrants, observed that immigrants had no inherent right to enter the United States, and that the government therefore had the right to reject those whose presence might lower living and cultural standards. For Williams and many of his contemporaries, the adulteration of the nation's population, like the adulteration of its milk or its medicine, was a legitimate concern of government. Good character, many Americans believed, was racially determined. Immigration restrictionists thought that good character was inherent in the resident Anglo-Saxon Protestant population but uncommon among certain resident groups, such as Native Americans and African Americans, and among the new immigrant groups from Asia, southern and eastern Europe, and the Caribbean.

Ellis Island early 1900s—ELLIS ISLAND MUSEUM LIBRARY

Ellis Island ferries, early 1900s—ELLIS ISLAND MUSEUM LIBRARY

I've heard stories of the roughness [of the inspectors]…the roughness consisted of somebody who did not make it. That was tough. That was worse than killing them. But we had to be honest enough. We had to go by the law…the ordeal they went through was not with the inspectors. It was with the doctors. —Jacob Auerbach, Immigration Inspector and staff positions at Ellis Island (1930-42).

1917 Congress confers American citizenship on "citizens of Puerto Rico."

1920 Attorney General A. Mitchell Palmer deports 600 aliens during the Red Scare.

1922 U.S. Supreme Court rules that Takao Ozawa, a Japanese immigrant, was not eligible for citizenship because he was not Caucasian.

Immigration station staff applied various tests to screen out the sick, convicts, political dissidents, and persons likely to require public assistance. The authorities believed the screening process should rest on the application of impartial judgment based on the facts, even if immigration authorities shared the prejudices of restrictionists, they did not think their prejudices determined inspection outcomes.

The Progressive Era saw the emergence of the expert as a key person in the reform process. The experts at Ellis Island included the commissioner of immigration, the inspectors and board of special inquiry members, and the medical doctors, assisted by an array of paid federal personnel, immigrant aid society staff, social workers, and interpreters. The system of experts and bureaucrats was supposed to operate honestly and fairly, even for the poorest or least qualified immigrant. When it became evident that abuses were occurring at Ellis Island, President Theodore Roosevelt, who prided himself on being a reformer, appointed William Williams as commissioner of immigration on the island in 1902 and charged him with cleaning up the mess. Williams completed the professionalization of the staff. He introduced the then new Civil Service system to Ellis Island to replace the old system under which jobs were given out in return for personal and political favors, and he established the principle that increases

Medical Examination at Ellis Island, early 1900s
—ELLIS ISLAND MUSEUM LIBRARY ARCHIVES

Inspection cards carried by immigrants going through processing at Ellis Island.—ELLIS ISLAND MUSEUM

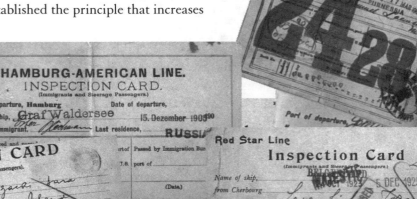

1922 The Cable Act states that a woman who had married an alien and so lost her citizenship could regain it unless she had married an Asian.

1923 In *U.S. v. Bhagat Singh*, the Supreme Court rules that Asian Indians are ineligible for citizenship because while they were Caucasian, they were not white.

1924 American Indians are recognized as U.S. citizens.

1927 Marcus Garvey, a Jamaican immigrant and leader of the United Negro Improvement Association, is deported.

1943 Chinese are granted naturalization rights.

in wages and job status would come from merit instead of favoritism. His goal was to make the system work efficiently, impartially, and fairly, according to federal law, and not necessarily to make it work compassionately.

Williams offered all immigrants equality of opportunity in passing through the inspection process, and willingly accepted the fact that some would be turned away and might suffer terribly as a result. Later commissioners were not as relentless as Williams but they preserved the goal of aiming at efficiency and impartiality above all. That attitude was perhaps easier to adopt for the higher-ups than for the staff who dealt with the immigrants every day.

Fiorello La Guardia, an interpreter at Ellis Island for several years immediately after the Williams tenure, observed many instances where the impartial application of the law seemed to cause much personal anguish. As he wrote in his autobiography, the rigorous enforcement of the immigration laws led to "many heartbreaking scenes," and during his three years on Ellis Island, he never became indifferent to "the mental anguish, the disappointment, and despair . . . [he] witnessed almost daily." La Guardia's pay seemed less important than the good he was doing, "the realization that a large percentage of the people pouring into Ellis Island would probably make good and enjoy a better life than they had been accustomed to where they came from."

Women from Guadalupe, 1911
—ELLIS ISLAND MUSEUM LIBRARY ARCHIVES

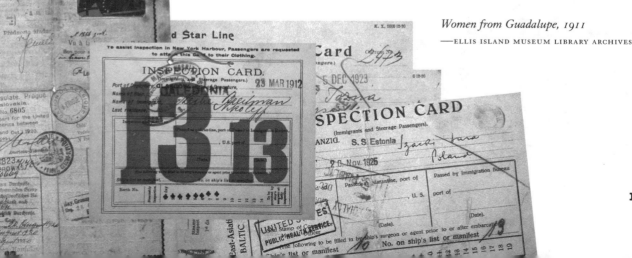

See there's the funny thing they did, you know. You have to have twenty-five dollars.
On the day before, the officer come around the ship. Who hasn't got the twenty-five dollars?
Well, some of them put up their hands. All right, we give you the twenty-five dollars.
They didn't just want to send anybody back, so they gave you—Just before you got ready to go out,
they gave you the twenty-five dollars. And when you got by the guy, they and another guy
pick up the twenty-five dollars. So you still landed with nothing, see?
—Ernest Becker, Germany

1946 Asian Indians are granted naturalization rights.

A Walk Through Ellis Island

3.5

3.5 THE IMMIGRANTS AT ELLIS ISLAND HAD ALREADY made the longest and most difficult part of the trip to the new land. They had decided to leave their familiar world and travel to a new one; they had gathered what information they could about conditions, travel costs, opportunities, and people to meet; and they had paid for transportation to a major port that offered scheduled service to the United States. Finally, they spent ten days to three weeks traveling in the uncomfortable steerage class across the sea. Ship tickets were usually the largest single cash expense of their journey, although rail passage in the United States, which could be purchased in advance, might also be substantial if they were traveling far.

The carriage of immigrants was a big business for the shipping industry which could count on filling the space taken by the cotton, wood, and crop cargoes they had brought to Europe with a different kind of return shipment—people traveling steerage class to the United States. Immigrants, then, were a form of cargo, and as such they were placed along with other internationally transported goods under the supervision of the Treasury Department. In 1903, immigration came under the direction of the newly created Department of Commerce and Labor, an appropriate recognition of the significance of immigrant labor to the American economy. Not until 1940 did the Department of Justice begin to oversee immigration, and it remains under its jurisdiction today.

Between the Decks in an Emigrant Ship— Feeding Time
—THE GRAPHIC, NOV. 30, 1872.

Ellis Island Ferries, ca. early 1900s

When we got to Ellis Island, they put the gangplank down.
And there was a man at the foot. And he was shouting at the top of his voice,
put your luggage here, drop your luggage here, men this way,
women and children this way. And then, looked at us, and said, well,
we'll meet you back at the mound of luggage and hope we find it again.
—Eleanor Lenhart, England

1948 The Supreme Court overthrows 1913 California land ownership law.

1950 The Internal Security Act requires all aliens to register annually with the INS

From the beginning of its oversight, the United States government sought to assure that unqualified immigrants would not arrive at federal processing stations with no means to return home. The federal government required steamship companies to begin the inspection process before an immigrant set foot on American soil. By U.S. policies, the shipping lines had to bear the cost of carrying excluded aliens back to their point of departure. Before sailing, again by U.S. law, the ship's stewards had to enter each passenger's name on a formal list along with information about each person. This was the ship's manifest, always used by captains entering a harbor as an inventory of their cargo. Now, it would become the document of record for all persons arriving at a U.S. immigration station.

Arriving at Ellis Island, early 1900s

After the long voyage, the ships entered New York harbor. A New York State quarantine inspector had to approve the passengers before they entered. Next a U.S. medical officer examined native-born Americans and first- and second-class passengers who could then move directly through customs to the mainland. All foreign passengers were examined by medical officers and immigration inspectors either aboard ship or on Ellis Island. The steerage passengers boarded ferries headed for Ellis Island. The ferry landed in a slip next to the main Ellis Island building, the one in which today's exhibits are housed. There, immigration officials would examine them for admission. The newcomers debarked with their baggage and their outer garments were tagged with their manifest number from the steamship, a card often seen in photographs of the period.

Arriving at Ellis Island, early 1900s

The Registry Room or "Great Hall" restored in 1990. — METAFORM INC. AND ... RMAYEFF AND GEISMAR INC.

After they walked into the building, they arrived first in the spacious Baggage Room, where the immigrants were advised to check their belongings. Most did as they were told, but some feared theft and insisted on carrying their belongings with them through the inspection process.

Next the immigrants walked single file up the grand staircase that led to the second floor Registry Room, the great hall that figures so prominently in all visual presentations of and visits to Ellis Island. As the immigrants made their way up the stairs, medical officers observed them in what came to be known as the six-second exam. Next came a more formal medical inspection. One of the most famous medical procedures was the exam for trachoma and other contagious eye diseases, which was often done with a buttonhook, a metal instrument used to button gloves. The Ellis Island Public Health Service physicians had discovered that this hook was more effective than any medical device in pulling the eyelids back to check for telltale signs of infection. Trachoma, a highly contagious disease, was, and remains, grounds for refusal of entry. The number of ailments and conditions to be checked increased with the years and reached fifty by 1917. Physicians marked those exhibiting deficiencies with a chalk mark on the outer garments, front or back: an *E* for eye problems, an *H* for possible heart problems, an *L* for lameness, and so on. About 20 percent of newcomers would receive one or more chalk marks, and they were detained for closer medical examination (**Document 35**).

Even the intelligence of the immigrants was tested, to comply with legislation that excluded retarded persons, then called idiots, imbeciles, or morons and other mentally deficient persons from entry. Physicians used various intelligence tests to evaluate persons who exhibited questionable mental traits or who were suspected of having mental problems. It was not always easy for the examiners to know for sure if odd behavior meant mental deficiency, resulted from stress, or arose from the fact that the examiners and the subject being examined usually spoke different languages and came from different cultures. For example, a test question asked: "Would you wash stairs from the top down or from the bottom up?" One

The Registry Room or Great Hall, early 1900s
— ELLIS ISLAND MUSEUM PHOTO ARCHIVES

Dormitories and Detention

We didn't know why we were there. We didn't know how long we were going to be there. —Herman Gold, Argentina

When you went to sleep you were afraid that maybe somebody was going to come during the night and pull you out and say, "Well, you're sick. Come on, we'll send you back...You lived in constant fear of being sent back." —Regina Sass Tepper, Polish Immigrant

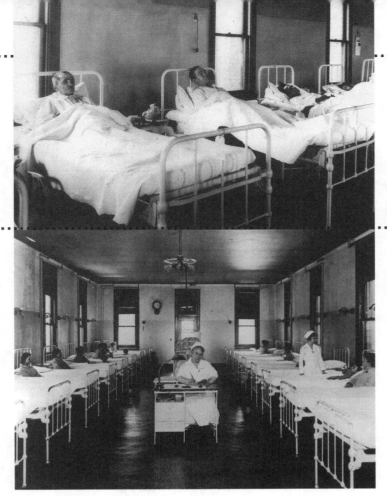

immigrant later reported that she replied: "I didn't come to America to wash stairs."

Anyone with obvious symptoms of mental or physical illness was sent to an examination room. This could cause panic among relatives and friends who did not understand why one of their number was being taken away. Some of the segregated immigrants passed the more detailed medical exam and returned to the main group. Others were held on the island in separate dormitories for children, women, and men, until their medical problem was cured or alleviated enough for entry to the United States. People who had common infectious diseases like whooping cough or even diphtheria usually

The Registry Room, after 1911 — ELLIS ISLAND MUSEUM LIBRARY ARCHIVES

Ellis Island Infirmary (top), Women's Ward (above), before 1914
— ELLIS ISLAND MUSEUM LIBRARY ARCHIVES

received treatment in the infirmary and were later released. Detention, whether for medical or legal reasons, or because an immigrant was waiting to be met by a family member, rarely lasted as long as two weeks. The most wrenching scene at the island happened when a child failed the medical exam, for then the entire family had to return to the port of origin, since children were not permitted to travel alone. Immigrants not cleared after closer examination were deported within days.

Immigrants who exhibited no obvious symptoms of physical or mental illness lined up for the legal inspection conducted by immigration inspectors, many of whom spoke foreign languages and came from foreign-born families. A tag was pinned on each person indicating the page and line of the

The biggest impression that I had was when they took us to the dormitories to see white linens, white tile, sparkling clean, almost a sterile sort of an environment.
—Morry Helzner, Russia

1952 The McCarran Walter Act overturns the 1790 naturalization law excluding non-whites from naturalization.

ship's manifest on which their name appeared. In the Registry Room the immigrant inspector assisted by interpreters when needed, and a registry clerk who called out the immigrants' names and recorded their responses, interrogated each immigrant to confirm the information declared on the manifest. The inspector could ask each immigrant's name, age, place of birth, occupation, port of embarkation, point of destination, and so forth. Over time immigration law required the inspector to ask several questions: Are you an anarchist? A polygamist? The questioning began, of course, with "What is your name?" and moved on to other questions designed to establish if the petitioner was coming to this country for a legitimate

Getting ready for inspection, early 1900s
—ELLIS ISLAND MUSEUM LIBRARY ARCHIVES

reason, had a proper moral character, and was unlikely to become a ward of the state, or a violent revolutionary. Examiners would be favorably impressed if the immigrant seemed to have paid employment already arranged, but on account of the contract labor issue, which remained alive throughout the peak years at Ellis Island, he was wary of petitioners who seemed to have been recruited to work in the United States, as opposed to those who had arranged a job through friends or relatives. They asked every adult immigrant if a job waited for them in the United States. A response of "No" might be enough to warrant denial of entry on the ground that they were likely to become a "public charge," a charity case. A response of "Yes" might make the inspectors see an example of engaging in contract labor, which was illegal. As La Guardia noted, "common sense suggested that any immigrant who came into the United States in those days . . . surely came here to work" yet, under the law, he could have no more "than a vague hope of a job" if he wanted to avoid trouble in answering the the inspectors' questions (**Document 36**). Answers to the inspector's questions had to match information on the manifest which the immigrants had provided to the shipping company before sailing. If the manifest information differed, questions might be raised about fitness for entry.

Immigrants found it advantageous in the questioning to show letters from friends and relatives already in the States. A prepaid railroad ticket indicated that the petitioner was moving on a planned route, not merely wandering about. The questioning lasted two or three minutes, and 80 percent or

more of the immigrants had no problem during it. Immigrants who gave answers that failed to satisfy the inspectors were sent to a special inquiry board, which determined if the immigrant was ineligible for admission on the grounds of being likely to become a public charge, or of being an anarchist, a polygamist, an immoral person, a convicted felon, and so on. Women faced unique restrictions even when they satisfied all the criteria for entry. Unmarried mothers and their illegitimate children were always excluded on grounds of moral turpitude and as potential public welfare charges. Single women could enter only if they were sponsored by U.S. residents, aliens or citizens as demonstrated through a

New Buildings for the Immigrant Station, Ellis Island
— HARPER'S WEEKLY, CA. 1900

telegram or other form of proof. Unaccompanied single women and children were detained until a relative could come and fetch them (**Document 37**).

The Federal Immigration Act of 1917 required that every immigrant over age fourteen be able to read. The test for literacy was relatively straightforward, consisting of a reading from a holy book on scriptures from the immigrant's culture. Jews had to read from the Torah in Hebrew or the language of their home culture, like Polish, Yiddish or Russian; Christians read from the Old and New Testament; Muslims from the Koran, and so forth. Whether the immigrant was reading well enough to constitute literacy was a matter for the individual inspector to decide. The literacy requirement was a product of American life, a print culture, and had little relevance to those immigrants who grew up in cultures of the spoken word and oral traditions. By imposing the literacy requirement, which many Americans thought would exclude ignorant and stupid people, the federal government was putting a premium on certain kinds of cultural traditions, mainly urban ones, to the detriment of others. Most immigrants found ways of passing the literacy test, even if they could barely read, and it does not often appear in immigrant recollections of Ellis Island.

Ellis Island and After 69

1990 1,536,483 legal immigrants were admitted into the U.S.
SOURCE: Priscilla Labovitz, *Immigration—Just the Facts*.

1994 804,416 legal immigrants were admitted into the U. S.
SOURCE: Priscilla Labovitz, *Immigration—Just the Facts*.

3.6

Detained aliens of many nationalities resided in the station's dormitory; they shared food and hospital facilities with other detainees from all over the world. Some would be released after a relative or friend arrived and declared sponsorship. Others detained for health reasons in the station's hospital left after brief hospital treatment. Still other detainees appeared before the Board of Special Inquiry to clarify whether or not they would be admitted at all. Composed of three inspectors appointed by the Commissioner of Immigration, the boards of inquiry interpreted the immigration law. Was a person insane and therefore incapable of self care? Would a senile old man's son provide for him as promised? Was a certain woman really a prostitute, a certain man really a labor contractor? National and international events could, of course, influence activities on Ellis Island. At times when Americans believed their national security threatened, after President McKinley's assassination by an anarchist, World War I, and the 1920's Red Scare, the boards of inquiry could expect to concern themselves more than usual with suspected radicals and revolutionaries.

There was a legal department on Ellis Island charged with assisting in interpretations of immigration law, but the board of inquiry was not in the strict sense of the term, a court. It had no judge, jurors, plaintiffs or criminals. The boards of special inquiry were independent tribunals. Their decisions were final and not subject to court review. If a board reached a decision in favor of deportation, immigrants had the right to appeal the decision to the official that oversaw immigration, the Secretary of the Treasury from 1891–1903 and the

Secretary of Labor and Commerce from 1903–1940. After 1940, due to the increasing concerns for national security, appeals as well as all other immigration issues were under the U.S. Attorney General and the Justice Department.

Of the immigrants processed at the island from 1892 through 1924, few, perhaps 20 percent, were detained; nearly 98 percent went through successfully, most of them in a single day of processing. Leaving the island was a simple matter, since immigrants needed no special papers from the U.S. or local governments to enter the country once they had passed through inspection. Passports were not required until 1921.

Ellis Island After the Peak Years

3.6 THE PEAK YEARS OF IMMIGRATION SERVICE FACILITIES like Ellis Island and Angel Island lasted until the early 1920s, when two developments sharply reduced the need for immigration stations. The first was a change in the method of processing migrants and the second was a series of sweeping federal laws that greatly reduced the size of annual immigration.

NEW PROCESSING METHODS

3.6.1 AS PART OF MAJOR CHANGES IN U.S. IMMIGRATION law during the 1920s, the site of inspection of migrants was moved from the United States to the place of departure. The new arrangement greatly reduced the size of U.S. facilities, which would no longer conduct medical or mental exams nor

1994 State with the largest number of legal immigrants from all foreign countries combined: California.
SOURCE: Priscilla Labovitz, *Immigration—Just the Facts.*

1994 State where fewest illegal immigrants lived: Wyoming.

European Immigrants, early 1900's

house immigrants who were ill or needed further examination. When restrictive immigration laws and the new processing methods took full effect, by the mid-1920s, the large facilities like Ellis Island began receiving far fewer arrivals. The number of arrivals virtually ceased altogether during World War II, when the island served as a detention facility for enemy aliens. After a brief flurry of activity during the late 1940s, when the European immigrant stream revived after the war, the Immigration and Naturalization Service ceased to process immigrants at Ellis Island.

RESTRICTING THE IMMIGRANT FLOW

3.6.2 EVEN WITHOUT THE CHANGE IN PROCESSING procedures, Ellis Island would have seen a major decline in activity owing to restrictive immigration laws passed in 1921 and 1924. The Progressive ideal of efficient control that informed the U.S. Immigration Service at Ellis Island and U.S. immigration policy always had a double-edged character, since it could be used either to enhance the migrant flow or to reduce it. Before World War I, when Americans still regarded their nation as in need of labor, federal policy controlled immigration in a way that kept the flow moving. After the war, a returning national concern with domestic issues, coupled with

rising acceptance of racialist attitudes, led Congress to pass laws that made immigrating to the U.S. difficult for all but a few categories of newcomers. The new laws drew on a lingering concern over the effect of mass immigration on the population profile of American society. Throughout the Ellis Island era, commentators on the American scene pondered what kind of nation was emerging from the constant influx of newcomers from all over the world (**Document 38**). By adopting a quota system that favored immigrants from the British Isles and western Europe, Congress attempted to retain a Protestant, northern European population. Mass immigration to the United States ended with the immigration acts of 1921 and 1924, which severely limited immigration from southern and eastern Europe and virtually ended it from Asia. Migration from Europe, which was about one million persons a year before 1924, was limited to 150,000 annually.

The decline in migration was not quite as severe as it might seem, however, for the new laws placed no quotas on migration from Western Hemisphere countries. Increased migration from Latin America, especially Mexico, replaced some of the labor force lost from the exclusion of Asians and the limitation of some other groups. Mexicans, who for generations had practiced circular migration to work on U.S. farms, ranches, and in mining and lumbering, found themselves even

For one thing, Ellis Island gave me a chance to stay here and live here and bring my children up here. And for that, I'm grateful to that little island.
—Pearl Pohrille, Germany

1875-1948 115,535 Arabs arrive in the U.S., many of them Christians.

1949-1976 154,000 Arabs arrive with Muslims exceeding Christians by 60%.

more welcomed by the cotton growers of Texas and the fruit and vegetable farmers of California. Not until the Great Depression of the 1930s, when unemployment reached historic highs, did Mexicans and other Western Hemisphere migrants find themselves subject to restrictive efforts.

Alongside international migration from south of its borders during the interwar years, the United States also experienced major internal migration by southern blacks and Appalachian whites, who followed the harvests in a pattern of circular migration or moved permanently from the countryside to the city to work in factories and other businesses. Many of the migrants to cities were following a pattern set during World War I, when labor demands by war-related industries opened up jobs for an array of previously excluded or underemployed Americans.

The Great Depression, which affected all industrialized societies, reduced economic opportunities in the United States so much that immigration fell to historic lows. Ellis Island officials, during the 1930s, actually processed many out-migrants, mainly Europeans who hoped to find better opportunities in their homelands. Instead of being an economic haven, the United States functioned as a place of political asylum for some of the

European Immigrants, early 1900s

German Jews fleeing Nazi persecution and for non-Jewish opponents of fascism, although many more would have entered had the federal government interpreted the immigration law less narrowly (**Document 39**).

WORLD MIGRATION INCREASES

3.6.3 WORLD WAR II VIRTUALLY HALTED VOLUNTARY MIGRATION but greatly increased the rate of forced or near-forced migration (**Document 40**). Armies and navies sent millions of people across the land and sea; national governments conscripted labor by force, including the labor of prisoners (Germany) and citizens (Soviet Union), who were transported to industrial centers and military sites. Military operations created refugees by the millions. Hundreds of thousands fled German-occupied Europe by leaving for Switzerland, Spain, Great Britain, North Africa, and other havens. The Japanese occupation of much of China dislocated millions of people who wanted to live free of foreign control. Some national governments began policies of colonization to consolidate their new conquests. The Nazis, for example, encouraged Germans to migrate to conquered lands in Poland and the Soviet Union.

A boy was screaming with joy, "Wake up, wake up, you can see the Statue of Liberty—You can see the Statue of Liberty—

Exhibit, the Statue of Liberty Museum (left) Exhibit of Ocean liners, the Ellis Island Museum (right) — METAFORM INC. AND CHERMAYEFF AND GEISMAR INC.

The end of war did not bring an immediate return to normalcy, for too much of the former world order had been disrupted. Economic devastation coupled with border realignments and the Cold War caused yet more migrations in the form of refugees and the exchange of populations to resolve political issues. Millions of Europeans had to find new homes after being forced out of their homelands by efforts to make ethnic composition match new political borders. Poland, for example, lost eastern territory to the Soviet Union but gained in the west from defeated Germany. Many residents of those areas were forced in or out in order to bring population characteristics in line with the new borders. The former German region of East Prussia, given to Poland by the Allies, saw its population change within a few years as Germans were forced out and Poles were encouraged to settle. More than one million displaced persons from Germany were resettled by international relief organizations: in the United States (330,000), Canada (125,000), Australia (180,000), Israel (140,000), and various European countries (270,000). German minorities of almost 3.5 million were expelled from Czechoslovakia, Hungary, Romania, and Yugoslavia and transferred to East and West Germany. Between 1948 and 1967 some 450,000 persons fled eastern Europe (**Document 41**).

Even larger population shifts were occurring in Asia. The struggle between the Chinese Communists and the Nationalists resulted in the flight of millions of Nationalist troops and supporters to Taiwan in the late 1940s. Many found their way to the United States, which had also become a haven for European refugees. The breakup of European colonial rule also contributed to a rise in the movement of people. In India the partition with Pakistan resulted in eight to nine million Hindus and Sikhs leaving Pakistan for India, and six to seven million Muslims leaving India for Pakistan. Another exodus occurred when nationalists drove the French out of the northern portion of Vietnam during the 1950s.

Not until the 1950s did wartime dislocation abate and world immigration resume its strongly economic nature. By then, conditions had begun to change in fundamental ways that still affect the nature of migration. A tremendous economic boom in the United States, western Europe, and parts of Asia stimulated migration: Turks came as "guest workers" in Germany, North Africans journeyed to France for work, and Koreans labored in Japanese industries. Meanwhile, many parts of the underdeveloped world were beginning to industrialize and experience population shifts from countryside to city that brought peasants into the cities, where they could get a taste of "modern" life and obtain job skills useful in the homeland or another land. Many peasants from southern Mexico, for example, moved north to the border towns, where there were jobs in American-owned factories, and then, later, moved north into the United States.

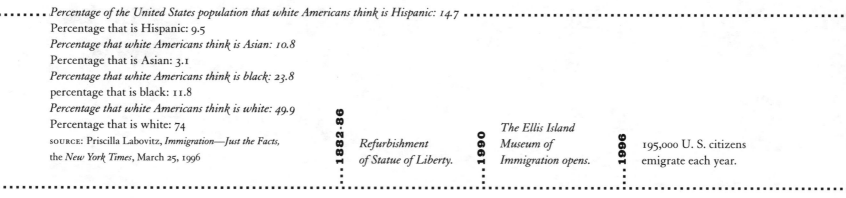

Percentage of the United States population that white Americans think is Hispanic: 14.7

Percentage that is Hispanic: 9.5

Percentage that white Americans think is Asian: 10.8

Percentage that is Asian: 3.1

Percentage that white Americans think is black: 23.8

percentage that is black: 11.8

Percentage that white Americans think is white: 49.9

Percentage that is white: 74

SOURCE: Priscilla Labovitz, *Immigration—Just the Facts*, the *New York Times*, March 25, 1996

1882·86 *Refurbishment of Statue of Liberty.*

1990 *The Ellis Island Museum of Immigration opens.*

1996 195,000 U. S. citizens emigrate each year.

THE FLOW RESUMES

3.6.4 THE UNITED STATES REMAINS A PRIME GOAL FOR THE world's migrants (**Documents 42, 43**). During the decades after World War II, immigration increased steadily and is now as high as in the heyday of Ellis Island. During the fiscal year ending September 1993, for example, almost 900,000 immigrants entered the United States, approximately the same number that came through Ellis Island in 1907, its peak year. Dramatic increases in immigration since the late 1960s, as well as a significant shift in the regions sending immigrants to the United States, are explained partly by changes in immigration policy. The restrictive character of the 1920s legislation remained undisturbed until the mid-1960s. Neither the 1952 McCarran-Walter Act (which maintained the 1920s quotas approach) nor a series of laws passed between 1952 and 1964 that favored those with special skills or with relatives in the United States upset the restrictive architecture of American immigration policy. Private bills introduced by

members of Congress petitioning for individual exceptions to the quotas were a common vehicle for obtaining admission, yet the quota system remained in place. The fact that two out of three immigrants between 1952 and 1965 entered under exceptions to the quota prompted calls for reform. Finally, a law in 1965 eliminated the national origins quotas and firmly established family reunification as a visa preference. The law permitted immigration from all nations, not from a select group, and opened the way for a large influx from Asia, the Caribbean, and Latin America. The law retained the idea of limiting immigrants by confining entries to twenty thousand per year for any single country outside the Western Hemisphere. For the first time the law imposed a limit on Western Hemisphere immigration to 120,000. Laws passed since 1965 have increased the numbers to be admitted to about 700,000, broadened acceptable job-related visas, made it more difficult to exclude political dissidents and homosexuals, and granted amnesty to thousands of illegal aliens.

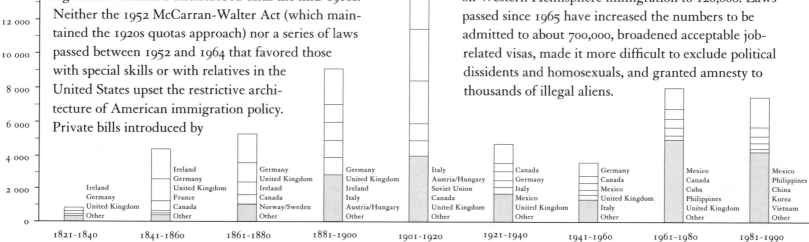

3.6.4a *Changing Origins of Immigrants to the U.S.* — 1990 STATISTICAL YEARBOOK OF THE I.N.S.

Region	1955-90	1955-64	1965-74	1975-84	1985-88	1989	1990
All regions	100.0	100.0	100.0	100.0	100.0	100.0	100.0
Europe	21.8	50.2	29.8	13.4	10.4	7.6	7.3
North and West	10.1	28.6	11.0	5.2	5.0	3.3	2.8
South and East	11.8	21.6	18.7	8.1	5.4	4.3	4.5
Asia	29.8	7.7	22.4	43.3	43.7	28.6	22.0
Africa	2.0	0.7	1.5	2.4	2.9	2.3	2.3
Colonials	0.6	0.4	0.7	0.8	0.7	0.4	0.4
North America	39.6	35.9	39.6	33.6	35.4	55.7	62.3
Caribbean	13.5	7.0	18.0	15.1	16.6	8.2	7.5
Central America	4.3	2.4	2.5	3.7	4.7	9.3	9.5
Other North America	21.9	26.4	19.0	14.8	14.1	38.3	45.3
South America	6.1	5.1	6.0	6.6	6.9	5.4	5.6

Most of the *new* immigrants of the 1970s, 1980s, and 1990s have come from countries that contributed little to earlier flows (the Irish and Italians are exceptions). The prosperity and political tranquility of western Europe caused a decline in emigration to the United States, reducing it to only 5 percent of newcomers in the 1980s. Northern Europe itself has become a magnet for immigrants from the Mediterranean region and also from Asian and Caribbean regions of the British Commonwealth. By 1975, no European country was among the five nations sending the largest numbers of immigrants to the United States: Mexico, the Philippines, South Korea, Cuba, and Canada. During the 1970s, Third World nations in Africa, Asia, the Caribbean, and—the largest—Latin America accounted for half or more of U.S. immigra-

tion. This historic shift reflects the relatively lower living standards in the new sending nations and the ability of Latin Americans, Asians, and Caribbeans to take advantage of family reunification provisions in immigration laws passed since 1965. Some regions of the country that have received especially large influxes of immigrants have attempted to control immigration through law, such as California's Proposition 187, passed by referendum in 1994 with a 59 percent majority, which denies certain healthcare and educational benefits to illegal aliens (**Document 44**).

Since the 1930s, women have constituted most of immigrants to the United States, a reversal of the historic pattern in which men dominated (**Document 45**). During recent decades, the increase in the relative proportion of women has

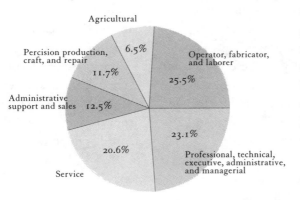

Agricultural
6.5%

Percision production, craft, and repair 11.7%

Administrative support and sales 12.5%

Operator, fabricator, and laborer 25.5%

23.1%

20.6%

Service

Professional, technical, executive, administrative, and managerial

3.6.4c *Immigrants Admitted to the U.S. by Occupation Groups, 1976–1990. Contemporary migration unlike the Ellis Island Era includes many skilled, white collar and professional workers*
— 1990 STATISTICAL YEARBOOK OF THE I.N.S.

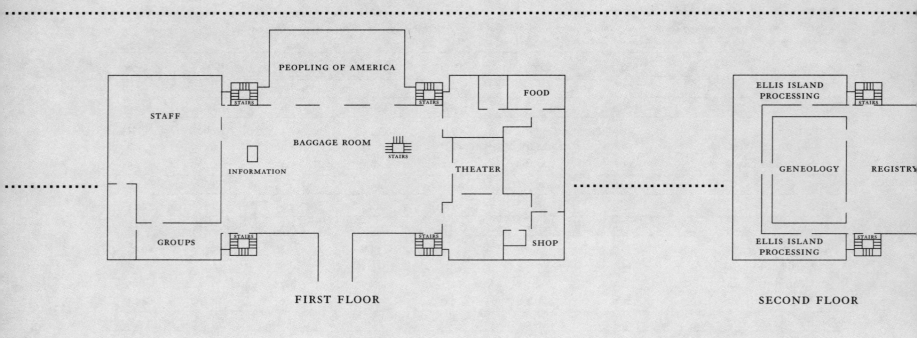

PEOPLING OF AMERICA

STAFF

BAGGAGE ROOM

INFORMATION

STAIRS

FOOD

THEATER

GROUPS

SHOP

ELLIS ISLAND PROCESSING

GENEOLOGY

REGISTRY

ELLIS ISLAND PROCESSING

SECOND FLOOR

resulted, in part, from federal legislation that exempts immediate family members of U.S. citizens—spouses, children, and parents—from numerical limits. The law favors wives of native-born and naturalized citizens who gain entry under family unification provisions. Economics joins with policy in explaining the reversal of the gender patterns of immigration. As indicated in the discussion in Part 1 concerning circular migration, increasing numbers of jobs in the service sector and the decline of heavy industry have created a labor market more favorable to both unskilled and professional women. Finally, employers often systematically hire female workers in order to keep wages down, a situation that increases demand for female immigrant laborers.

Migration patterns have reflected worldwide economic, social, and political developments. Increasingly, however, the types and numbers of immigrants are determined by the regulations of the receiving country. Although some professionals came to the United States during the transatlantic migrations of the last century, they were neither favored nor excluded as a matter of federal policy. Over the past decade, however, pro-

fessionals from countries such as India have come in large numbers to the United States, following immigration laws, dating from 1965 and later, that favor the educated. Third World professionals and skilled workers, who constitute about one-fourth of today's immigrants to the United States, represent the "brain drain" that so many developing nations lament. From Central America during the 1980s, in contrast, came war refugees who crossed the Mexican border without legal papers. The fact that many of these Central Americans were illegal entrants while 90 percent of those who came in the great European migrations were legally admitted resulted from changes in federal policy rather than a change in the nature of migration (**Document 46**).

Today air travel has replaced the steamship as the major long-distance carrier of migrants, and an elaborate highway system has replaced railroads to bring migrants to their final destinations. New transportation technology has speeded the pace of movement and also redirected its flow, often away from the historic central cities that once drew immigrants. The movement of many businesses and jobs to

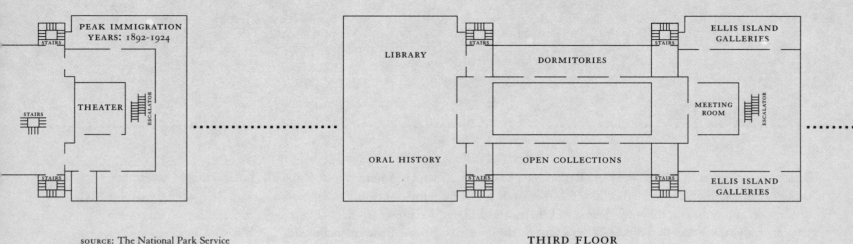

PEAK IMMIGRATION YEARS: 1892-1924

STAIRS

THEATER

STAIRS

ESCALATOR

STAIRS

LIBRARY

DORMITORIES

ELLIS ISLAND GALLERIES

STAIRS

STAIRS

MEETING ROOM

ESCALATOR

ORAL HISTORY

OPEN COLLECTIONS

ELLIS ISLAND GALLERIES

STAIRS

STAIRS

SOURCE: The National Park Service

THIRD FLOOR

3.7

the periphery of older cities marks a change in economic patterns that has altered employment opportunities for everyone, newcomer and native-born. In former times, immigrant populations initially congregated in ethnic neighborhoods, but today, they may settle on the fringes of major metropolitan centers, as in northern Virginia, near Washington, D.C., for example, where many newcomers from South and Southeast Asia have settled.

Ellis Island's Rebirth

3.7 THE RISE OF THE "NEW" MIGRATION OF THE POSTWAR YEARS had little to do with Ellis Island, which was ordered closed in 1954 by President Eisenhower's Attorney General Herbert Brownell. The Immigration Service removed the last remaining aliens on November 12, 1954, and finally abandoned it on March 15, 1955, when the General Services Administration assumed control (1955–65). After a fruitless effort to sell Ellis Island, the buildings began slowly to deteriorate. The millions of immigrants who had passed through the island, along with

their children, seemed to care just as little about the island's fate. They were too busy doing what the immigration station's founders and staff had hoped they would do: assist in building the country and becoming part of the resident population.

It took the tremendous economic boom of the postwar years, which finally blossomed in the 1960s and 1970s, to give Americans the pause they needed to think about their immigrant origins. The civil rights movement also contributed, by raising issues of racial and ethnic identity and rights that helped fuel debates over national identity. African Americans and Native Americans took renewed pride in their cultural heritage and expanded the scope of their legal rights, which highlighted the quite different heritages of European and Native Asian Americans.

Out of the growing sense of racial and ethnic identity came a new sense of interest in the immigrant experience, including the moment of arrival in the new land. For the thousands of Americans who could trace their family history to a person who had passed through Ellis Island, the facility in New York Harbor came to represent an entire experience and perspective.

The Statue of Liberty-Ellis Island Foundation Inc., a non-profit organization, was founded in 1982 to raise funds for the restoration and preservation of the Statue of Liberty and Ellis Island. Under the leadership of Lee Iacocca and working in conjunction with the National Park Service, the sole adminis-trator of the sites, the Foundation has restored the Statue and the Main Building at Ellis Island and created the Ellis Island Immigration Museum which opened in September, 1990, restored additional buildings on Ellis Island's north side, and established a $20 million endowment to sustain both monu-ments throughout the years. The largest restoration and preservation project in American history, it was funded entirely at a cost of $170 million by the American people. Over twenty million private citizens contributed to the effort.

The Foundation's current efforts include The American Immigrant Wall of Honor® and the creation of the The American Family Immigration History Center™, both at Ellis Island. (See "About the Statue of Liberty-Ellis Island Foundation, Inc.").

The interpretive plan for the Ellis Island Museum docu-mented the historic function of the island as an immigrant processing center, but a major exhibit on the Museum's first floor *The Peopling of America* exhibit, contextualizes that story by documenting immigration to the United States from all the world's continents including Africa, Asia, and South America over the course of American history. The American Immigrant Wall of Honor®, the largest wall of names in the world, dramatically testifies to the emotional significance which Americans ascribe to the intersection between their family histories and national history. Almost every nationality is represented here. Those who endured forced migration from Africa are included as are Native Americans and the earliest European colonists. George Washington's great grandfather, John F. Kennedy's grandparents, the families of Cicely Tyson and Barbara Streisand stand along side the ancestors of thousands of other American family ancestors. These interpretive and fund-raising strategies represent an effort to make Ellis Island a truly inclusive national symbol.

The United States and other parts of the developed world are still magnets to people seeking a better life. The numbers entering the United States today are higher than they have been in any decade since the early 1900s. Twenty-five hundred arrive each week at Kennedy International airport in New York City alone. Today's migrant arrives already approved for admission by a United States official abroad. At debarkation points in the United States, immigration officers check papers —not the ship's manifest as in the old days but a computer-generated "green card," an alien registration document bear-ing the immigrant's signature, a print of the right index fin-ger, and a photo of the right earlobe. Although the entry process has been modernized, however, immigrants still echo the hopes and fears of their Ellis Island predecessors. Today or yesterday, and probably tomorrow too, people look for something better. They always have and always will. People have always moved.

4

Documents

These documents describe various kinds of immigration as they were experienced by individuals. Maps, charts, and graphs chronicle large–scale movements of people described in earlier sections of the guide. Questions designed to facilitate learning at home, in the classroom, or at the museum are included at the end of the section, beginning on page 163.

Documents

4.1 Part 1 of this guide explored five ways of classifying immigration and migration from an historical and global perspective. The categories of migration relate to important themes including family history, slavery and wage labor, colonization and settlement of the New World, and gender. The discussion also suggested the relationships that people use to exercise control over their lives and patterns of migration.

1.4 World History and the Social Organization of Migration

The following documents on forced, voluntary, circular, chain, and colonizing migration capture moments in world history experienced by a variety of immigrant groups.

Document 1

Major World Migrations, 1700–1810. The slave trade was one of the great migrations of world history. Far more Africans than Europeans came to the Americas before 1810.

Source: Adapted from Kevin Reilly, *The West and the World: A History of Civilization*, 2d ed. (New York: HarperCollins College, 1989), Vol. 2, 55.

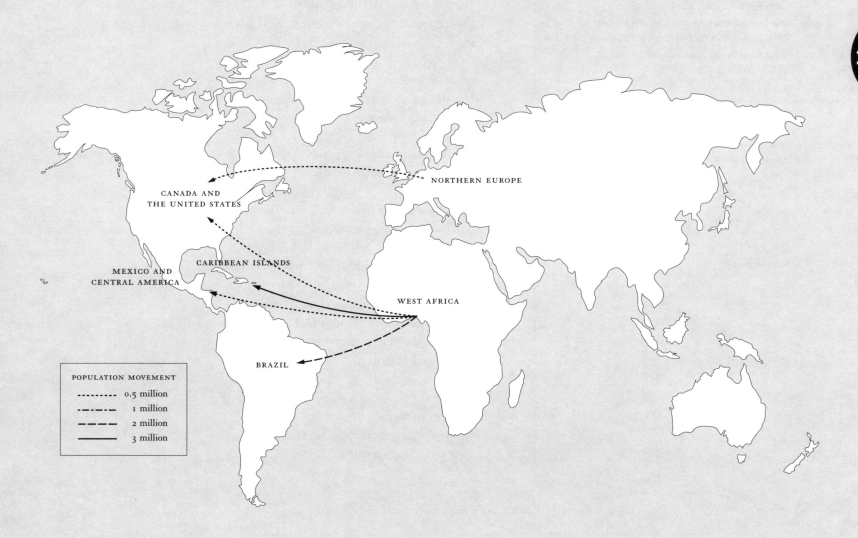

CANADA AND
THE UNITED STATES

NORTHERN EUROPE

MEXICO AND
CENTRAL AMERICA

CARIBBEAN ISLANDS

WEST AFRICA

BRAZIL

POPULATION MOVEMENT

·········· 0.5 million

·—·—·— 1 million

— — — 2 million

———— 3 million

1.4.1 Forced Migration

Document 2

Gustavus Vassa, an African-born slave from Benin, in what is now Nigeria, published this story of his captivity in 1789, when he was 33 years old. After his arrival in the United States, he was a slave in Virginia and Philadelphia. His Philadelphia master provided him with some education and sent him to work on trading ships to the West Indies and on Caribbean plantations. In later years, he became an antislavery activist in England.

Source: *The Interesting Narrative of the Life of Olaudah Equiano, or Gustavus Vassa, the African; by Himself, 1789*, edited by Arna Bontemps, *Great Slave Narratives* (Boston: Beacon Press, 1969), 4–5, 11, 20, 26–34, reprinted by permission of Beacon Press, Boston, ©1969 .

That part of Africa, known by the name of Guinea, to which the trade for slaves is carried on, extends along the coast above 3,400 miles, from Senegal to Angola, and includes a variety of kingdoms. Of these, the most considerable is the kingdom of Benin.... I was born in the year 1745, situated in a charming fruitful vale, named Essaka. The distance of this province from the capital of Benin and the sea coast must be very considerable, for I had never heard of white men or Europeans, nor of the sea.... When our people go out to till their land, they generally take their arms with them for fear of a surprise.... From what I can recollect of these battles, they appear to have been irruptions of one little state or district on the other, to obtain prisoners or booty. Perhaps they were incited to this by those traders who brought...European goods...amongst us. Such a mode of obtaining slaves in Africa is common; and I believe more are procured this way, and by kidnapping, than any other. When a trader wants slaves, he applies to a chief for them and tempts him with his wares. It is not extraordinary if, on this occasion, he yields to the temptation with as little firmness, and accepts the price of his fellow creature's liberty with as little reluctance as the enlightened merchant. Accordingly, he falls on his neighbors and a desperate battle ensues. If he prevails and takes prisoners, he gratifies his avarice by selling them....

One day, when all our people were gone out to their works as usual and only I and my dear sister were left to mind the house, two men and a woman got over our walls and in a moment seized us both and, without giving us time to cry out or make resistance, they stopped our mouths and ran off with us into the nearest wood…. my sister and I were then separated while we lay clasped in each other's arms. It was in vain that we besought them not to part us; she was torn from me and immediately carried away, while I was left in a state of distraction not to be described. I cried and grieved continually; and for several days did not eat anything but what they forced into my mouth…. I continued to travel, sometimes by land, sometimes by water, through different countries and various nations, till, at the end of six or seven months after I had been kidnapped, I arrived at the sea coast….

The first object which saluted my eyes when I arrived on the coast, was the sea, and a slave ship which was then riding at anchor and waiting for its cargo. These filled me with astonishment, which was soon converted into terror when I was carried on board. I was immediately handled and tossed up to see if I were sound, by some of the crew; and I was now persuaded that I had gotten into a world of bad spirits, and that they were going to kill me. Their complexions, too, differing so much from ours, their long hair, and the language they spoke (which was very different from any I had ever heard) united to confirm me in this belief. Indeed,

such were the horrors of my views and fears at the moment that, if ten thousand worlds had been my own, I would have freely parted with them all to have exchanged my condition with that of the meanest slave in my own country. When I looked round the ship, too, and saw a large furnace of copper boiling, and a multitude of black people of every description chained together, every one of their countenances expressing dejection and sorrow, I no longer doubted of my fate; and, quite overpowered with horror and anguish, I fell motionless on the deck and fainted. When I recovered a little, I found some black people about me who, I believed, were some of those who had brought me on board and had been receiving their pay; they talked to me in order to cheer me, but all in vain. I asked them if we were not to be eaten by those white men with horrible looks, red faces, and long hair. They told me I was not, and one of the crew brought me a small portion of spirituous liquor in a wine glass but, being afraid of him, I would not take it out of his hand. One of the blacks, therefore, took it from him and gave it to me, and I took a little down my palate, which, instead of reviving me as they thought it would, threw me into the greatest consternation at the strange feeling it produced, having never tasted any such liquor before. Soon after this, the blacks who brought me on board went off, and left me abandoned to despair.

I now saw myself deprived of all chance of returning to my native country…. and I even wished for my former slavery in preference to my present situation.… I was not long suffered to indulge my grief; I was soon put down under the decks and there, I received such a salutation in my nostrils as I had never experienced in my life; so that, with the loathsomeness of the stench and the crying together, I became so sick and low that I was not able to eat, nor had I the least desire to taste anything. I now wished for the last friend, death, to relieve me; but soon, to my grief, two of the white men offered me eatables; and, on my refusing to eat, one of them held me fast by the hands and laid me across, I think, the windlass and tied my feet while the other flogged me severely. I had never experienced anything of this kind before.… In a little time after, amongst the poor chained men, I found some of my own nation which, in a small degree, gave ease to my mind. I inquired of these what was to be done with us? They gave me to understand we were to be carried to these white peoples' country to work for them. I then was a little revived and thought, if it were no worse than working, my situation was not so desperate but still I feared I should be put to death, the white people looked and acted, as I thought, in so savage a manner; for I had never seen among any people such instances of brutal cruelty.… I could not help expressing my fears and apprehensions to some of my countrymen; I asked them if these people had no country, but lived in this hollow place (the ship)? They told me they did not, but came from a distant

one. "Then," said I, "how comes it in all our country we never heard of them?" They told me because they lived so very far off.… I then asked where were their women?…. They answered…they were left behind. I asked how the vessel could go? They told me they could not tell; that there was cloth put upon the masts by the help of the ropes I saw, and then the vessel went on; and the white men had some spell or magic they put in the water when they liked in order to stop the vessel. I was exceedingly amazed at this account and really thought they were spirits. I therefore wished much to be from amongst them for I expected they would sacrifice me; but my wishes were in vain.…

The stench of the hold, while we were on the coast was so intolerably loathsome, that it was dangerous to remain there for any time.… The closeness of the place and the heat of the climate added to the number in the ship, which was so crowded that each had scarcely room to turn himself, almost suffocated us. This produced copious perspirations, so that the air soon became unfit for respiration from a variety of loathsome smells and brought on a sickness among the slaves, of which many died—thus falling victims to the improvident avarice, as I may call it, of their purchasers. This wretched situation was again aggravated by the galling of the chains, now became insupportable, and the filth of the necessary tubs, into which the children often fell and were almost suffocated. The shrieks of the women, and the groans of the dying rendered the whole a scene of horror almost inconceivable....

At last, we came in sight of the island of Barbadoes.... we plainly saw the harbor... and we soon anchored....

We were conducted immediately to the merchant's yard, where we were all pent up together.... We were not many days in the merchant's custody before we were sold after their usual manner, which is this: On a signal given (as the beat of a drum), the buyers rush at once into the yard where the slaves are confined and make their choice of that parcel they like best.... In this manner, without scruple, are relations and friends separated, most of them never to see each other again. I remember, in the vessel in which I was brought over, in the men's apartment, there were several brothers who, in the sale, were sold in different lots; and it was very moving on this occasion to see and hear their cries at parting. O, ye nominal Christians! might not an African ask you—Learned you this from your God, who says unto you, "Do unto all men as you would men should do unto you?"....

I, and some few more slaves...were shipped off in a sloop for North America.... I was constantly grieving and pining and wishing for death rather than anything else.

We were not many days in the merchant's custody before we were sold after their usual manner... In this manner, without scruple, are relations and friends separated, most of them never to see each other again.

The forme of binding a servant

Document 3

An indentured servant's contract, presented here with its unfamiliar 17th-century spellings, is typical of indentures coming to Maryland during the colonial era.

Source: Courtesy of the Maryland State Archives Special Collections (Huntingfield Corporation Collection). MSA SC 1399–526, *A Relation of the Lord Baltimore's Plantation in Maryland*, Maryland State Archives: *Documents for the Classroom* MSA SC 2221–19–12–2.

The forme of binding a servant,

This indenture made the_____ day of_____ in the _____ yeere of our Soveraigne Lord King Charles.... betweene _____ of the one party, and_____ on the other party, Witnesseth, that the said _____ doth hereby covenant, promise, and grant, to and with the said _____ his Executers and Assignes, to serve him from the day of the date hereof, untill his first and next arrival in Maryland; and after for and during the tearme of _____ yeeres, in such service and imployment, as he the said _____ or his assignes shall there imploy him, according to the custome of the Countrey in the like kind. In consideration whereof, the said _____ doth promise and grant, to and with the said _____ to pay for his passing, and to find him with Meat, Drinke, Apparell and Lodging, with other necessaries during the said terme, and at the end of the said terme, to give him one whole yeeres provision of Corne, and fifty acres of Land, according to the order of the countrey. In witnesse whereof, the said _____ hath hereunto put his hand and seale, the day and yeere above written.

Sealed and delivered in the presence of _____.

LONDON

These are to certify,
That Samuell Harris of the parish
of St. Faiths, London, Joyner,
Aged Twenty Four Years, came before
me one of His Majesty's Justices of
Peace, and Voluntarily made Oath,
That he this Deponant is not Married,
no Apprentice nor Covenant, or
Contracted Servant to any Persons,
nor listed Soldier or Sailor in
His Majesty's Service, and is free
and willing to serve William Burge or
his Assigns Four Years in Virginia,
His Majesty's Plantation in America,
and that he is not perswaded, or
enticed so to do, but that it is his own
Voluntary Act.

Sworn the 18th January 1734
before Richd. Brocas.

**Samuel Harris of the parish
of St. Faiths, London...
Aged Twenty Four Years...
is free and willing to serve
William Burge... in Virginia...**

Document 4

Each person who left England for
the colonies under an indenture
arrangement had to certify before a
Justice of the Peace that he or she
was free to enter into the contract.

Source: Jack Kaminkow and
Marion Kaminkow, *A List of Emigrants from
England to America, 1718–1759* (Baltimore:
Magna Charta Book Co, 1964), xvix.

Every master or mistress shall provide for their servants so imported or indented competent diet, clothing, and lodging. And shall not exceed the bounds of moderation in correcting them beyond their demerits.

Document 5
The following excerpt, a typical colonial law on indentured servants, is from North Carolina, 1715. It explains how the master and servant would proceed should either party break the contract's terms.

Source: Walter Clark, ed., *The State Records of North Carolina*, 16 vols. (11–26), (Releigh: State of North Carolina, 1895–1906), 23: 62–66.

Every Christian servant whether so by importation or by contract made in this government that shall, at any time or times absent him or herself from his or her master's or mistress' service without his or her license first had [sic] shall make satisfaction by serving after the time by custom or indenture or contract for serving is expired, double the time of service lost or neglected by such time or times of absence and also such longer time as the court shall see fit to adjudge in consideration of any further charge or damages accruing to the master or mistress by such time or times of absence as aforesaid….

If any Christian servant shall lay violent hands on his or her master or mistress or overseer, upon proof thereof made, shall for every offence suffer such corporal punishment as the court shall think fit to adjudge. And as an encouragement for Christian servants to perform their service with fidelity and cheerfulness….

Every master or mistress shall provide for their servants so imported or indented competent diet, clothing, and lodging. And shall not exceed the bounds of moderation in correcting them beyond their demerits. And that it shall and may be lawful for any servant having just cause of complaint to repair to the next magistrate who is hereby empowered, required and directed to bind over such master or mistress to appear and answer the complaint the next precinct court and there to stand to and abide by such orders and judgment as the court shall think fit to pass thereon….

Every Christian servant shall be allowed by their master or mistress at the expiration Of his or her time of service three barrels of Indian corn and two new suits of apparel of the value of five pounds at least or, in lieu of one suit of apparel, a good well-fixed gun, if he be a man servant.

COLUMBUS, GA, ...186–

Document 6

After the abolition of slavery, southern farmers had to explore alternative means to recruit labor. The proposal below was used by a contractor who provided Scottish laborers and women servants to southern farm owners. Note that unlike indentured servitude or slavery, the relationships described here (between laborer and contractor and between contractor and employer) are based upon exchanges of cash and, in this instance, require laborers to pay their passage.

Source: Special Collections Library, Duke University, Broadside Collection (Georgia Broadsides).

Mr...

Dear Sir:

I have had some experience for the last fifteen years in the employment of Foreign Labor in my orchards and I am satisfied that the Scotch are the most reliable in the fulfillment of their contracts, and most readily adapt themselves to the mode of living at the South; unlike the Dutch, they require neither soup nor sourkrout, and are extremely economical and industrious.

I have arranged with a reliable Scotchman in Aberdeen to export as many as I shall have a demand for, and to select men who are of good character at home, and who will come, *not because they are vagrants at home, but because they desire to better their condition*. Three thousand have recently gone to Texas, engaged for three years at £30, equal to about $210 in currency, for Farm hands, about $300 for Gardeners, and $125 for women as House Servants or Farm Hands. The contracts must be made in gold, and I will deliver them according to direction, at the above rate, to serve three years. That is to say:

Farm Hands .... at £30 to 35
Gardeners .... at £40 to 45
Women for House Servants or Farm Work .... at £15 to 20

Or less if they can be engaged for less. I will charge only the actual cost.

Each order must be accompanied with $100 in currency, to pay their transportation, of which an exact account will be kept; which sum, so far as it is expended for transportation, will be charged by the employer to the Emigrant, and deducted out of the wages. Twenty dollars will be retained by me, for my trouble and expense, for each laborer exported, and the balance, if any, will be retained by me to the employer.

Where persons are willing to employ laborers with families, a cabin and wood will have to be furnished. The ages of the children allowed by the employer will be stated, and $40 additional must be sent for the passage of each child: should it not take so much, the balance will be returned. In contracts for persons with families, of course the passage of the children will be charged to the wages of the laborer, and the support of the children will be at the laborer's expense, while the hands that labor will be furnished by the employer with lodgings, three and a half pounds of bacon and one peck of meal, each, per week, or the money value of the same, at the option of the laborer.

April is the most favorable time for employing hands in reference to the sea voyage and their labor management at home.

Persons ordering hands will give a full statement of the services required, and leave to my discretion the employment of a proper person to fill the place. I shall send out for a number for myself and my neighbors, and feel satisfied that the arrangements which I have made will secure a reliable and useful class of citizens.

Respectfully,

N.B. I am satisfied from experience that one good Scotch laborer will do more work, and do it better, than two of our former slaves or three of the present freedmen.

N.B. I am satisfied from experience that one good Scotch laborer will do more work, and do it better, than two of our former slaves or three of the present freedmen.

Document 7

In 1948, when Europe was still flooded with refugees displaced by World War II, the United Nations adopted this declaration and began to develop a body of international human rights law that made the right to migrate fundamental. The declaration attempted to assure the individual's right to asylum from political or religious persecution.

Source: *The Universal Declaration of Human Rights* (New York: The United Nations, 1948).

UNIVERAL DECLARATION OF HUMAN RIGHTS

Adopted and proclaimed by General Assembly resolution 217 A (III) of 10 December, 1948

PREAMBLE

whereas recognition of the inherent dignity and of the equal and inalienable rights of all members of the human family is the foundation of freedom, justice and peace in the world....

whereas Member States have pledged themselves to achieve, in co-operation with the United Nations, the promotion of universal respect for an observance of human rights and fundamental freedoms,

whereas a common understanding of these rights and freedoms is of the greatest importance for the full realization of this pledge,

> *Now, therefore,*
> *The General Assembly*

Proclaims this Universal Declaration of Human Rights as a common standard of achievement for all peoples and all nations....

ARTICLE I

All human beings are born free and equal in dignity and rights. They are endowed with reason and conscience and should act towards one another in a spirit of brotherhood.

Everyone is entitled to all the rights and freedoms set forth in this Declaration, without distinction of any kind, such as race, color, sex, language, religion, politics or other opinion, national or social origin, property, birth or other status.

Furthermore, no distinction shall be made on the basis of the political, jurisdictional or international status of the country or territory to which a person belongs, whether it be independent, trust, non-self-governing or under any other limitation of sovereignty.

ARTICLE XIII

1. Everyone has the right to freedom of movement and residence within the borders of each State.

2. Everyone has the right to leave any country, including his own, and to return to his country.

ARTICLE XIV

1. Everyone has the right to seek and to enjoy in other countries asylum from persecution.

2. This right may not be invoked in the case of prosecutions genuinely arising from non-political crimes or from acts contrary to the purposes and principles of the United Nations.

ARTICLE XV

1. Everyone has the right to nationality.

2. No one shall be arbitrarily deprived of his nationality nor denied the right to change his nationality....

Everyone has the right to seek and to enjoy in other countries asylum from persecution.

1.4.3 Circular Migration

Document 8

This document outlines the obligations that an employer promised to honor in exchange for the labor of Puerto Ricans who came to the Philadelphia area to work as farm harvesters. Laws forbidding or requiring permits for the importation of contract labor do not apply to Puerto Ricans, who are U.S. citizens. After World War II, when East Coast farmers and agricultural processors experienced labor shortages, the government of Puerto Rico cooperated with the U.S. Employment Service to recruit thousands of sugarcane workers to come to the continental United States during the season from May to November. Most returned to Puerto Rico after the completion of their work contracts.

Source: Friend Neighborhood Guild Papers, urb 32, box 6x, Floder 219, Urban Archives, Temple University, Phila., PA., Record Group 64, Box 219, 1950–51.

INSTRUCTIONS FOR UTILIZING OF PUERTO RICAN AGRICULTURAL WORKERS

A. An employer must place an order with the local Employment Service office for workers.

B. Local office must establish need for outside workers.

C. Puerto Rican workers are available under the terms of a signed agreement. The agreement provides, among other things, that the employer must:

1. Sign an agreement with each employee and post a performance bond.

2. Arrange for transportation of the workers, and provide subsistence en route.

3. Assure workmen's compensation coverage for workers.

4. Guarantee minimum employment of 160 hours in each four-week period during the life of the agreement.

5. Provide suitable housing at no cost to the worker.

6. Pay prevailing rates for similar work in the community plus a bonus to workers completing the period of the work agreement....

Employers must post a performance bond.... The form of the bond required is the usual performance bond with which the Puerto Rican offices of the various insurance and surety companies are familiar....

The employer must arrange for transportation of workers from San Juan, Puerto Rico to the place of employment....

If the work agreement is for 13 weeks or more, transportation is advanced by the employer and withheld from the employees' earnings....

[The employer must provide] medical care....

Workmen's compensation coverage must be obtained for each worker....

Housing and living conditions:...where the employer houses and feeds the workers, the housing shall consist of place of abode approved by the appropriate state authority, including at least bed or cot, mattress, and blankets. Three meals a day shall be furnished...at a charge not to exceed $1.50 per day to the workers....

The employee will be paid the wage either on an hourly or piece-work basis prevailing in the area, but never less than the rate set forth in the work agreement....

Non-discrimination—Neither the white nor the colored Puerto Rican is accustomed to race discrimination at home. It should be understood by every local office and every prospective employer of Puerto Rican labor that the Government of Puerto Rico will not approve working agreements from communities in which the workers would be subjected to discrimination. The Government of Puerto Rico will not discriminate because of race, color or creed in the recruitment of workers for an employer.

> It should be understood by every local office and every prospective employer of Puerto Rican labor that the Government of Puerto Rico will not approve working agreements from communities in which the workers would be subjected to discrimination.

1.4.4 Chain Migration

Documents 9a and b

Letters sent to the editor of the *Chicago Defender*, an African American newspaper, demonstrate how print media stimulated and supported chains of migration from South to North during the World War I era. Northern employers facing a war-caused labor shortage advertised for workers in the *Defender*. The letters show that the migration experience of southern Blacks was similar to that of European immigrants who also migrated when they learned of job opportunities through letters, immigrant newspapers, or word of mouth. Notice the difference in the way the male and the female writer present themselves and their credentials. Like many Blacks who attended segregated schools in the South, these individuals were not fully literate. The lack of education did not, however, dampen their ambitions to improve life for themselves and their families. The woman who seeks work writes in her southern dialect. The misspellings are as they appear in the original documents.

Source: Emmett J. Scott, *Journal of Negro History*, 4, no.3 (July 1919), 305, 316.

ALGIERS, LA. MAY 16-17

Sir:

I saw sometime ago in the Chicago Defender, that you needed me for different work, would like to state that I can bring you all the men that you need, to do anything of work. or send them, would like to Come myself Con recommend all the men I bring to do any kind of work, and will give satisfaction; I have bin foreman for 20 yrs over some of these men in different work from R.R. work to Boiler Shop machine shop Blacksmith shop Concreet finishing or puting down pipe or any work to be did. they are all hard working men and will work at any kind of work also plastering anything in the labor line, from Clerical work down, I will not bring a man that is looking for a easy time only hard working men, that want good wages for there work, let me here from you at once.

JACKSONVILLE, FLA., MAY 22, 1917

I wish to go North....
I am brown skin
and just meaden size.

Chicago Defender:

I wish to go North haven got money enuff to come I can do any kind
of housework laundress nurse good cook has cook for northern
people I am 27 years of age just my self would you kindly inderseed
for me a job with some rich white people who would send me a
ticket and I pay them back please help me. I am brown skin
and just meaden size.

MENDOZA, 13 NOVEMBER 1901

Document 10

The Sola family of Biella in northern Italy sent two sons to Argentina who became part of a migration chain. In this letter, eighteen-year-old Oreste, the oldest brother, writes home describing all of the family and hometown acquaintances he had encountered in Argentina. The letter illustrates how originating towns and villages sent their inhabitants out to Argentina and other parts of the world. It also documents the way in which immigrants exported their earnings to the Old Country.

For additional information on Italians in Argentina see Part 2.5.2.

Source: Samuel L. Baily and Franco Ramella, eds., *One Family, Two Worlds: An Italian Family's Correspondence across the Atlantic, 1901-1922* (New Brunswick: Rutgers University Press, 1988), 38–40.

Dearest Father, Mother, brother, and sister,

This morning Secondino [a friend from Biella] arrived as you already indicated he would in your letter of 14 October. He had a very good trip, and he made everyone happy to see him healthy and cheerful—as we are, Carlo, Cichina, and Luigi [also friends from Biella]....

I have been in Mendoza for about three months, and I am happy that Secondino is here now, too. But I don't plan to stay fixed here. I would like to go to Peru with Beretta or to Cuba, where dear Cousin Edvino is staying, since I know that those who are there are doing well now. It wouldn't be bad here except you aren't sure about employment or about anything, especially for the type of work I do. So you can't even be sure of staying in one place. Before leaving I am waiting to get the address of Beretta. I thought that I could send something, instead I had to make some purchases. Be patient. I think of our family conditions too often to be able to think of anything else. Excuse me if I have been slow in writing. It's because I hoped to get a particular job, and I wanted to let you know. I was waiting for the decision of the company. The job went to another, also Italian, with whom nobody could compete. But let's leave the subject of work because here there are so many professions and so many trades that you can't say what you are doing. Today it's this and tomorrow it's that. I tried to go into the construction business for myself, but it didn't work out. So much effort and expense. Now I am doing something else, and I shall change again soon....

From what I make out of Dad's letter, he says that he was planning to send me some clothes when I get established here. Excuse me, dear parents, your sacrifices are already excessive. Now it is my job to pay them back at least in part, and I shall do everything possible to that end. But excuse me I am old enough now to earn my bread. I beg you not to be offended about this. If later I be in a position to, I shall send you money and everything. But for now, first of all, I have clothes to wear. I have already purchased here two suits and four pairs of trousers. So don't be upset then. Rather, I repeat, as soon as I am able, I'll see that you get something. Now I cannot; it has gone badly for me before I got started. When I shall again be the way I was in the beginning—but I don't know when because here [in] America [things] can change from one day to the next—you will have some repayment....

I am working as a smith and various things for the Great Western Railway of Argentina. But since they don't pay me as I want and I have to be first a blacksmith, then work as a planer, then at the lathe, I don't like it. At the first other job that comes along, I'm off. When I find something better, I don't want to work as a laborer for low wages anymore....

Your most loving son and brother,
Oreste Sola

Excuse me, dear parents, your sacrifices are already excessive...If later I be in a position to, I shall send you money and everything.

Documents 11a and 11b

Asian women often entered the immigration chain as "picture brides," that is, through marriages arranged by mail. Mail-order marriage was an effective way of providing spouses for Asian men settled in the Americas who were excluded from relationships with native-born women because of cultural differences and racial discrimination. To many native-born Americans, however, the picture bride tradition seemed akin to buying a wife through a catalogue.

Source: Eileen Sunada Sarasohn, ed., *The Issei: Portrait of a Pioneer, An Oral History*, 55–56; 31–34. Copyright 1983 by The Issei Oral History Project, Inc. Pacific Books, Publishers, Palo Alto, Calif.

Document 11a

In the following document Mrs. Ai Miyasaki, a Japanese immigrant who had met her future husband before she immigrated to the United States from Kumamoto Ken in 1916, tells an oral historian about less fortunate women, known as picture brides.

There were mostly picture brides on the ship—young girls, couples, men who came to Japan to find brides. Filipinos were on board also. The picture brides were full of ambition, expectation, and dreams. None knew what their husbands were like except by the photos. I wondered how many would be saddened and disillusioned. There were many. The grooms were not what the women thought they were. The men would say that they had businesses and send pictures which were taken when they were younger and deceived the brides. In reality, the men carried blanket rolls on their backs and were farm laborers. The men lied about their age and wrote they were fifteen years younger than they actually were.

The women were disillusioned and wanted to go back. There were many incidents of infidelity. Those women dressed fancy and worked in clubs and would find a man and run away with him. Then the husband would come with a pistol and shoot them. If children were born, the women had no choice but to bear the ordeal. Many Issei [first generation Japanese] people were in that situation. They suffered. I heard from many Issei people about their tragic life. Many were not compatible. Their ideas were different. Not only material but emotional hardships had to be borne. Many Issei mothers suffered much, but they could not afford to go back to Japan. Their expectations were great, so the disappointment was as great. I was fortunate because I had met my husband before I came here. So many imagined their prospective groom to be a certain type of great man. In our town in that era, the men all wore white clothes and dressed very nicely in the summer. Here, in America, the men usually had only one dingy black suit, worn-down shoes, shaggy hair…and to have seen someone like that as you came off the ship must have been a great disappointment. It was only natural to feel that way.

I took a look at his picture and told myself that I was to marry him.

Document 11b

Mrs. Rioy Orite, a native of Hiroshima Ken, came to the United States in 1914 after her marriage. Her description of her marriage reveals the complexity of personal and social relations underlying traditionally arranged marriages in Japan. Excepting the Japanese practice of a bride's family "adopting" her husband if they had no male heir, traditional European, Latin American, and Middle Eastern societies organize arranged marriages similarly. Mr. and Mrs. Orite raised a family and remained together until his death.

My husband had been living in the United States before his younger brother joined him. One family among my relatives wanted to adopt a child, but they couldn't find anybody. Orite's elder brother was married to a lady who was a relative of mine. Thus, his younger brother was recommended and then called back from the United States. When the younger brother returned to Japan, I met him briefly at a temple celebration. The younger brother said that his elder brother wanted to marry. He wondered if I would marry his brother. The proposal went smoothly. Since Orite's younger brother had been adopted by my aunt, we didn't have to trace Orite's lineage for we knew his family background already. All agreed to our marriage, but I didn't get married immediately. I was engaged at the age of sixteen and didn't meet Orite until I was almost eighteen. I had seen him only in a picture at first. Ours was a picture marriage. Being young, I was unromantic. I just believed that girls should get married. I felt he was a little old, about thirty, but the people around me praised the match. I took a look at his picture and told myself that I was to marry him. His brother in Tokyo sent me a lot of beautiful pictures [taken in the U.S.]. I was more excited about visiting a lot of places than about getting married. My name was entered in the Orites' *koseki*. Thus we were married.

Not having my husband with me, I lived off and on with both my parents and Orite's parents. Although my mother had decided to let me go to the States, she was worried about my going to a foreign country alone. She was willing to let me go if Orite returned to pick me up; otherwise, she was against the idea. She talked to the Orites, and they wrote him a letter. He returned in November, the following year. Everybody in his family was surprised, for he'd come back all of a sudden. I greeted him and gave him an address of welcome. Then he went straight into his father's bedroom. His father was eighty years old then. Being old, he just ate and stayed in bed. Not having seen each other for such a long time, the son and the father were all excited. My husband had brought bundles of bills, money which he had patiently earned for his father. He said, "Father, I have been working for a long time in order to make you happy. I'll give this to you." Both insisted that the other should keep the money....

My husband and I made a New Year's visit to my family. We were to stay overnight, but my husband wanted to go. I decided to stay overnight because they were my parents, and he went back home ahead. He picked up his younger brother on the way, since they were planning a short trip the following day. When they got home, they found every door locked. Orite got in through his father's bedroom. There he saw his mother sitting by his father's bed. She was worried about his father because he was breathing very heavily. Soon after Orite got back home, his father died. My husband was lucky. He was present at his father's deathbed. We came to the States after he'd concluded the funeral service and a forty-ninth-day memorial service for his father. I said to him, "You'll have nothing to regret concerning Japan even if you die in America for you have concluded your filial duty."

My husband and I left home the day following the memorial service. Our neighbors brought lunches with them and came to see us off. We went to an inn with the food and had a farewell party there. Then my husband and I got on a train. My father saw me off at the train station. My mother, who was still young then, had given birth to my younger brother right before I left and couldn't come for it was too soon after the delivery.

My husband's eldest brother saw us off too. He said, "Don't stay in the States too long. Come back in five years and farm with us." My father said, "Are you kidding? They can't learn anything in five years. They'll even have a baby over there for five years won't be enough time to do anything. Be patient for twenty years." Hearing those words, I was so shocked that I couldn't control my tears. My father told me to return to Japan if I wasn't able to adjust to things.

1.4.5 Colonizing Migration

Document 12

The following excerpts from a June 1880 Congressional debate express the U.S. justification for relocating a tribe of Native Americans, the Ute people. White miners wanted the Ute reservation opened for exploitation of its rich deposits of metals. The justification for relocating the Ute people, as described in the excerpts, amounted to a government-sponsored resettlement of Ute. After the federal government purchased reservation land, miners and settlers moved in, an instance of colonizing migration that had the approval of the government.

Source: *Congressional Record, House*, 46th Cong., 2nd Sess., June 7, 1880, 4259–62.

REPRESENTATIVE HASKELL. Mr. Speaker, if there is no other member of the House who desires to speak against this bill, I wish to present to the House as briefly as I am able the causes that have led to this Ute agreement, and the main features of the bill.

It will not be necessary for me to enter into any description of the Ute outbreak, and the conflict between the Indians and the troops out of which this agreement grew. It is a well-known fact that our policy of maintaining large Indian reservations immediately in front of the advancing tide of civilization has been found to be a poor policy, and one which we cannot sustain. It has been found thus with this Ute Reservation. A large territory embracing over twelve millions of acres of the richest mineral lands of Colorado has been allowed to be occupied exclusively by less than four thousand Utes. Within twenty miles of the eastern boundary of this reservation is a city of forty thousand inhabitants. Looking longingly across the borderline of that reservation are hundreds and thousands of venturous miners who desire to secure possession of the immense mineral wealth that it contains, and this is what led to the conflict originally between the United States and the Indians. The Interior Department became well advised that it would be utterly impossible to prevent a conflict between the Indians and the miners desiring to enter upon these lands for the sake of prospecting for minerals, and in view of the fact that an outbreak had occurred they sent for and brought on here the head chiefs of the Ute Nation, in order that a peaceful conference could be had which might avert the impending danger of an Indian war and bring about a peaceful settlement of the difficulty.

The Ute chiefs came here and met in council. They were not held in duress. They met the officers of the Interior Department and agreed to sell to the United States this reservation upon certain stipulated terms. They agreed to sell to the United States their reservation and to take up individual selections upon the best farming lands of the reservation. They are to receive $50,000 per annum as a perpetual annuity; they are to be provided with schools; they are to be made subject to the laws of the land. Their lands, however, are to be made inalienable, so that speculators and land-sharks cannot, by means of incumbrances, leases, or other methods, obtain control of their property hereafter for a period of twenty-five years.

There are, Mr. Speaker, before this Congress of the United States, in my judgment, but two roads open. One is to accept this bill, which is the result of a compromise and an agreement between the Government and the Indians, satisfactory to both.. .or we are to abandon this bill and undertake to maintain in that rich mineral district of Colorado a great Indian reservation of twelve millions of acres, against the on-rushing tide of civilization and of adventurous miners. In other words, we are to accept this treaty of peace.... or we are to engage in an Indian war that will result simply in the extermination of the Indians. There is no other course open. Already the miners are clustered on the borders of the reservation ready to enter. It is a mountainous country that would require three times the force the United States has at its disposal to protect and defend. It is a mountainous country in which, if we went to war, there would be simply a reproduction on a larger scale of those terrible scenes in the lavabeds when we captured the Modocs. In other words, it means the absolute extermination of the Indian at a great cost of blood and treasure to the United States, or it means the peaceable solution of the question by which the Government buy their land, pay them year by year a fair stipend, care for their little ones in school, protect them under the laws of the land, put whites and Indians side by side under the same law, and teach the red men the arts of civilization by actual contact with the civilized man himself.... I yield now for two minutes to the gentleman from Colorado.

MR. BELFORD. Mr. Speaker, this bill is not what the people of my state desire, but yet I propose to vote for it, because I regard it as the only way out of the war which will inevitably happen if Congress ignores the consideration of this question.... it shows how utterly futile is the attempt to civilize and educate these Indians....

MR. ATKINS: I wish to ask the gentleman from Colorado a question, and that is whether the value of the lands to be ceded to the United States will reimburse the Government what is paid out to these Indians under this bill?

MR. BELFORD:...Every man who has gone through the reservation says it is exceedingly rich in gold and silver.... If you pass this bill you at once open up a tract of country almost as large as New England; a country abounding in great material wealth, and fitted to become the home of a million active and enterprising citizens. You give the sanction of the Government to the act of the miner in taking up a claim; you open a way by which he can acquire title to land; and you apprise the Indian that he can no longer stand as a breakwater against the constantly swelling tide of civilization. The passage of this bill is the reclamation of eleven millions of acres of land from the domain of barbarism. It enlarges the possible achievements of the white man by enlarging the field in which he can labor. It settles for all time the doctrine which has received illustrations in the past that an idle and thriftless race of savages cannot be permitted to guard the treasure vaults of the nation which hold our gold and silver, but that they shall always be open, to the end that the prospector and miner may enter in and by enriching himself enrich the nation and bless the world by the results of his toil.

...an idle and thriftless race of savages cannot be permitted to guard the treasure vaults of the nation which hold our gold and silver...

Migration and the New World

Documents

4.2

The following documents continue the themes discussed in Part 2 of the text. World migration patterns, migration to the New World, the causes for migration to the United States, and American reactions to the presence of foreign–born residents and ethnic minorities are described.

2.2 Sending and Receiving Regions

See also 1.4.1, Forced Migration, and 1.4.2, Voluntary Migration.

Document 13

Major World Migrations, 1830–55.
This map show the impact of the Irish
potato famine from 1846 to 1851 and the
replacement of Africans by northern
Europeans in the Americas.

Source: Information from Kevin Reilly, *The West and
the World: A History of Civilization*, 2d ed. (New York:
HarperCollins College, 1989), Vol. 2, 237.

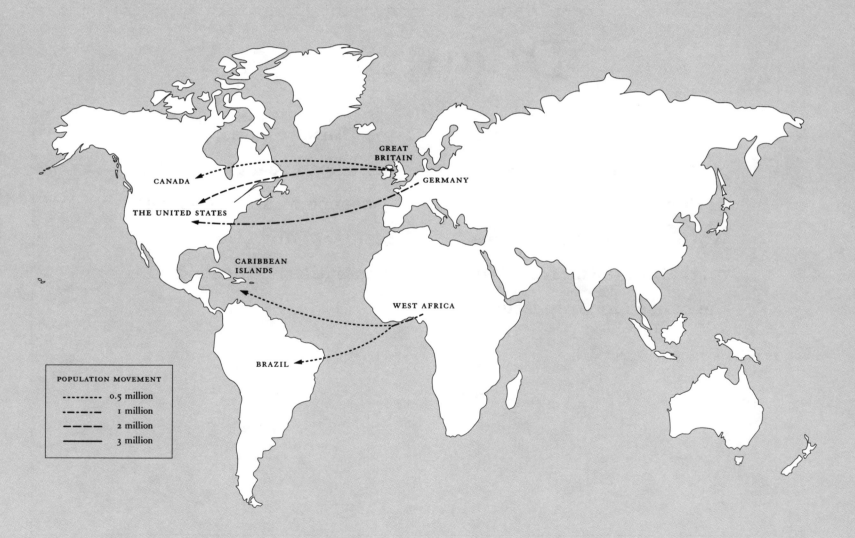

POPULATION MOVEMENT

- ·········· 0.5 million
- ·-·-·-· 1 million
- – – – 2 million
- ——— 3 million

Document 14

Destination of Immigrants, 1881–1924. This chart demonstrates that the United States was the world's major receiving nation for immigrants in that era.

Sources: William S. Bernard, ed., *American Immigration Policy* (New York: Harper and Brothers, 1950), 202; U.S. Immigration and Naturalization Service, *1990 Statistical Yearbook of the Immigration and Naturalization Service* (Washington, D.C.: U.S. Government Printing Office, 1991), 15.

TOTAL NUMBER 45 954 633

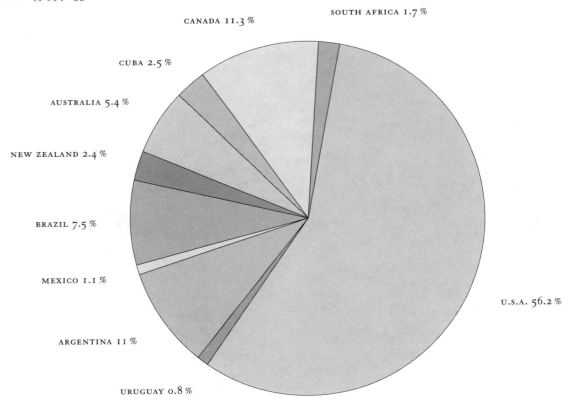

SOUTH AFRICA 1.7 %

CANADA 11.3 %

CUBA 2.5 %

AUSTRALIA 5.4 %

NEW ZEALAND 2.4 %

BRAZIL 7.5 %

MEXICO 1.1 %

ARGENTINA 11 %

URUGUAY 0.8 %

U.S.A. 56.2 %

Document 15

Major World Migrations, 1860–85. This map illustrates migration patterns that came into being because of demands for labor in receiving nations. The out-migration from northern Europe to North and South America and the huge movement from India to Burma were labor migrations. For the most part, the India to Burma flow was a circular migration of seasonal labor.

Source: Information from Kevin Reilly, *The West and the World: A History of Civilization, 2d ed.* (New York: HarperCollins College, 1989), Vol. 2, 238.

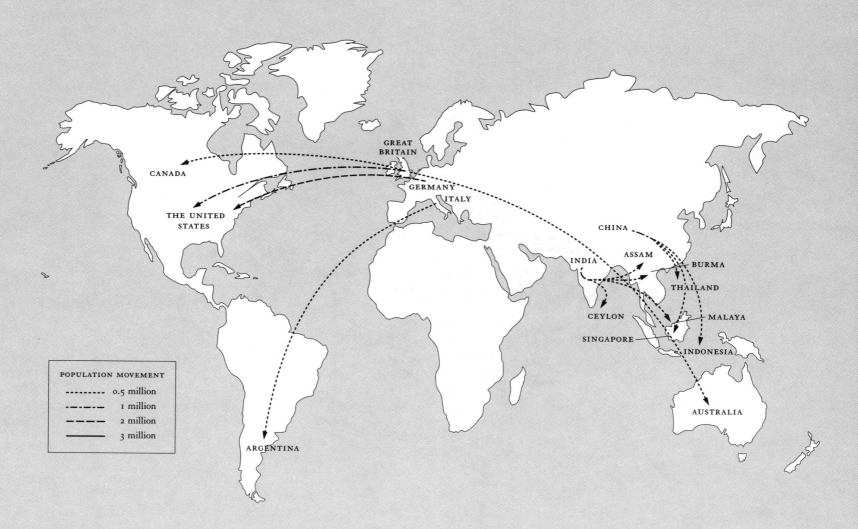

POPULATION MOVEMENT

- - - - - - - - - 0.5 million
- · - · - · - 1 million
- - - - - 2 million
——————— 3 million

2.3 Colonization of the New World

Document 16

Because the colonial effort succeeded in creating what is now the United States, we tend to forget that the founders of Virginia and other colonies had to persuade potential settlers and investors of the value of their effort. Promoters of Virginia colony produced the following document, here presented with its original seventeenth-century spellings. It enumerates propagation of the Christian faith, defense of the King's economic and political interests, and sound investment potential as reasons for settling Virginia.

Source: Lord De la Ware, Sir Thomas Smith, Sir Walter Cope, and Master Waterson, *A True and Sincere declaration of the purpose and ends of the Plantation begun in Virginia* (London, 1610), from *The Old Dominion in the Seventeenth Century: A Documentary History of Virginia, 1606–1689*, edited by Warren M. Billings, 14–15., ©1975 by the University of North Carolina Press. Published for the Institute of Early American History and Culture. Used by permission of the publisher.

It is Reserved and onely proper to *Divine Wisdome* to forsee and ordaine, both the *endes* and *wayes* of every action. In *humaine prudence* it is all [that] can be required, to propos *Religious* and *Noble* and *Feasable* ends....

Upon which grounds, We purpose to deliver roundly and clearly, our *endes* and *wayes* to the hopeful Plantations begun in Virginia.... The Principal and *Maine Endes* (out of which are easily derived to any meane understanding infinitlesse, and yet great ones) were first to preach and baptize into *Christian Religion,* and by propagation of the *Gospell,* to recover out of the Armes of the Divell, a number of poore and miserable soules, wrapt up unto death, in almost *invincible ignorance,* and to endeavour the fulfilling, and accomplishment of the number of the elect, which shall be gathered from out all corners of the earth; and to add our myte to the Treasury of Heaven, that as we pray for the coming of the Kingdome of Glory, so to express in our actions, the same desire, if God, have pleased, to use so weak instruments, to the ripening and consummation thereof.

Secondly, to provide and build up for the publike *Honour* and *Safety* of our *Gratious King* and his *Estates* (by the favor of our Superiors even in that care) some small Rampier of our owne, in this opportune and general summer of peace, by transplanting the rancknesse and multitude of increase in our people; of which there is left no vent, but age; and evident danger that the number and infinitness of them, will out-grow the matter, whereon to worke for their life and sustentation, and shall one infest and become a burthen to another. But by this provision they may be seated as a Bulwarke of defence, in a place of advantage, *against a stranger enemy,* who shall in great proportion grow rich in treasure...

Lastly, the appearance and assurance of *Private commodity* to the *particular undertakers,* by recovering and possessing to themselves a fruitful land, whence they may furnish and provide this Kingdome, with all such necessities and defects (Copper, Iron, Steel, Timber for ships, yards, masts, cordage, sope ashes) [marginal note in original—Ed.] under which we labour, and are now enforced to buy, and receive at the curtesie of other Princes, under the burthen of great Customs, and heavy impositions, and at so high rates in trafique, by reason of the great waste of them from whence they are now derived, which threatens almost an impossibility long to recover them, or at least such losse in exchange, as both the Kingdome and Merchant, will be weary of the deerenesse and peril. These being the true, and essential ends of this Plantation....

Document 17

Edward Johnson (1598–1672) migrated
to Boston in 1630, returned to England for his
family, and left his homeland again in the
midst of religious controversy about the
relative importance of divine selection versus
good works as the cause of personal salvation.
The Puritans maintained that only God
determined individual salvation.

Active in New England public life,
Johnson became a selectman, military captain,
and a deputy to the General Court of
Woburn, a town he helped to establish.
He published his *Wonderworking Providence
of Sions Savior in New England* anonymously
in London in 1654. The religious motivations,
notably, the desire to return the Christian
church to a pure state uncorrupted by
"popery," or Roman Catholic influences, and
idolatry, motivated Johnson and others,
according to his account, to migrate to the
New World. Johnson himself was not a
clergyman, yet the religious motivations
behind colonization are clear in his account.

Source: Perry Miller and Thomas Johnson, eds.,
The Puritans (New York: American Book Company,
1938; rev. ed. New York: HarperTorch books, 1963),
143–47.

WONDER-WORKING PROVIDENCE
OF SIONS SAVIOR BEGING,
A RELATION OF THE FIRST PLANTING IN
NEW ENGLAND,
IN THE YEARE, 1628.

BOOK I. CHAP. I.
*The Sad Condition of England, When This People
Removed.*

When England began to decline in Religion…. and
instead of purging out Popery, a farther compliance
was sought not onely in vaine Idolatrous Ceremonies,
but also in prophaning the Sabbath, and by Procla-
mation throughout their Parish churches, exasperating
lewd and prophane persons to celebrate a Sabbath like
the Heathen to *Venus*, *Baccus* and *Ceres*; in so much
that the multitude of irreligious lascivious and popish
affected persons spred the whole land like *Grashoppers*,
in this very time Christ the glorious King of his
Churches, raises an Army out of our *English* Nation,
for freeing his people from their long servitude under
usurping Prelacy; and because every corner of
England was filled with the fury of malignant adver-
saries, Christ creates a New *England* to muster up the
first of his Forces in; Whose low condition, little
number, and remotenesse of place made these adver-
saries triumph, despising this day of small things, but
in this hight of their pride the Lord Christ brought
sudden, and unexpected destruction upon them. Thus
have you a touch of the time when this worke began…

*The Commission of the People of Christ
Shipped for New England, and First of Their
Gathering into Churches.*

At your landing see you observe the Rule of his
Word…. Let the matter and forme of your
Churches be such as were in the Primitive
Times before *Antichrists* Kingdome prevailed
plainly poynted out by Christ and his Apostles,
in most of their Epistles to be neither Nationall
nor Provinciall, but gathered together in
Covenant of such a number as might ordinarily
meete together in one place….

CHAP. XII

*On the Voluntary Banishment, Chosen
by This People of Christ, and Their Last Farewel
Taken of Their Country and Friends*

And now behold the several Regiments of these
Souldiers of *Christ*, as they are shipped for his
service in the *Western* World, part thereof being
come to the Towne and Port of *Southampton* in
England, where they were to be shipped, that
they might prosecute this designe to the full….
making sale of such Land as they possesse, to
the great admiration of their Friends and
Acquaintance, who thus expostulate with them.
What, will not the large income of your yearly
revenue content you, which in all reason cannot
chuse but be more advantagious both to you and
yours, than all that Rocky Wildernesse, whither
you are going, to run the hazard of your life?

Have you not here your Tables filled with great
variety of Foode, your Coffers filled with Coyne,
your Houses beatufilly built and filled with all
rich Funderniture?…have you not such a
gainfull Trade as none the like in the Towne
where you live?…

Ah! my much honoured friend, hath Christ
given thee so great a charge as to be Leader of his
People into that far remote, and vast Wildernesse,
I, oh, and alas thou must die there and never shall
I see thy Face in the flesh againe, wert thou called
to so great a taske as to passe the pretious Ocean,
and hazard thy person in Battell against thousands of Malignant Enemies there? There were
hopes of thy return with triumph, but now after
two three, or foure moneths spent with daily
expectation of swallowing Waves, and cruell
Pirates, you are to be Landed among barbarous
Indians, famous for nothing but cruelty, where
you are like to spend your days in a famishing
condition for a long space; Scarce had he uttered
this, but presently hee lockes his friend fast in his
armes, holding each other thus for some space of
time, they weepe againe, But as *Paul* to his
beloved flock: the other replies what doe you
weeping and breaking my heart? I am now prest
for the service of our *Lord Christ*, to re-build the
most glorious Edifice of Mount Sion in a
Wildernesse, and as *John* Baptist, I must cry
prepare yee the way of the Lord, make his paths
strait, for beholde he is comming againe, he is
comming to destroy *Antichrist*, and give the whore
double to drinke the very dregs of his wrath.

2.4.2 Agriculture and Migration

Document 18

After Congress passed legislation forbidding the importation of contract labor in 1885, it investigated to determine how and if the laws were being violated. Antonio di Dierro, a migrant from an Italian agricultural village, testified concerning abuses of contract laborers.

Source: U.S. House of Representatives, *Testimony Taken by the Select Committee of the House of Representatives to Inquire into the Alleged Violation of the Laws Prohibiting the Importation of Contract Laborers, Paupers, Convicts, and other Classes* (House of Representatives, 1888, Misc. Doc., 50 c., I s. No. 572, vol.15, #2579, 100–05).

What caused you to think or consider the question of emigrating to the United States?

Where were you born?

In a village called the Cildona, in the province of Campo Basso.

Did you live there until you emigrated to America?

Yes, sir.

When did you arrive in this country?

The 27th of April.

What year?

This year....

What was your occupation in Italy?...

Farm work....

What caused you to think or consider the question of emigrating to the United States?

There was a man who was collecting and persuading people to come here, and I heard of it and I joined the others....

What was this man's name?

Giovanni Di Chicchio.

This man was persuading emigrants to come to the United States?

He was persuading them to come to this side and he gave good news about work.

Did you have a personal interview with Di Chicchio? Did you see him personally?

Whoever happened to be in the village he would coax them all and approach them and talk to them about coming to this side.

Did he have an office in the village where you lived?

He resided in the same village....

What was his business?

He had no occupation except employing men, and he had some property; he had no other occupation excepting the employment of men.

The employment of men for what purpose?...

Employing people for farm work around about the same district.

Did he also employ people to work in the United States?

All I know is the men when he met them he used to talk

to them about coming to America; he said: "You will
find good wages there, and if you can't find anything
there you can always come back."

*What did he say about what the rate of wages were
and whether they were steady or not?*

He wrote something to us to the effect that there
would be plenty of work, the moment we landed,
at a dollar and a half.

Did Di Chicchio write to you?

Yes sir....

State the contents of that paper as near as you can remember it.

He undertook to give us work as soon as we landed in
America, and if he did not give us work he undertook
to give us food.

*Did you finally make up your mind to emigrate
to the United States?*

Yes sir; I was persuaded from these representations to
come here.

*Would you have come here if it had not been for the
representations of Di Chicchio?*

I would never have thought of coming out had
I not been persuaded by this man.

*When you finally made up your mind to emigrate what
did you do?*

Well, when I made up my mind I had nothing to do;
I had only to undertake the repayment of
200 francs and start.

Did you have any money yourself at all?

Not a cent.

Did you have any property, real or personal?

Nothing, sir.

*Who was it that offered to advance your passage
money to the United States?*

This man, Giovanni Di Chicchio.

*In consideration of Di Chicchio paying this passage to the
United States what did you agree to do?*

In consideration of the advancing of the money to pay
for the passage, I undertook to return 200 francs.

Return it to whom?

This Di Chicchio came with us as far as Albany
on this side.

*I asked you the question who you were to return
the 200 francs to?*

Di Chicchio himself.

After you made the arrangement in Italy what next took place?

I left the village together with twenty-four other
countrymen of mine.

*Did you further agree to labor for Di Chicchio at any
particular place in the United States?*

Di Chicchio said he had work in America where
he was going to take these men.

How much did he agree to pay you?

One dollar and forty cents, or $1.50, according
to circumstances.

A day?

Yes, sir.

*Do you know what the price of a passage ticket was from your
town to New York?*

He did not mention it to us, and I don't
know it now....

Did you subsequently go to work in Albany?

Six or seven days after my arrival, Di Chicchio found
some work for us and we went to work....

How long did you work there?

About twenty days, as near as I can remember.

During that twenty days where did you board?

We lived where Di Chicchio did.

Did Di Chicchio pay for your board and charge it to you?…
    He had board at his house and we had to take
    it from him.

By MR. GUENTHER:

How did you return to New York?
    By steam-boat.
Who paid your fare?
    I paid it, sir.

By MR. OATES:

Where did you get the money from?
    At the end of the fortnight—they paid every
    fortnight up there—and at the end of the fortnight,
    I cashed some money. All I had left was $3; $2
    I paid for the steamboat for myself and friend,
    and we had one left amongst the two when
    we landed in New York from Albany.
How much money did you receive for your work in Albany?
    About $21 or $22, at $1.25 a day.
*Were you paid for this work; did you receive the money
for the twenty-one days' work?*
    Yes, sir; at $1.25.
Was it paid to you?
    I cashed, after a fortnight and a half, $22, at
    $1.25, from the boss, and then I had to settle
    with Di Chicchio..
*How much had you left when you paid Di Chicchio
for the board?*
    I had $3 left out of the $22 paid….
How much do you still owe Di Chicchio?
    …that would be $35 still unpaid.

By THE CHAIRMAN:

*Have you any money today or any property of any kind or
description?*
    Nothing, not a cent.
How do you live?
    Pick wood and on charity; picking sticks….
Are you willing to work today?
    Yes, sir; if I can find it.
At what price?
    The usual price.
*Suppose you could not get the usual price, would you be
willing to work for 50 or 75 cents a day if you could
not get any better pay?*
    No, sir; I would rather go back and starve there than
    to starve here on half that. So long as I can't make
    a $5 bill to send to my mother and father in Italy,
    there is no use working….
When you came here did you intend to stay here always?
    I came with the intention of remaining a few seasons
    if I found work.
*If you did not find work, what did you expect to do—
to go back to Italy?*
    Yes, sir.

By MR. GUENTHER:

*If I should want you to work for me for three days
at 75 cents a day, would you do it?*
    No, sir.
Why not?
    I always dream of going back rather than to work
    at that price….
Then you rather beg than work for 75 cents a day?…
    …I would rather beg.

Document 19

Decennial Immigration to the United States
from Europe, 1820–1919. These statistics, culled
from the U.S. Census, describe changing sources
of European migration to the United States.

Source: Niles N. Carpenter, "Immigrants and Their
Children," U. S. Bureau of the Census, Monograph No. 7
(Washington, D. C.: Government Printing Office, 1927),
324–25.

	1820	1830	1840	1850	1860	1870	1880	1890	1900	1910
Millions of people	0.1	0.5	1.4	2.7	2.1	2.7	5.2	3.7	8.2	6.3
% of total from:										
Ireland	40.2	31.7	46	36.9	24.4	15.4	12.8	11	4.2	2.6
Germany*	4.5	23.2	27	34.8	35.2	27.4	27.5	15.7	4	2.7
U.K.	19.5	13.8	15.3	13.5	14.9	21.1	15.5	8.9	5.7	5.8
Scandinavia	0.2	0.4	0.9	0.9	5.5	7.6	12.7	10.5	5.9	3.8
Canada**	1.8	2.2	2.4	2.2	4.9	11.8	9.4	0.1	1.5	11.2
Russia*					0.2	1.3	3.5	12.2	18.3	17.4
Austria-Hungary*					0.2	2.2	6	14.5	24.4	18.2
Italy					0.5	1.7	5.1	16.3	23.5	19.4

* Continental European boundaries prior to the 1919 settlement.
** British America to 1867, Canada includes Newfoundland;
Canadian immigration was not recorded between 1886 and 1893.

2.4.3 Industrialization and Settlement Patterns

Document 20

Urbanization in the United States, 1830.
This map shows the major areas to which most
nineteenth-century immigrants were drawn.

Source: David Ward, *Cities and Immigrants* (New York:
Oxford University Press, 1971), 27, Fig.1–5,
"Urbanization in the United States, 1830."
Reprinted by permission of Oxford University Press.

●	200 000+
●	100 000 - 200 000
•	50 000 - 200 000
•	25 000 - 50 000
•	10 000 - 25 000
•	5 000 - 10 000
– – –	MORE THAN TWO PEOPLE PER SQUARE MILE

Document 21

Urbanization in the United States, 1910.
This map, which shows major areas of urban
settlement in 1910, indicates that most
immigrants settled in cities.

Source: David Ward, *Cities and Immigrants* (New York:
Oxford University Press, 1971), 42, Fig. 1–9,
"Urbanization in the United States, 1910."
Reprinted by permission of Oxford University Press.

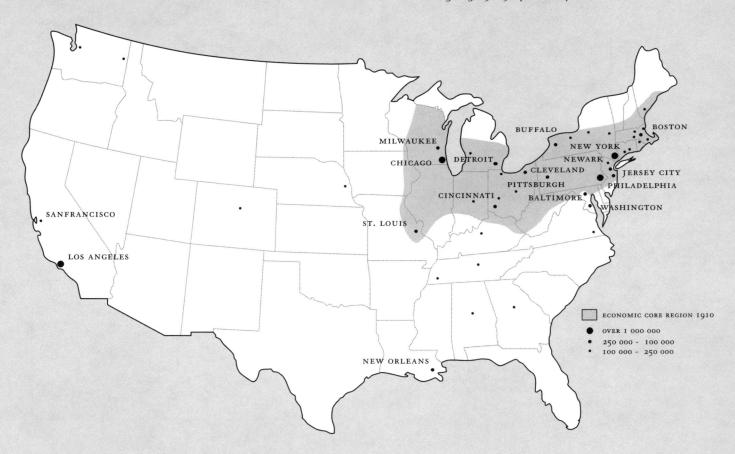

PERCENTAGE URBAN POPULATION

UNDER 30   30-50   50-70   OVER 70

BUFFALO

MILWAUKEE

CHICAGO   DETROIT

BOSTON

NEW YORK

NEWARK

CLEVELAND   JERSEY CITY

PITTSBURGH   PHILADELPHIA

CINCINNATI   BALTIMORE

SAN FRANCISCO   WASHINGTON

ST. LOUIS

LOS ANGELES

ECONOMIC CORE REGION 1910

● OVER 1 000 000

• 250 000 - 100 000

· 100 000 - 250 000

NEW ORLEANS

Document 22

Industrialization was not simply a matter of machines taking over what human hands had done. It also meant great population movements from countryside to city and the separation of young workers from their families. Sarah Rice had just reached adolescence when she migrated from her father's farm and hometown to work in a textile mill in Connecticut. Her letter tells us that leaving home was not easy.

Source: Vermont Historical Society. Reprinted by permission of Vermont Historical Society.

MASONVILLE, SUNDAY, FEBRUARY 23, 1845

Dear Father:

I now take my pen in hand to let you know where I am and how I came here and how my health is. I have been waiting perhaps longer than I ought to without letting you know where I am and yet I had a reason for so doing. Well knowing that you were dolefully prejudiced against a cotton factory, and being no less prejudiced myself, I thought it best to wait and see how I prospered and also whether I was going to stay or not. I well knew that if I could not make more in the mill than I can doing housework I should not stay. Now I will tell you how I happened to come. The Saturday after New Years I came to Masonville in Thompson, Connecticut, with James Alger to visit his sister who weaves in the mill. We came Saturday and returned to Millbury on Monday. While here I was asked to come back and learn to weave. I did not fall in with the idea at all because I well knew that I should not like it as well as housework and knowing that you would not approve of my working in the mill. But when I considered that I had got myself to take care of, I knew I ought to do that way I can make the most and save the most. I concluded to come and try, promising Mrs. Waters that if I did not like it I would return the first of April.

I have wove 4 weeks and have wove 6.89 yds. We have one dollar and 10 cents for a hundred yards. I wove with Oliver Alger one week to learn and I took 2 looms 2 weeks and now I have 3 looms. I get along as well as anyone could expect. I think that very likely before the year is out I shall be able to tend 4 looms and then I can make more. 0. and P. Alger make three dollars a week besides their board. We pay 1.25 for our board. We three girls board with a Widow Whitemore. She is a first rate homespun woman. I like it quite as well as I expected but not as well as housework. To be sure it is a noisy place and we

I should not want to
spend my days in a mill
unless they are short
because I like a farm
too well for that.

are confined more than I like to be. I do not wear out my clothes and shoes as I do when I do housework. If I can make 2 dollars per week besides my board and save my clothes and shoes I think it will be better than to do housework for nine shillings. I mean for a year or two. I should not want to spend my days in a mill unless they are short because I like a farm too well for that. My health is good now. And I say now that if it does not agree with my health I shall give it up at once. I consider if my health is gone I am done at once. I have been blessed with good health always ever since I began to work out. I have not been confined to my bed but one day since I was sick with mumps the time Grandmother Rice died. I was very sick one day when I was at Mrs. Waters.

Dear Father, in my last letter I told you I had morally reformed. Yes I trust I have and bless God that he unsealed my eyes to see where I was standing, and where I have been since I became a backslider. The name haunts me. It all seems like a dream. Pray for me, Father, that if I ever enjoyed Religion I may enjoy it again and do as much good as I have hurt in the cause and the great God assisting me I will try to pray for myself. I feel I am perfectly willing to give up all into the hands of God and will try to lead a better life than I have done.

I want you to write as soon as you get this. Address your letter to Masonville, Thompson, Connecticut. Give my love to Mother & to all our folks. Tell Brother to write. I have not written to Hiram yet. I want to know where Ephraim is and how you all do Father.

Good bye
Sarah Rice

Document 23

Major World Migrations, 1890–1915. This map shows the great increase in world population movements to the United States during the Ellis Island era. Note the huge numbers of Europeans migrating to the United States. The United States restricted immigration from China in 1882.

Source : Kevin Reilly, *The West and the World: A History of Civilization*, 2d ed. (New York: HarperCollins College, 1989), Vol. 2, 240, "Major World Migrations, 1870–1915."

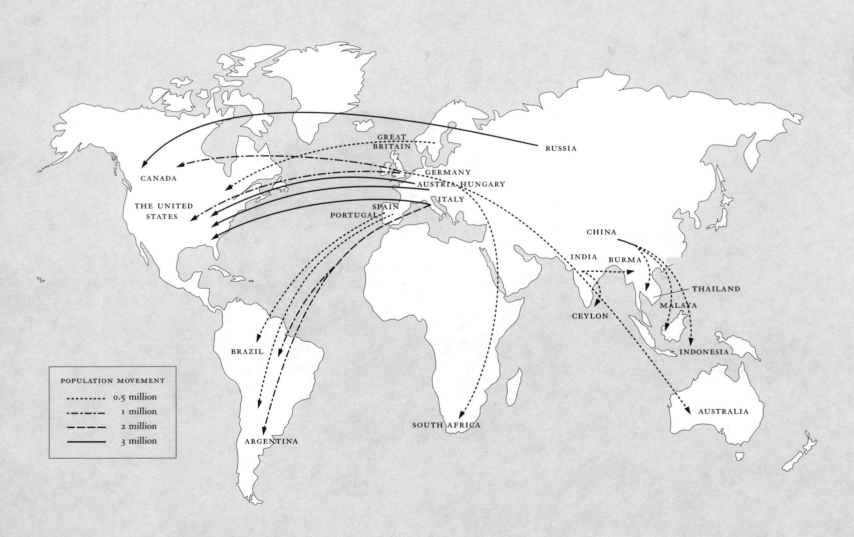

POPULATION MOVEMENT

.... 0.5 million
–·–·–·– 1 million
– – – – 2 million
———— 3 million

2.4.4 Worldwide Effects

Document 24

Chinese Expatriates in Asia in 1922. The United States was not the only point of
arrival for great numbers of the world's immigrants; Chinese immigration to southeast
Asia was also significant. The stream of Indian migrants to the area around Ceylon
and Burma, Malaya, Fiji, and Natal was a form of colonizing migration with contract
labor; the British East India Company exported Indian labor to those areas.

Source: Department of History, Rutgers the State University of New Jersey (New Brunswick, N.J.,
1985). Based on U.S. Census information.

TOTAL NUMBER - 7, 882, 676

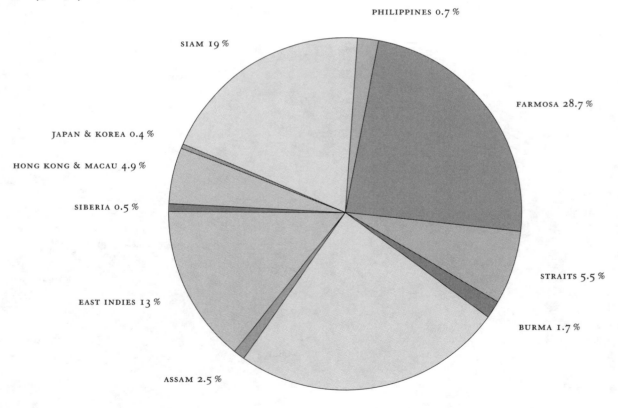

PHILIPPINES 0.7 %

SIAM 19 %

FARMOSA 28.7 %

JAPAN & KOREA 0.4 %

HONG KONG & MACAU 4.9 %

SIBERIA 0.5 %

STRAITS 5.5 %

EAST INDIES 13 %

BURMA 1.7 %

ASSAM 2.5 %

JAVA 23.2 %

Document 25

Chinese Living in the Americas in 1922. This chart demonstrates that other receiving nations were accepting Chinese immigrants early in the twentieth century. Despite exclusion laws, the United States still received a majority of Chinese who came to the Americas.

Source: Department of History, Rutgers the State University of New Jersey (New Brunswick, N.J., 1985). Based on U.S. Census information.

TOTAL NUMBER - 255, 146

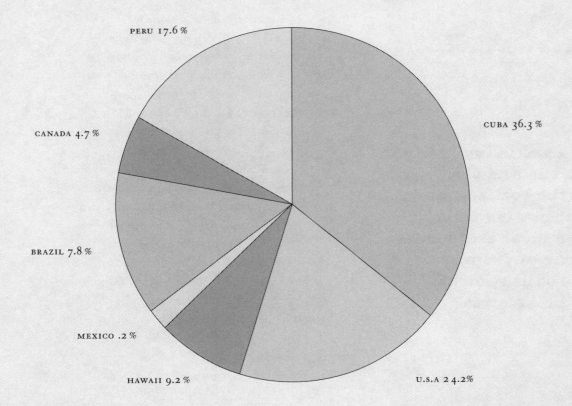

PERU 17.6 %

CANADA 4.7 %

CUBA 36.3 %

BRAZIL 7.8 %

MEXICO .2 %

HAWAII 9.2 %

U.S.A 24.2%

2.5 Reactions to Mass Immigration

See also 2.6, A Range of Views about Immigration.

Document 26

German emigration to the United States, which followed the Irish, peaked during the 1850s and 1860s, driven mainly by politics in the form of a failed liberal revolution in 1848 that caused thousands of Germans to seek a life elsewhere (see **Document 13**, "Major World Migration, 1830–55"). Although the Germans, like the Irish, suffered from stereotyping in the United States, they were a more affluent group to begin with and quickly established themselves in business. This newspaper article is written by a Scottish observer.

Source: "German Emigration," *Chamber's Edinburgh Journal* (June 20, 1846), 387–89, in Stanley Feldstein and Lawrence Costello, eds., *The Ordeal of Assimilation: A Documentary History of the White Working Class* (New York: Anchor Books, 1974), 10–14.

...there are many restrictions and the young, the restless, and the imaginative thirst for their ideal freedom, and many of them seek for the realisation of Utopia in America.

The dread of destitution is a motive to emigrate in Germany, as in England; but not a principal motive.... In Westphalia, for instance, a great number of small proprietors have lately sold their lands, and sailed for America—each of whom, it is reckoned, has taken with him at least thirty pounds' worth of goods and money....

The one great cause of this almost national movement is the desire for absolute, political, and religious freedom; the absence of all restrictions upon the development of society; and the publication of opinions which cannot be realised at home....

There is nothing that can be called oppression on the part of the governments; the mass of the people are well satisfied with their rulers—and with reason, for the actual executive has been generally excellent; but there are many restrictions and the young, the restless, and the imaginative thirst for their ideal freedom, and many of them seek for the realisation of Utopia in America. Complete religious equality is a still more powerful want in a country where Catholics and Protestants are so nearly balanced, and where the state of parties is such, that the minority in faith, though nominally equal in law must always live under the shade of an alien creed. This of itself has urged many across the Atlantic....

The most important point connected with the subject is the influence which such an annual influx of a foreign population, speaking the same language and nearly all professing the same (the Roman Catholic) faith, cannot fail to exercise upon the future destinies of the United States.... The great object of each family that successively arrives, is to fix itself as near as possible to its relatives, if it has any; if not, to its countrymen. Every settlement thus becomes the nucleus of a pure German circle which is born, marries, and dies within itself, and with the least possible admixture of Anglo-Americans.... Chance or preference directed the first settlers towards Pennsylvania. To Pennsylvania, accordingly, the stream has steadily set ever since; and the result is, that the *German* population of that state already balances the Anglo-Saxon; and stands in the adjoining state of Ohio, as three to seven. Next to these, the greatest number is found in Maryland, Indiana, Illinois, and Missouri, neither going far to the north or south of the same parallel. In most of these states, the debates in the houses of representatives and the laws are printed alike in German and English.

Every settlement thus becomes the nucleus of a pure German circle which is born, marries, and dies within itself, and with the least possible admixture of Anglo-Americans....

2.5.1 The Irish Influx

See **Document 13**, "Major World Migrations 1830–55," and **Document 19**, "Decennial Immigration to the United States from Europe, 1820–1919."

2.5.2 Example: Italian Migration
The U.S.A. Compared to Argentina

For a more detailed discussion of Italians in New York City and Buenos Aires, see Samuel L. Baily, "The Adjustment of Italian Immigrants in Buenos Aires and New York, 1870–1910," *American Historical Review*, vol. 88, no. 2, (April 1983), 281–305.

Document 27

Italian Emigration to U.S. and Argentina, 1861–1970. This chart suggests how the United States compares to Argentina as a receiving nation for immigrants.

Source: Department of History, Rutgers the State University of New Jersey (New Brunswick, N.J., 1985). Based on U.S. Census figures.

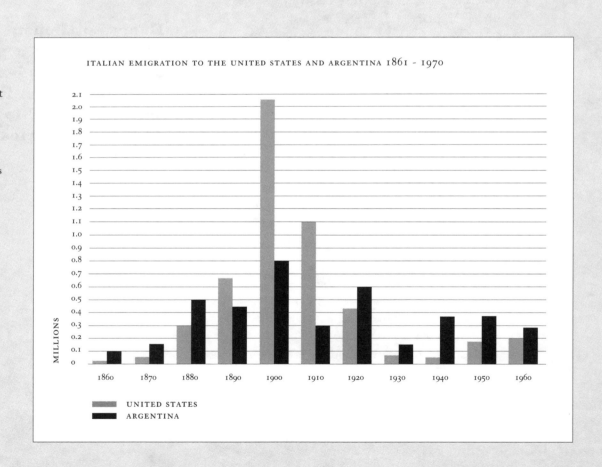

ITALIAN EMIGRATION TO THE UNITED STATES AND ARGENTINA 1861 - 1970

2.6 A Range of Views about Immigration

Document 28

"The mortar of assimilation—and the one element that won't mix." This cartoon, published in *Puck*, a popular magazine that often satirized U.S. politics, portrays a number of immigrant and minority groups.

Source. Puck, 1889.

THE MORTAR OF ASSIMILATION — AND THE ONE ELEMENT THAT WON'T MIX.

Immigrants who came to the United States did not view themselves in the same way as resident Americans did. In 1865, an English immigrant coal miner described his own work and living habits in a British newspaper.

Source: Durham *Chronicle*, in Charlotte Erickson, ed., *Emigration from Europe, 1815-1915: Select Documents* (London: Adam and Charles Black, 1976), 203–4.

> ...the motive of employers and capitalists in sending agents among you is plain. It is to overstock the labour market, and thereby reduce wages.

31 MARCH, 1865

A Durham miner, John Watson, formerly of Wrekenton, has been out in Jefferson County, Ohio, eight years. Watson writing from America, and addressing the working men of the North says: "Employers and capitalists, and others interested in getting cheap labour, have sent agents and commissioners among you, who, by advertisements in newspapers and publications would make the English miner and English working man believe that America is at the present time little short of a terrestrial paradise, that here, if the millennium has not already arrived, it certainly is close at hand. No, the motive of employers and capitalists in sending agents among you is plain. It is to overstock the labour market, and thereby reduce wages. They may tell you we are making very high wages, which some of us may do but they don't tell you that all things we have to buy are high also. I worked over 20 years in the coal mines of Durham and Northumberland; therefore I am well acquainted with all the evils you have to contend with. I have worked eight years in the coal mines of this country so I think I may claim to be able to judge of a miner's life here and in England. In England you have a house and fuel for next to nothing—about 13s a year; you have medical attendance gratis in case of accidents, and at some places 5s per week; you have besides, what no amount of money can buy you, your friends and your relations living about you, and very likely you have a snug little reading room where you can spend your leisure hours pleasantly and profitably. On the other hand here I have paid the last year over 90 dollars for house rent, and about 40 dollars for coal; here is no medical attendance, except you pay for it; here is no smart money, here are no reading rooms where you might pass away an hour if you had it to spare, which you might not after you have worked 12 or 14 hours a day, if you are so lucky as to get work."

Document 30

These song lyrics, published in 1869 in a workingman's newspaper, represent a common view of white workers toward Chinese immigrants. Most trade unions of the period favored total exclusion of the Chinese. One exception, the Colored National Labor Union, founded soon after the Civil War, opposed only Chinese labor imported under contract.

Source: *Workingman's Advocate* (August 21, 1869), rpt in Philip S. Foner, *American Labor Songs of the Nineteenth Century* (Urbana: University of Illinois Press, 1977), 110.

JOHN CHINAMAN

A Song by R.W. Hume

What have you gone and done?
    To rouse that Eastern Goblyn Grim,
I'm sure it is no fun

Wherever you can put him now
    I'm sure I cannot see,
    Unless in Boston Bay so deep,
You ask him down to tea.

The servants in our palaces
    Must now be smart and spry;
And keep their rooms all dusted clean—
    And put their chignons by,
For Foo Choo has his eyes on them,
    He knows what he's about,
He'll do their work at half the price—
    Nor ask a Sunday out.

Now James, rub up your harness,
    And brush your master's coats
Polish your band and buttons well,
    And don't purloin the oats
Or Ho Sam Ling, in half a wink
    Will turn you out to graze,
Where you'll have time enough to think
    Upon your wicked ways.

...Come friends, we'll have to leave this land
    To nobles and to slaves,
    For, if John Chinaman comes in,
    For us — there's only graves.

Your sturdy tillers of the soil.
    Prepare to leave full soon,
For when John Chinaman comes in
    You'll find there is no room.
Like an Egyptian locust plague,
    Or like an eastern blight,
He'll swarm you out of all your fields,
    And seize them as his right.

Let the mechanic pack his traps,
    And ready make to flit;
He cannot live on rats and mice,
    And so he needs must quit.
Then, while he can with babes and wife,
    Let him in peace retire,
Lest in the shadowed future near,
    His children curse their sire.

At the full cost of bloody war,
    We've garnered in a race,
One set of men of late we've freed,
    Another takes his place.
Come friends, we'll have to leave
this land
    To nobles and to slaves,
For, if John Chinaman comes in,
    For us—there's only graves.

Document 31

Novels were an important form of popular entertainment in the early part of the twentieth century, before the arrival of radio, television, and cinema. One of the popular villains was Dr. Fu-Manchu, a wily, scheming, evil man who came to represent the American caricature of the Oriental. Introduced in 1913 by writer Sax Rohmer, Dr. Fu-Manchu became the basis for the stereotyped Chinese characters who were later portrayed in films and radio, including the beloved detective, Charlie Chan, who also exhibited the mysteriousness that Americans believed characterized the Chinese.

Source: Sax Rohmer, *The Insidious Dr. Fu-Manchu* (New York: Pyramid Books, 1961), 85–89. Originally published by P. F. Collier & Sons Inc., 1913.

My head throbbed madly; my brain seemed to be clogged—inert, and though my first, feeble movement was followed by the rattle of a chain, some moments more elapsed ere I realized that the chain was fastened to a steel collar—that the steel collar was clasped about my neck.

I moaned weakly.

"Smith!" I muttered, "Where are you? Smith!"…

Groping in the darkness, my hands touched a body that lay close beside me. My fingers sought and found the throat, sought and found the steel collar about it.

"Smith," I groaned; and I shook the still form. "Smith, old man, speak to me! Smith!"

Could he be dead? Was this the end of his gallant fight with Dr. Fu-Manchu and the murder group? If so, what did the future hold for me—what had I to face?

He stirred beneath my trembling hands.

"Thank God," I muttered, and I cannot deny that my joy was tainted with selfishness. For, waking in that impenetrable darkness, and yet obsessed with the dream I had dreamed, I had known what fear meant, at the realization that alone, chained, I must face the dreadful Chinese doctor in the flesh….

Footsteps sounded on the flagged passage. A blade of light crept across the floor towards us. My brain was growing clearer. The place had a damp, earthen smell. It was slimy—some noisome cellar. A door was thrown open and a man entered carrying a lantern. Its light showed my surmise to be accurate, showed the slime covered walls of a dungeon some fifteen feet square— shone upon the long yellow robe of the man who stood watching us, upon the malignant, intellectual countenance.

It was Dr. Fu-Manchu.

At last they were face to face—the head of the great Yellow Movement, and the man who fought on behalf of the entire white race. How can I paint the individual who now stood before us—perhaps the greatest genius of modern times?

Of him it had been fitly said that he had a brow like Shakespeare and a face like Satan. Something serpentine, hypnotic, was in his very presence. Smith drew one sharp breath, and was silent. Together, chained to the wall, two medieval captives, living mockeries of our boasted modern security, we crouched before Dr. Fu-Manchu. He came forward with an indescribable gait, cat-like yet awkward, carrying his high shoulders almost hunched. He placed the lantern in a niche in the wall, never turning away the reptilian gaze of those eyes which must haunt my dreams forever. They possessed a viridescence which hitherto I had supposed possible only in the eye of the cat—and the film intermittently clouded their brightness— but I can speak of them no more.

I had never supposed, prior to meeting Dr. Fu-Manchu, that so intense a force of malignancy could radiate—from any human being. He spoke. His English was perfect, though at times his words were oddly chosen; his delivery alternately was guttural and sibilant.

"Mr. Smith and Dr. Petrie, your interference with my plans has gone too far. I have seriously turned my attention to you."…

"You have presumed," continued Fu-Manchu, "to meddle with a world-change. Poor spiders— caught in the wheels of the inevitable! You have linked my name with the futility of the Young China Movement—the name of Fu-Manchu! Mr. Smith, you are an incompetent meddler—I despise you! Mr. Petrie, you are a fool—I am sorry for you!"

He rested one bony hand on his hip, narrowing the long eyes as he looked down on us. The purposeful cruelty of the man was inherent; it was entirely untheatrical. Still Smith remained silent.

"So I am determined to remove you from the scene of your blunders!" added Mr. Fu-Manchu.

"Opium will very shortly do the same for you!" I rapped at him savagely.

"That is a matter of opinion, Doctor," he said. "You may have lacked the opportunities which have been mine for studying that subject—and in any event, I shall not be privileged to enjoy your advice in the future."

"You will not long outlive me," I replied. "And

our deaths will not profit you, incidentally, because"—Smith's foot touched mine.

"Because?" inquired Fu-Manchu softly. "Ah! Mr. Smith is so prudent! He is thinking that I have *files*!" He pronounced the word in a way that made me shudder. "Mr. Smith has seen a *wire jacket*! As a surgeon its functions would interest you!"...

"Oh God of Cathay!" he cried, "by what death shall these die—these miserable ones who would bind thine Empire, which is boundless!"

Like some priest of Tezcat he stood, his eyes upraised to the roof, his lean body quivering—a sight to shock the most unimpressionable mind.

"He is mad!" I whispered to Smith. "God help us, the man is a dangerous homicidal maniac!"

Nayland Smith's tanned face was very drawn, but he shook his head grimly.

"Dangerous, yes, I agree," he muttered; "his existence is a danger to the entire white race which, now, we are powerless to avert."...

From somewhere above us—I could not determine the exact direction—came a low, wailing cry, an uncanny thing of falling cadences... which seemed to pour ice into my veins....

"What is it? Who uttered It? What does it mean?"

"I don't know what it is, Petrie, nor who utters it. But it means death!"

I had never supposed, prior to meeting Dr. Fu-Manchu, that so intense a force of malignancy could radiate— from any human being.

Document 32

This witness interrogation by immigration officials concerning a Chinese merchant, Chu Hoy, and **Document 33** show the impact of Chinese exclusion laws, which forbade Chinese laborers from returning to the United States in circular migration. Chu Hoy, a merchant who wanted to return to the United States after a trip to China, found that the exclusion law directed toward laborers affected his movements, too.

Source: The National Archives and Records Administration, North East Region, New York City.

KWONG SUN CHONG & CO.,
30 MOTT ST., NEW YORK CITY.
New York, September 17,1904

Chu Hoy.
Class, Departing Merchant
E. G. Sperry, Inspector
T. W. Wallace, Interpreter
Levi R. H. Dick, Stenographer

Chu Kew York, witness, after being by me duly sworn, deposes and says:

Q. What is your name?
A. Chu Kew York.

Q. What is your occupation?
A. Merchant.

Q. Of what firm are you a member?
A. Kwong Sun Chong & Co., 30 Mott St., New York.

Q. How long have you been a member of this firm?
A. About 8 years.

Q. Are you to be the manager after Chu Hoy leaves?
A. Yes.

Q. Do you recognize that photograph (exhibits photograph of Chu Hoy)?
A. Yes, that is Chu Hoy.

Q. How long have you known him?
A. I have known him a long time.

Q. What has he been doing since you've known him?
A. Been in this firm....

Q. How much interest has he?
A. $1,500.

Q. What is the nature of the business conducted by this firm?
A. Chinese groceries and clothing.

Q. Do you manufacture your clothing here?
A. Yes.

Q. Does Chu Hoy ever have anything to do with manufacturing the clothing?
A. No....

Q. Has this firm any connection with any gambling or opium smoking joints?
A. No.

Q. What is the value of the stock you have on hand at the present time?
A. About 8 or $9000....

(Records of this office show that Chu Hoy went to China via Seattle during the month of September or October, 1904)

Q. Do you know whether Chu Hoy is married?...
A. Yes, sir, I know he is married....

Q. Did you ever see his wife?
A. Yes, sir.

Q. Do you know her name?
A. Why, it isn't customary for Chinese to know the names of the women.

Q. Did she have natural or bound feet?
A. Bound feet.

Q. Do the daughters have natural or bound feet?
A. I don't know.

Q. Where did you see Chu Hoy's family?
A. In the same village as my own—in his house.

Q. What is the name of your village?
A. Har Low village, Sun Woey district, China....

Q. Is your wife living?
A. She is in China...

Q. Have you any children?
A. I have two wives—by one I have one daughter and by the other one I have a son and daughter...

Q. Do your two wives live in the same house?
A. Yes, sir...

Q. Did you frequently go to the home of Chu Hoy during your visits in China?
A. Yes, sir, I used to go there occasionally.

Q. Has Chu Hoy any brothers?
A. He has one younger brother.

Q. What is his name.
A. Chu Hei.

Q. Do the daughters have natural or bound feet?

A. I don't know.

Q. Was he ever in the U.S.?
A. Yes, sir.

Q. Is he here now?
A. He went to China in the first of the fourth month, this year.

Q. Where did he live in the United States?
A. He was in my store.

Q. Is he a member of that firm?
A. Yes, sir.

Q. Did he file papers in this office when he went out?
A. No, sir, he was very sick at the time and had to take his departure very suddenly...

Q. Is that your photograph? (Photograph shown is that of witness attached to his affidavit, signed by him and dated December 4th, 1899, which affidavit was filed with the Collection of Customs at Plattsburg, at the time this witness departed for China and was a part of the record in the case of this witness when he returned to the United States through Malone in 1901.)
A. Yes, sir.

Chinese and Immigrant Inspector

(Signed:) E. G. Sperry

Document 33

Exit visa issued in 1898 to Chu Yuk Jan. The visa allowed Mr. Chu to gain return entry to the United States after his visit to his Chinese homeland

Source: The National Archives and Records Administration, North East region, New York City.

He conducted such business for more than one year...and... during such time he was not engaged in the performance of any manual labor.

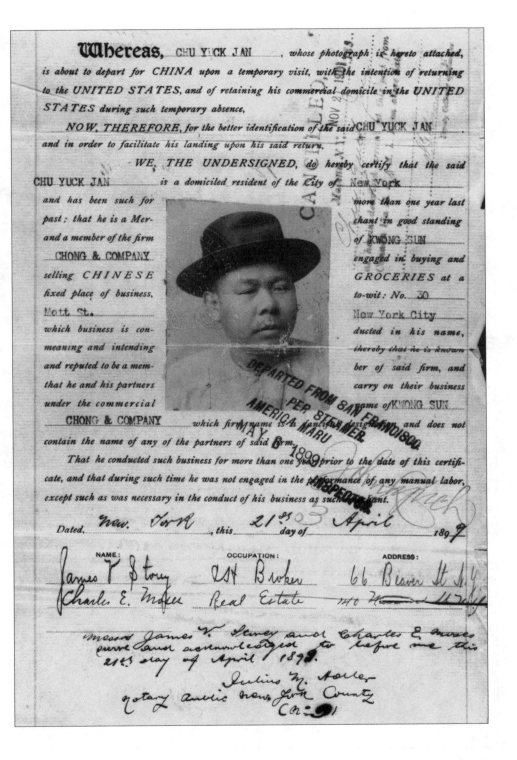

Ellis Island and After

Documents

Part 3 discussed Ellis Island as an immigrant–processing center within the broader context of U.S. immigration policy and American attitudes to immigrants. The examinations administered to immigrants at Ellis Island were explained as an outcome of Progressive Era politics and beliefs. Part 3 closed with a discussion of contemporary immigration.

The following documents explore these themes and suggest their consequences to the immigrants.

3.4 Progressive Ideals and Attitudes

Document 34

A letter that the Commissioner of Immigration wrote in 1921 to his superior, the Secretary of Labor, reveals many Progressive Era ideals. Note that the commissioner recommended moving the inspection process to the immigrant's place of origin, a change that came when the 1924 Quota Act went into effect.

Source: Chief Clerk's File, 2/174 B, RG 174, in Harlan D. Unrau, *Historic Resource Study (Historical Component), Vol. II, Ellis Island National Monument* (Washington, D.C.: U.S. Department of the Interior, National Park Service, 1984).

October 5, 1921
Honorable James J. Davis, Secretary of Labor
Washington, D. C.

My Dear Mr. Secretary,
Complying with your direction…I am reciting some of the reforms that have been effected during my administration at Ellis Island.

On assuming the duties as Commissioner on June 1, 1920, I was determined to humanize such portion of the Immigration Service as might come under my direction. My whole administration has been directed along that line so far as consistent with the highest degree of efficiency and the proper enforcement of the Immigration Laws.

I directed my energies at the outset toward a physical clearing up of all buildings, grounds and equipment at this station and included in my efforts the steerage quarters of ships and the railroad stations….

I made my own observations and inspections of the island. I found a guard keeping watch at the…door. When I asked him why he did not keep the door open to let some air in to the immigrants, he said that they ask too many questions. I told him he should be thrown out in the Bay with a stone about his neck. When I opened the door, the hot, foul sultry air almost pushed me backward. There were several hundred immigrants in the room and seats for not more than fifty. Men, women and children were standing all day or sitting on the dirty floor….

In the dining room for the immigrants where we serve as many as 10,000 meals some days, there was not a drop of drinking water for the immigrants…. They were as thirsty as wolves….

As a result of personal investigation and inspection of immigrant carrying steamships, a complete change for the better

Ellis Island is not only the "gateway of the nation" but it is the nation's great kindergarten of Americanization, and what they receive on the island they will live out in the nation.

has been effected in the steerage quarters. Many of the boats were almost uninhabitable on account of the filth, lack of light and want of ordinary accommodations. It is true that the steerage of some of the ships is better than the first cabin of others, but many of the ships should never be allowed to stick their nose in a civilized port. Men and women using the same toilet rooms, no tables, immigrants sitting on the floor eating with a spoon out of buckets.... no privacy whatever for women and children....

I found immigrants sleeping on the tiled floors without cover and without bedding. Hundreds of men, women and children would sleep all night in this way. I induced the Department to approve of purchasing 10,000 blankets from the War Department at cost, thus affording blankets for bedding and for covering the immigrants who are made to suffer the hardship of inadequate equipment....

I then supplied them with reading matter, games and other forms of amusement which helped them to while away what seemed to be an indeterminable detention....

I have arranged moving picture shows for every other night on the big Registration floor. These pictures are constructive and educational in character with a film here and there of comedy. It is remarkable how the immigrants enter into the movies....

I have always believed in humane practices. If we sleep immigrants on cold tiled floors without covering, give them impure food, rob them, curse them and handle them worse than cattle, then they go out into the nation and practice what they have received here on the island. Ellis Island is not only the "gateway of the nation" but it is the nation's great kindergarten of Americanization, and what they receive on the island they will live out in the nation.

Americanization is not the work of pressure—it is the work of patience. You can no more cram Americanization down an

alien's throat than a minister can cram religion down our throats....
Let the immigrant know that his work is appreciated, that this
Government is his friend and that this country is his opportunity,
then and then only will the foreigner make his best contribution to
our American life and labor....

There is much to be done at Ellis Island yet. As you well
know, it cannot all be done in a year's time. Dishonest employees
who were exploiting aliens and their friends, taking money from
them illegally, were eradicated from the service. Charges, where
warranted, have been preferred and their cases referred to the
Federal District Attorney for proper action. Fines and
imprisonment have been imposed....

I do believe that our nation is committing a gross injustice for
which some day it must render an account, in allowing these
hundreds of thousands of people to sell all they have, sever all
connections, come four thousand miles out of the heart of Europe
and other countries, only to find after passing the Statue of Liberty
that they must go back to the country whence they came. Our
inspection and examination should be conducted on the other side,
thus saving thousands of people the suffering we see at this island
daily which is indescribable and that would melt a heart of granite.
The last great final day of assize will disclose no sadder scenes than
separation and deportation is producing at this station.
Examination on the other side is ten thousand times better than
rejection on this side.

Ever cordially and faithfully yours,
Signed: Commissioner

**Our inspection and
examination should be
conducted on the other
side, thus saving
thousands of people
the suffering we see
at this island daily
which is indescribable
and that would melt
a heart of granite.**

Document 35

The examinations that immigrants faced at Ellis Island were the final tests after a long journey. The medical examination came first. In 1917, E. H. Mullan, a surgeon and U.S. Public Health Official, described the physical and mental examination process at Ellis Island.

Source: E. H. Mullan, "Mental Examination of Immigrants: Administration and Line Inspection at Ellis Island," *Public Health Reports*, 33, no. 20 (May 18, 1917), 733–46.

3.5

Pompadours are always a suspicious sign. Beneath such long growth of hair are frequently seen areas of favus....

MENTAL EXAMINATION OF IMMIGRANTS
Administration and Line Inspection at Ellis Island by E. H. Mullan, Surgeon, United States Public Health Service

Immigrants not traveling in the cabin, who enter the United States at the port of New York, are first brought to Ellis Island in order to undergo an examination to determine their fitness for admission.

The average immigrant remains at Ellis Island two or three hours, during which time he undergoes an examination by the Public Health Service in order to determine his mental and physical condition, and by the Immigration Service in order to find out whether he is otherwise admissible....

As the immigrant approaches the officer gives him a quick glance. Experience enables him in that one glance to take in six details, namely, the scalp, face, neck, hands, gait, and general condition, both mental and physical. Should any of these details not come into view, the alien is halted and the officer satisfies himself that no suspicious sign or symptom exists regarding that particular detail. For instance, if the immigrant is wearing a high collar, the officer opens the collar or unbuttons the upper shirt button and sees whether a goiter, tumor, or other abnormality exists.... Likewise, if the alien approaches the officer with hat on he must be halted, hat removed and scalp observed in order to exclude the presence of favus, ringworm, or other skin diseases of this region of the body. Pompadours are always a suspicious sign.

Beneath such long growth of hair are frequently seen areas of favus…. Where the alien carries luggage on his shoulder or back, it may be necessary to make him drop his parcels and to walk 5 or 10 feet in order to exclude suspicious gait or spinal curvature. Immigrants at times carry large parcels in both arms and over their shoulders in order that the gait resulting from shortened extremity or ankylosed joint may escape notice. In like manner they maneuver in attempting to conceal the gaits of Little's disease, spastic paralysis, and other nervous disorders. All children over 2 years of age are taken from their mother's arms and are made to walk….

Many inattentive and stupid-looking aliens are questioned by the medical officer in the various languages as to their age, destination, and nationality. Often simple questions in addition and multiplication are propounded. Should the immigrant appear stupid and inattentive to such an extent that mental defect is suspected an X is made with chalk on his coat at the anterior aspect of his right shoulder. Should definite signs of mental disease be observed, a circle X would be used instead of the plain X. In like manner a chalk mark is placed on the anterior aspect of the right shoulder in all cases where physical deformity or disease is suspected.

In this connection B would indicate back; C, conjunctivitis; CT, trachoma; E, eyes; F, face; Ft., feet; G, goiter; H, heart; K, hernia; L, lameness; N, neck; P, physical and lungs; Pg, pregnancy; Sc., scalp; S, senility. The words hand, measles, nails, skin, temperature, vision, voice, which are often used, are written out in full.

The alien after passing the scrutiny of the first medical officer passes on to the end of the line, where he is quickly inspected again by the second examiner. This examiner is known in service parlance as "the eye man." He stands at the end of the line with his back to the window and faces the approaching alien. This position affords good light, which is so essential for eye examinations….

He looks carefully at the eyeball in order to detect signs of defect and disease of that organ and then quickly everts the upper lids in search of conjunctivitis and trachoma. Corneal opacities, nystagmus, squint, bulging eyes, the wearing of eye glasses, clumsiness, and other signs on the part of the alien, will be sufficient cause for him to be chalk-marked "Vision." He will then be taken out of the line by an attendant and his vision will be carefully examined….

Roughly speaking, from 15 to 20 per cent of the immigrants are chalk-marked by the medical officers, and it is these chalked individuals who must undergo a second and more thorough examination in the examination rooms of the Public Health Service. Those aliens marked X and circle X are placed in the mental room. All other marked aliens are placed in the two physical rooms, one for men and the other for women….

If the Italian responded to questions as the Russian Finn responds, the former would in all probability be suffering with a depressive psychosis.

Every effort is made to detect signs and symptoms of mental disease and defect. Any suggestion, no matter how trivial, that would point to abnormal mentality is sufficient cause to defer the immigrant for a thorough examination....

Experience enables the inspecting officer to tell at a glance the race of an alien. There are, however, exceptions to this rule. It occasionally happens that the inspecting officer thinking that an approaching alien is of a certain race brings him to a standstill and questions him. The alien's facial expression and manner are peculiar and just as the officer is about to decide that this alien is mentally unbalanced, he finds out that the alien in question belongs to an entirely different race. The peculiar attitude of the alien in question is no longer peculiar; it is readily accounted for by racial considerations. Accordingly, the officer passes him on as a mentally normal person. Those who have inspected immigrants know that almost every race has its own type of reacting during the inspection. On the line if an Englishman reacts to questions in the manner of an Irishman, his lack of mental balance would be suspected. The converse is also true. If the Italian responded to questions as the Russian Finn responds, the former would in all probability be suffering with a depressive psychosis.

Document 36

After the medical inspection, the inspectors at Ellis Island asked a series of questions already posed to the immigrants by the shipping companies. The inspectors asked the same kinds of questions to see if the answers matched. Inconsistent responses might result in further examination. The objective was to exclude people who might become public charges, act immorally, or cause social unrest.

Source: Ira Wolfman, *Do People Grow on Family Trees?: Genealogy for Kids and Other Beginners: The Official Ellis Island Handbook* (New York: Workman Publishing, 1991).

Are you going to join a relative?

Are you a polygamist?

1. What is your name?

2. How old are you?

3. Are you married or single?

4. What is your calling or occupation?

5. Are you able to read or write?

6. What is your nationality?

7. Where was your last residence?

8. Which U.S. seaport have you landed in?

9. What is your final destination in the United States?

10. Do you have a ticket to your final destination?

11. Did you pay for your passage over? If not, who did?

12. Do you have money with you? More than $30? How much? Less? How much?

13. Are you going to join a relative? What relative? Name and address?

14. Have you ever been to the United States before? Where and when?

15. Have you ever been in prison, in a poorhouse, or supported by charity?

16. Are you a polygamist?

17. Are you under contract, expressed or implied, to perform labor in the United States?

18. What is the condition of your health, mental and physical?

19. Are you deformed or crippled? If so, by what cause?

Document 37

Edward Corsi, once a director of Ellis Island, describes what happened to women whose husbands, families, or friends interrupted migration chains by not coming to claim their female relatives.

Source: Edward Corsi, *In the Shadow of Liberty, The Chronicle of Ellis Island* (New York: The MacMillan Co., 1935; rpt Arno Press, 1969), 73–81.

...we could not let her loose on the streets of a strange city looking for her husband.

To make things run fairly smoothly in that mixed crowd of poor, bewildered immigrants, we would tag them with numbers corresponding to numbers on their manifest, after they had been landed from the barges and taken in the building.

Here in the main building, they were lined up—a motley crowd in colorful costumes, all ill at ease and wondering what was to happen to them. Doctors put them through their medical inspection, and whenever a case aroused suspicion, the alien was set aside in a cage apart from the rest, for all the world like a segregated animal.... These methods, cruel as they seem had to be used, because of the great numbers and the language difficulties....

A woman, if she came alone, was asked a number of special questions: how much money she had; if she were going outside of New York; whether her passage had been paid by herself or by some charitable institution. If she had come to join her husband in New York or Brooklyn, we could not let her loose on the streets of a strange city looking for her husband. This also applied to all alien females, minors, and others who did not have money but were otherwise eligible and merely waiting for friends or relatives. We generally had more of this class than we could handle. One Sunday morning, I remember, there were seventeen hundred of these women and children kept in one room with a normal capacity of six hundred. How they were packed in! It had to be seen to be appreciated. They just couldn't move about, and whenever we wanted to get one out it was almost a major operation....

With so many people packed together under such conditions, it was naturally impossible for them to keep clean, for the clean ones were pressed against aliens infected with vermin, and it was not long before all were contaminated....

There were times, of course, when all our efforts to locate the immediate relative failed. Sometimes a married woman had come to join her husband, or a young woman to marry her fiancee, and the man could not be located. Perhaps he had died, or moved, or the correspondence hadn't reached him—who knows? In any event, the results were tragic indeed, as I well know from personal experience. There was no way of soothing these heartbroken women who had traveled thousands and thousands of miles, endured suffering and humiliation, and who had uprooted their lives only to find their hopes shattered at the end of the long voyage. These, I think, are the saddest of all immigration cases.

Sometimes these women were placed in the care of a social agency which agreed to be responsible to the Commissioner [of Immigration], caring for them or placing them in some appropriate occupation. But if everything possible had been done, and the missing husband or fiancee still could not be traced, the poor alien, despite all her tears, had to be returned to her native country.

...if everything possible had been done, and the missing husband or fiancee still could not be traced, the poor alien, despite all her tears, had to be returned to her native country.

Document 38

In an effort to preserve the white, Anglo-Saxon culture of the United States, Congress passed the National Origins Act of 1924, which limited entry and established quotas that favored northern and western Europeans. The notion that quotas could solve social problems was popular during the Progressive Era, and it was not restricted to immigration law. In 1922 the president of Harvard University spoke out in favor of quotas for Jewish admission to his school as a way of reducing anti-Semitism. Many Harvard students agreed with him.

Source: *The Nation* (Sept. 6, 1922), 225–27.

Fair Harvard's fairness is excitedly being called into question...the college has become a hot-bed of anti-Jewish feeling.

Harvard Student Opinion on the Jewish Question
By William T. Ham

Fair Harvard's fairness is excitedly being called into question by those who imply, if they do not assert, that the college has become a hot-bed of anti-Jewish feeling.

What are the facts? Opportunity to get at them offered itself at the end of the college year when, in a class in the department of Social Ethics, Dr. Richard C. Cabot gave the following as a part of the examination:

> *Discuss as fairly as you can this question:*
> *For the good of* all *persons concerned, is a college ever ethically justified in limiting to a certain percentage the number of any particular race who are admitted to the freshman class each year?*

The students concerned were from the three upper classes. For a year they had been considering the ethics of human relationships, of property, of veracity, of freedom and restraint, confidence and suspicion.... of the eighty-three men examined, forty-one believed in the justice of a policy of race limitation under certain circumstances. Thirty-four held that such a policy was never justified. Eight stayed on the fence. Of this last group, one name was Jewish. Seven of those who opposed restriction had Jewish names. Those who favored it were all Gentiles.

All the proponents of limitation made the assumption that the number of Jews in Harvard College was increasing out of all proportion to the increase in the number of other races, and argued that this boded ill for the future of the institution. "Harvard is an American college, devoted to American ideals, maintained for the good of the greatest number. If it becomes top-heavy from an over-supply of some one race, it serves neither that race nor America." "Harvard must maintain a cosmopolitan balance. Restriction, not to preserve a mere aristocratic tradition, but to keep the proportions on which fruitful educational contact depends, is justifiable and democratic." Not all the restrictionists took this ground. Three maintained that "a college is a private institution and can sell its goods or not, as it sees fit, to whomever it pleases." One asserted that the overseers of a college have no more to do with the public weal than the directors of a bank. One even went so far as to compare Harvard College to an automobile, "which I am obliged to lend to all comers simply because they would like to ride in it." For the most part, however, the restrictionists agree that "while the endowed college is a private corporation, it has a public function, recognized by the state.... "

There is unanimous agreement in this group that a college education is more than a matter of "academic knowledge..." "Admission to the college cannot be based on mere knowledge...." "Were it merely a matter of scholarship, there would be no objection to Jews at all." But "they do not mix."...

Now why is it that the presence of the Jew is so inimical to this highly desirable "atmosphere" that is the cynosure of endowment-givers and their sons? The restrictionists agree that it is because of the objectionable personal character of the Hebrew. They bristle with accusations, the general effect of which is to make him seem as hard to live with as a porcupine. A few say that he is in this condition irredeemably; the rest imply that if he would only improve his manners and get new ancestors, his chances would be better. "The Jewish race makes 'Take away' its motto, rather than 'Give and take.' They are governed by selfishness. They care nothing for the friends they make save as future business acquaintances; to them the social side of college life is only so much twaddle." "They want property for power rather than for use. Even in the gymnasium they take possession of the apparatus, not by using it, but by sitting on it." "Expediency is their standard of action; traditions mean nothing to them."—this of the Chosen People! . . .

But in contrast to this grudging view are those, even among the restrictionists, who assert that the Jew is superior. "It is a fact," one remarks, "that on the average the Hebrews are brighter than the rest of us."...One of the more careful papers differentiates between two general types of Hebrew: (1) "Those who, with the Chinese, are the intellectual leaders of all universities, who have grown beyond a particular race, being of universal intellect, and (2) those who are domineering, eager for advancement, pushing, disliked even by other members of their own race."...

A few of the restrictionists have a black outlook upon the race question. "Race prejudice," avers one, "is

inevitable." Two students find a parallel to Jewish
exclusion in measures adopted to keep out
Orientals. One of these does not confine his sus-
picions to the Jews, but would also exclude the
Irish "or what amounts to the same thing, the
Catholics." The latter by the way "long ago saw
the folly of forcing themselves on the American
college, and built institutions of their own."...

As to the future of the college itself, restriction
is the first step on a path that leads to barrenness.
The true way of the educational institution,
according to these papers, is to bring about contact
... and to foster a competition which shall be a
replica on a higher plane, of the racial competition
which the student must meet when he goes on to
democratic life....

The final objections to a policy of restriction
have to do with difficulties involved. How can any
racial percentage be fixed so as to be equitable?
Should not a policy such as this apply to all races,
rather than to one only?...Is not the anti-Jewish
feeling the un-American element in the situation,
rather than the Jews themselves?

**How can any racial
percentage be fixed so as
to be equitable?**

Document 39

The immigration quota acts became so enmeshed in bureaucratic thinking that they hindered humanitarian efforts to save Jews from Nazi persecution during the late 1930s. In 1939, when Americans learned of Nazi persecutions and jailings of Jews in German-occupied territories, Congressional leaders proposed the Wagner-Rogers Bill, which would have added twenty thousand German Jewish children under age fourteen to the German immigration quota set by law. In this letter to Sen. Richard Russell, Secretary of State Cordell Hull offers reasons against admitting the children. His letter, recorded in Congressional hearings, explains why Jews could not easily immigrate to the United States during the years of the Holocaust.

Source: "Admission of German Refugee Children," Joint Hearings before a Sub-Committee on Immigration, U.S. Senate and a Subcommittee of the Committee on Immigration and Naturalization, House of Representatives, April 20, 1939, 2–3.

Dear Senator Russell: I refer again to your communication of February 10, 1939, requesting the views of this Department with respect to Senate joint Resolution 64, a joint resolution to authorize the admission into the United States of a limited number of German refugee children.

While I am very mindful of the plight of many German children today and am in sympathy with the laudable objective of joint Resolution 64 to relieve the suffering of these children, there are features of this proposed resolution of which, I am sure, your committee will wish to give particular attention. These features relate both to technical and administrative aspects of the resolution....

The children whose admission is proposed by Senate joint Resolution 64 are to be admitted in addition to existing quotas, but they are required to be otherwise eligible. In this connection you will recall that section 3 of the Immigration Act of February 5, 1917, excludes, among other classes of aliens, "all children under sixteen years of age unaccompanied by or not coming to one or both parents, except that any such children may, in the discretion of the Secretary of Labor, be admitted if in his opinion they are not likely to become a public charge and are otherwise admissible." Presumably many of the children will neither be accompanying their parents nor proceeding to join them in the United States. Section 3 of the Immigration Act of February 5, 1917, also excludes from admission "persons whose ticket or passage is paid for by any corporation, association, society, municipality, or foreign government, either directly or indirectly." Many of the children undoubtedly will be financially assisted in obtaining transportation or passage to the United States.

Children fourteen years of age or under, who reside, or at any time since January 1, 1933, have resided in any territory now incorporated in Germany, subject to certain conditions, are entitled to the benefits of the resolution.... it will be remembered that country of birth and not country of residence is a basic feature of the quota system in the act of 1924. While a departure from this basic principle for a period of two years and for the humanitarian purpose of relieving suffering might not be regarded as a precedent, your committee, I am sure, will give consideration to this feature of the resolution because of the possibility of its opening the door to similar or more radical departures from the quota system established by the existing law....

While I can assure you and your committee of the wholehearted support of our consular officers and of this Department in complying with the provisions of the resolution, if it should become law, the issuance of 10,000 immigration visas in addition to an estimated 30,000 immigration visas now being issued annually in that country will inevitably necessitate increased clerical personnel, unfamiliar with the law and regulations, as well as additional office accommodations.

Section 11 (f) of the Immigration Act of 1924 limits the monthly issuance of immigration visas in quotas of 300 and over to 10 percent of the annual immigration quotas. This statutory provision regulates the rate at which visas are issued as well as the flow of immigrants arriving at ports of entry. Assuming that added personnel and office accommodations were to be made available, a monthly limitation on the issuance of visas to the refugee children would be essential as a measure of control to insure proper administrative action with respect to the applications of these children as well as to those provided by the present quota law.

... the issuance of 10,000 immigration visas in addition to an estimated 30,000 immigration visas now being issued annually in that country will inevitably necessitate increased clerical personnel...as well as additional office accommodations.

3.6.3 World Migration Increases

Document 40

Major World Migrations, 1930-55. This map documents how world migration patterns were altered by restrictive U.S. immigration policies of the 1920s and by World War II.

Source: Information from Kevin Reilly, *The West and the World: A History of Civilization*, 2d ed. (New York: HarperCollins College, 1989), Vol. 2, 364, "World Migrations, 1930–55."

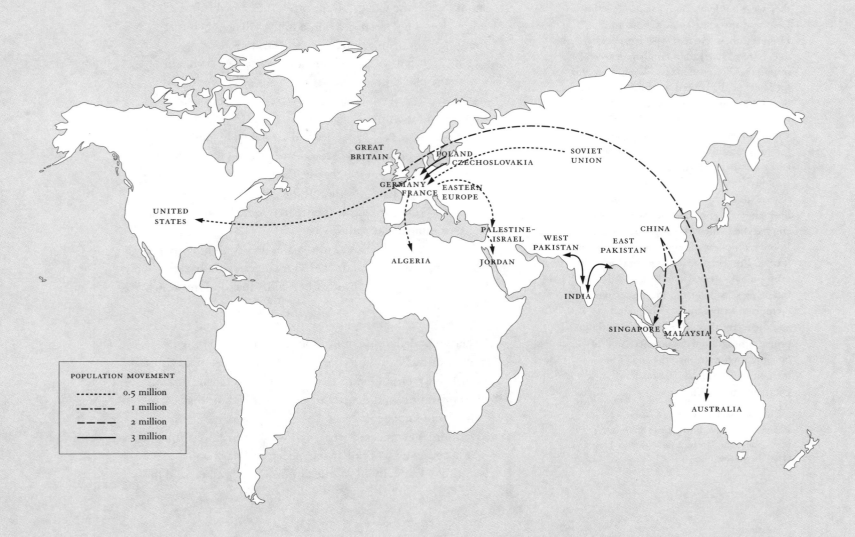

POPULATION MOVEMENT

· · · · · · · 0.5 million

· — · — · 1 million

– – – – 2 million

———— 3 million

GREAT BRITAIN · POLAND · CZECHOSLOVAKIA · SOVIET UNION · GERMANY · FRANCE · EASTERN EUROPE · UNITED STATES · ALGERIA · PALESTINE-ISRAEL · JORDAN · WEST PAKISTAN · EAST PAKISTAN · CHINA · INDIA · SINGAPORE · MALAYSIA · AUSTRALIA

Document 41

Susan Suleiman, the daughter of a rabbi, and now a professor of French literature at Harvard University, left Hungary as a refugee in 1949 at the age of ten. Her family had escaped the Holocaust because they were able to obtain false papers indicating that they were not Jews. But in 1948, after the Communist regime came to power in Hungary, they, like many people, decided to emigrate. The Rubin family had several important choices to make. Should they aim for Israel or the United States? If the United States, how could they be sure of gaining entrance, and how long would they be willing to wait? Should they join other refugees residing in displaced-persons camps and wait their turn there for entry to the United States? They chose to go to Haiti where Susan's uncle, a U. S. resident, had business connections. From there, they later entered the United States through Miami. In the six months of residence in Haiti, Susan learned French, the language to which her professional career would be devoted. The following selection from Professor Suleiman's memoir describes the risks her family took and the terror they felt as refugees without proper immigration documents. As Prof. Suleiman writes toward the end of her memoir, "survival, adaptation, [and] luck" got them through their journey.

Source: Reprinted from *Budapest Diary: In Search of the Motherbook*, by Susan Rubin Suleiman, 3–7. By permission of the University of Nebraska Press, 1996. ©1996 by Susan Suleiman.

We were sitting in a cornfield waiting for the sun to set. Mother, Daddy, and I and our guides, a man and a woman who had given us directions from the train station. They knew the border country well and would lead us across once night had fallen.

"You must walk fast, silently," the man told us. "We should reach the village on the other side shortly after midnight. You'll sleep in a house in the village, then first thing in the morning you'll take the bus to Košice."

At nightfall we started our walk. After the cornfields, where the plants grew tall, we had to cross a series of flat, freshly harvested fields entirely covered with stubble. Walking on the stubble was horrible: the sharp ends dug into the thin soles of my shoes and scratched my ankles. I was hanging on to Daddy's hand and gritting my teeth to keep from crying out. Mother walked on his other side.

Suddenly I felt him stumble; he gave a sharp, low cry. "I've twisted my ankle," he whispered to the guide, who had come running at the sound.

"Can you go on? You must go on, there's nothing we can do for you here," the guide said. "Or you can turn back."

"No turning back," my father said. "Just find me a stick I can lean on."

The guide handed him his own thick stick and my father limped along, leaning from time to time on my mother or me. I could see he was in pain, each step an effort. Poor Daddy, he still had a bandage on his stomach from his ulcer operation, and the strain was surely bad for his heart. What would happen to us?

Midnight came and went, and we were still in the fields. The August sky was full of stars, deep and dark and beautiful. Gradually I lost track of time and walked as if in a trance. We entered woods, then walked on a road. The sky had faded; it was almost dawn. By the time we arrived in the village, a pale gray light outlined the houses and fences. Every house seemed to have a dog, and every dog seemed to smell our arrival: furious barking accompanied us as we followed our guides down the single street. Finally we reached the house where beds were waiting. "You mustn't sleep long," the guide said. "The dogs have alerted people, you should leave here as quickly as possible." The bus to Košice left at 7 a.m.; we would be on it.

An hour of dead sleep, a cup of hot milk, and we were being herded toward the bus. "We're in Slovakia," my mother whispered to me. I had not yet had time to think about that. Now it became obvious, for everyone on the bus spoke a language different from our own. I could see the guide talking to the bus driver, looking at us. The bus driver nodded, smiled, said something. The guide came over: "The bus passes a police station, but it's never stopped. You should have no trouble getting to Košice. Good luck."

And what would we do in Košice? I wondered. How far we still were from America! The bus rumbled along, only half full at this hour. We sat bleary-eyed among the peasant women taking their wares to market. We had no papers. If by some chance the police stopped the bus, we were done for.

I was beginning to doze off when the bus screeched to a halt. Two men got on, wearing uniforms and carrying guns in holsters. The bus driver accompanied the policemen, talking, as they walked through the bus checking papers. When they stopped in front of us, the driver pulled my mother to his side: "She's my wife," he said in a foreign language—yet we understood him. "All right, but the gentleman and the little girl will have to get off." Next thing I knew, I was following Daddy and one of the policemen into a small building, then into an office with dark wood floors. I knew I was starting in a real-life drama, yet I felt almost nothing. It was as if everything were happening to someone else.

No sooner had we entered the room than the second policeman came running. The two policemen conferred, then I was heading back toward the bus with one of them: my mother had set up such a ruckus, she told me a few minutes later, that they had to let me go. It was all beyond me: How could they believe she was the driver's wife and also believe I was her daughter if Daddy was my father? Didn't they realize he and I were related? Why had the bus been stopped, when it never was? What would happen to Daddy?

I don't remember our arrival in Košice. We must have gotten off the bus, carrying almost nothing by then, and found our way to a building, a school perhaps, where a large number of Jewish refugees were gathering to leave on a convoy to Israel. My mother spoke to the man in charge....

In the middle of the night I was awakened by voices in the room; then a light went on, and I heard a man's voice say "Rubin." My mother sat up.

"Here I am," she called. The man in charge approached; he was followed by two other men carrying a stretcher. On the stretcher lay my father.

For a wild moment I thought he was dead. But he was not even asleep; he was smiling at my mother and me.

Later he told us the story. After I had been taken out and he was left alone in the room with the two policemen, they made him sign a piece of paper. He would be taken back over the border, they told him, like all the other Hungarians. This was a popular border crossing; the police were used to returning people. Many simply crossed the border again, they told him with a laugh. They spoke some Hungarian.

After a while my father said to them: "I'm a religious Jew, a rabbi, and I would like to pray. Do you mind?"

"No, go ahead."

He took out his tefilin, the little black leather box and leather straps he put on his arms and forehead every morning, and stood in front of a wall. He put on the tefilin and started to pray, swaying back and forth slightly as he always did. Suddenly, as he prayed, he let himself fall backward and lay stretched out on the floor. The policemen rushed over to him; he appeared to have lost consciousness. After a short while he came to.

"I'm recovering from an operation," he told them. "See there's still a bandage on my stomach." He opened his shirt to show them the bandage. "I also have a bad heart," he added.

The policemen looked at each other, then at him. He understood they were afraid he might die in the station.

"Is there any way you could send me to my wife and daughter in Košice?" he asked them, still on his back....

That's how he ended up on a stretcher.... The main thing is that we were together again. Next morning we boarded a train for Bratislava—again without papers.... We spent a day with my aunt Ica, my father's youngest sister, who had married a Czech doctor. They had both been active in the Resistance and were committed Communists (that would change soon after, when they discovered even the Party had its anti-Semitic streak). My aunt told my father: "Take the first train out of here, no matter where it's going. They're cracking down; you won't make it if you wait."

My father had planned for us to spend the night at his sister's and take the morning train to Vienna. Instead we left that night on a train bound for Trieste. The train was carrying a convoy of Jewish refugees on their way to Israel and was sealed: no stops along the way. My parents did not want to go to Israel. As we neared Vienna, my father fainted again (I assumed it was an act). My mother called for help. The train made an unscheduled stop and he was carried off on a stretcher, my mother and I accompanying him. After a few days in the hospital he was released. We declared ourselves officially homeless. We were free.

3.6.4 The U.S. Flow Resumes

Document 42

Yearly Immigration to the United States,
1880–1940. This chart documents the
changing sources of immigration to the
United States in the 60-year period before
World War II.

Source: Department of History, Rutgers. The State
University of New Jersey (New Brunswick, N.J.,
1985). Based on U.S. Census information.

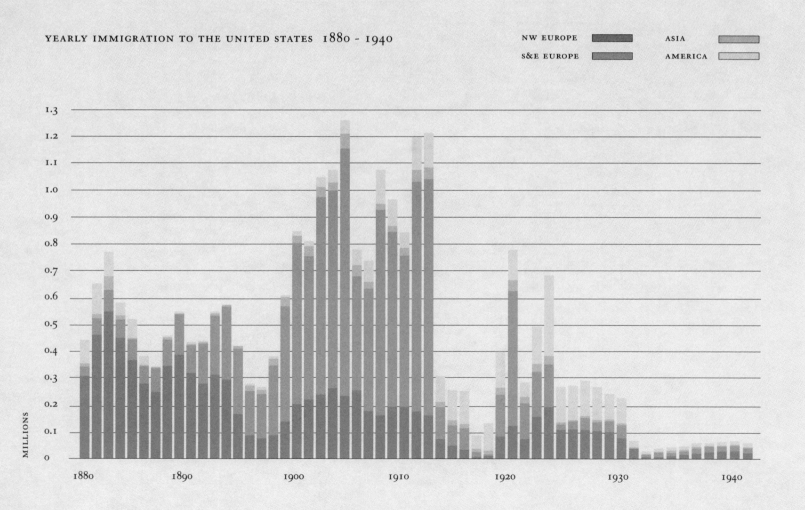

YEARLY IMMIGRATION TO THE UNITED STATES 1880 - 1940

NW EUROPE   ASIA

S&E EUROPE   AMERICA

Document 43

Post World War II Immigration to U.S.
This chart shows that recent immigration to
the United States is approaching the high
numbers of the Ellis Island era. The sources
of immigration, however, are changing.

Source: Department of History, Rutgers the State
University of New Jersey (New Brunswick, N.J.,
1985). Based on U.S. Census information.

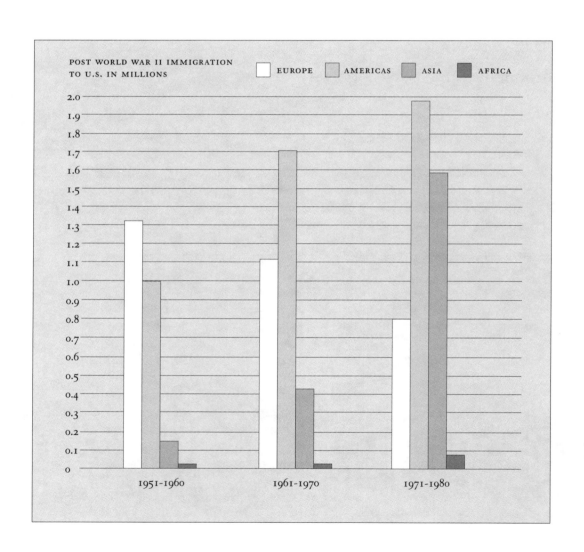

Document 44

In 1994, California's voters approved a referendum measure, Proposition 187, which denied certain public services to illegal aliens. State and federal judges declared most of the provisions of Proposition 187 unconstitutional.

Source: Associated Press, printed in *Raleigh [N.C.] News & Observer* (December 15, 1994), 8A.

U.S. District Judge Mariana Pfaelzer granted a preliminary injunction blocking almost all of Proposition 187's bans against allowing illegal aliens to use public schools, public health services, and public social services.

Federal Judge Blocks Prop. 187

Los Angeles

The voter-approved measure to deny almost all state services to undocumented immigrants was blocked Wednesday by a judge who said it appears to conflict with the federal government's authority. U.S. District Judge Mariana Pfaelzer granted a preliminary injunction blocking almost all of Proposition 187's bans against allowing illegal aliens to use public schools, public health services, and public social services.

Pfaelzer let stand two of the proposition's more minor provisions: one prohibiting undocumented immigrants from attending state colleges and another banning the sale and use of false immigration documents. The higher education ban had already been blocked by a state judge.

The judge said the measure, approved by 59 percent of California voters on November 8, denies health and social services to some immigrants who may be entitled to receive them under federal law. It could also pressure some immigrants into leaving the country when they have the right to remain, Pfaelzer said.

The judge said only the federal government has the authority to determine who can enter and remain in the United States.

The health care provision, in particular, has serious implications, Pfaelzer said, because it could put the public health at risk. "The loss of medical services for illegal aliens could result in greater health risks for the general population," she said.

The ruling "restores decency and common sense to the state of California," said Mark Rosenbaum, legal director for the American Civil Liberties Union of Southern California, which is representing opponents of the measure.

Charlton Holland, assistant state attorney general, said he was disappointed in the ruling, but declined further comment.

Pfaelzer issued her ruling after a 2-hour hearing. The injunction will remain in effect until a trial to determine disputed facts in the case can be held. But unlike a temporary restraining order issued previously, the state can appeal the injunction to higher courts.

Critics claim that Proposition 187 violates federal laws and the constitutional rights of immigrants.

Pre-Proposition 187 state law entitles illegal immigrants to a public education but makes them ineligible for most health and welfare programs. They can receive emergency health care, including childbirth, under federal law, and prenatal and long-term care under state law.

Document 45

Distribution of Alien Immigrants by Sex, 1831–1989. A three-dimensional version of this chart appears in *The Peopling of America* Exhibit on the first floor of the Ellis Island Museum. It shows that after the 1920s, women outnumbered men in arrivals to the United States.

Source: This table was constructed by Reed Ueda, *Postwar Immigrant America: A Social History* (Boston: Bedford Books of St. Martin's Press, 1993), 157, from the following sources: Imre Ferenzci and Walter F. Willcox, *International Migrations* (New York: National Bureau of Economic Research, 1929–1931), Vol. 1, 211; U. S. Bureau of the Census, *Statistical Abstract of the United States, 1942*, 123; *Statistical Abstract of the United States, 1954*, 106; *Statistical Abstract of the United States, 1984*, 93; *Statistical Yearbook of the Immigration and Naturalization Service, 1985*, 46; *Statistical Yearbook, 1989*, 24.

Years	% Males	% Females
1831–35	65.6	34.4
1836–40	63.3	36.7
1841–45	58.3	41.7
1846–50	59.8	40.2
1851–55	57.8	42.2
1856–60	58.1	41.9
1861–65	59.5	40.5
1866–70	61	39
1871–75	60.4	39.6
1876–80	62.8	37.2
1881–85	60.5	39.5
1886–90	61.6	38.4
1891–95	61.2	38.8
1896–1900	61.6	38.4
1901–05	69.8	30.2
1906–10	69.7	30.3
1911–15	65	35
1916–20	58.3	41.7
1921–24	56.5	43.5
1925–29	60	40
1930–34	45.2	54.8
1935	44	56
1936–40	45.2	54.8
1941–45	41	59
1946–50	40.3	59.7
1951–60	45.9	54.1
1961–70	44.8	55.2
1971–81	46.9	53.1
1982–85	50.4	49.6
1986–89	50.2	48.8

Document 46

Major World Population Movements, 1960–85. This map shows the
importance of Asian and Latin American migration to the United States,
the postwar German magnet in Europe, and the pull of some of the oil-
producing countries.

Source: Information from Kevin Reilly, *The West and the World: A History of
Civilization*, 2d ed. (New York: HarperCollins College, 1989), Vol. 2, 366, "Major
World Migrations, 1960–1985."

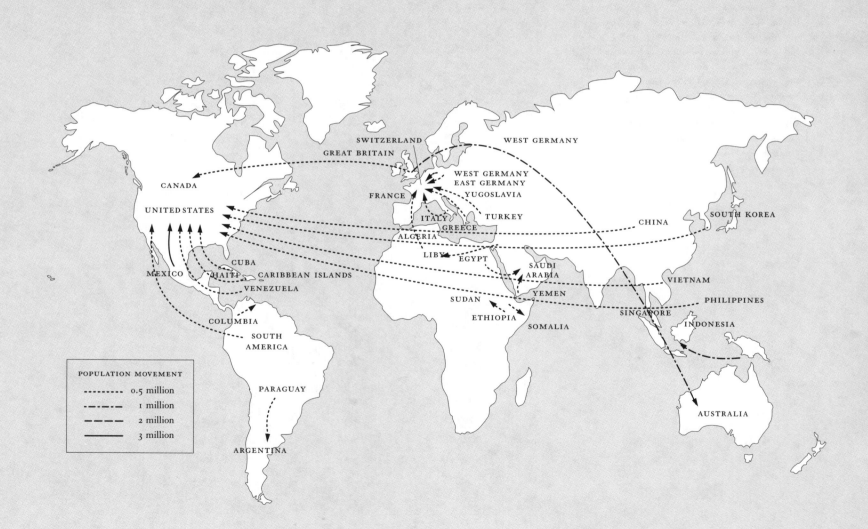

4.4 Documents: Questions and Activities

This section of the guide is intended for teachers and learners.
The general reader or families visiting Ellis Island and other immigration sites
may also wish to read this section for discussion and thought.

Part 1: Migration and Examples from World History

ASK STUDENTS TO EXAMINE THEIR OWN FAMILY BACKGROUNDS to see how they illustrate the various kinds of migration that have existed throughout history: forced and voluntary, circular, chain, and colonizing; as well as internal and external migration. The documents and these exercises related to Part 1 will help students understand the migration process as well as their own histories.

1.3 Family Histories, as Case Studies

The ethnic backgrounds of students in classrooms across the nation differ, reflecting the immigrant history of each locale. Asking students to think about themselves and their family roots, however, leads them to understand that the seemingly personal decisions to migrate, and immigration movements themselves, are part of a continuing worldwide historical process. Students may begin to think about themselves, their peers, and their immediate world in a more sophisticated way. Immigration history and individual family histories, seen within the broad context of world history, bring the student to examine notions of choice and social organization. Even the seemingly fixed categories of slave and free labor can be examined in a different light. Slaves and free laborers were not only bound or free persons, but free or forced immigrants, drawn to the Americas and elsewhere by the same demand for labor. Finally, the idea of immigration itself is refined to include forced and voluntary migrations, as well as persons who remain permanently in the receiving country and persons who return to their homeland. Migration is revealed as a much more complex process than it initially appears to be.

A teacher has many ways to integrate family histories, and the broader histories of human migration which they represent, into the curriculum. Teachers of traditional U.S. history and European history who normally spend time on major themes like industrialization and urbanization can easily enrich these discussions by connecting them to immigration history and to the employment histories of particular families. Industrialization in the United States created a demand for labor; the demand for labor drew people away from agricultural areas to urban places where manufacturing was conducted. Today's labor market draws a broad spectrum of workers, from trained professionals to service personnel. These workers, whether Europeans or Chinese from abroad or African American freemen and women from the South, are all migrants seeking to improve their chances for a better economic situation. Did anyone in a student's family move to find work? Did they remain in their new places?

This guide offers many pedagogical examples. Teachers will find it possible to apply these tools to the specific study of immigration and to courses and sections of courses in world history, American and European history, economics, political science, and geography. They can also use these concepts in helping students construct their own family histories. The answer to the question, "How did my family and I get here?" may have a different, richer meaning to students and their classmates whose families migrated to America under very different circumstances but, nonetheless, shared as much in common as families on the move.

Following are some questions to help students discover the history of their family's migration. Some students will not be able to answer questions about their family's past; they can be asked instead to act as researchers and to interview another student or person in their community. Students can use these questions in conjunction with the documents to understand which category of migration best describes a given family's history:

- *Did anyone in your family immigrate?*

- *Who was the first to move and why?*

- *When?*

- *Did they join relatives or bring relatives after their arrival?*

- *Are they still in contact with relatives or friends who remained behind?*

- *Do they go to see them often?*

- *How did they find work and when?*

- *How did the experiences of the men differ from those of the women?*

- *Can you draw a tree that indicates the migration history of your family?*

1.4 World History and Social Organization of Migration

Ask students to read the documents related to this section and comment upon which kinds of migration they find preferable. Which is possible under a given set of historical circumstances? Which allows the most freedom of choice? How does being a man or a woman influence possibilities and means of migration? Ask students to assume the roles of the various migrants described and to discuss their circumstances with each other.

Document 1

Which migration streams represent forced and voluntary migration? Which migration included the greatest number of people? Why? Explain the stream of African migration to the United States, the Caribbean, and Brazil.

See also **Document 13**, which documents voluntary and slave migrations for a later period, 1830-55, after the U.S. government prohibited the importation of slaves.

Document 2

What did Vassa think about white men? How did he compare the white man's enslavement of Africans to slavery as practiced in his own country?

Document 3

What is the nature of the contract described? What are its special terms and conditions? Would you sign it? Why?

Document 4

What kinds of prior agreements would inhibit that right to enter into a contract? Did European slave traders enter into such contractual relations with Africans?

Document 5

Slavery and indentured servitude operated on different assumptions about individual rights. How did the indentured servant's rights differ from those of a slave? How were these rights protected?

Document 6

What comparisons does the author of the document make concerning the different ethnic groups he mentions?
Is his thinking based upon stereotypes? Does it remind you of any present day stereotypes of foreign-born workers? What clues indicate the document was written after the Civil War?

Document 7

How does the Universal Declaration define human rights? How do these definitions affect the rights of migration? Do U.S. citizens enjoy all these rights?

Document 8

Note the special protection, including a provision against racial discrimination, which earlier foreign-born immigrants who were not U.S. citizens did not enjoy. What do you suppose was the reason for this official policy against racial discrimination? What special protection did these laborers enjoy?

See also **Docs. 32** and **33**, which relate to Chinese immigration and the Chinese exclusion laws. These laws prohibited reentry of Chinese immigrant laborers into the United States after they had made a return trip to China. Thus, the laws inhibited circular migration. As these two documents show, Chinese who wished to participate in circular migration had to demonstrate that they were not laborers but relatively well-off businessmen, who could support themselves and contribute to the nation's wealth if they did return to the United States.

Document 9

On the basis of these two letters, explain how the experiences of southern blacks differed from the experiences of migrating Puerto Ricans. How did the historical timing of the migrations of these two groups affect their experiences?

Document 10

What problems did Oreste find most difficult in his new home? What and who enabled him to survive? How did his family and relations help in his adjustment?

Document 11a

Imagine how the male and female partners felt in these marriages. Discuss the marriages from each perspective.

Document 11b

Both Mr. and Mrs. Orite came from relatively prosperous families. What difference do you think this made in their immigration process? Compare Mrs. Orite to the "picture brides" described in the previous document. What role did the bride's and the groom's family appear to play in each situation?

Document 12

Explore how Native Americans who were relocated onto reservations differed from people we conventionally think of as immigrants. How would you evaluate the Congressman's ethical values concerning Indians? Does any similarity underlie his thinking and that of immigration restrictionists? What did he mean by civilization?

Part 2: Migration and the New World

PART 2 STRESSED THE IMPORTANCE OF CONSIDERING BOTH THE sending and the receiving countries in the migration process, which requires discussion about conditions abroad that have led to mass migration to the Americas. Using the migration patterns and categories presented in Part 1, this section explores immigration in the history of the Americas and the world. The themes in Part 2 give teachers of U.S. history and world history a new way to present chronological periods from the European Age of Exploration to the twentieth century, and they also open the way for using the subject of immigration to explore contemporary social and economic issues, including current controversies about immigration policy and refugee policy in the United States and abroad.

Examples from the five centuries of migration that followed the first voyage of Columbus to the Western Hemisphere also help relate immigration and migration to major changes in transportation, agriculture, and the means of production—changes commonly lumped in the term Industrial Revolution—and demonstrate the close relationship between immigration and demands for labor. To explore how Americans regarded the newcomers, Part 2 discussed the massive Irish immigration to the United States; and, to show how conditions in the receiving country might affect the evolution of the immigrant community, it compared Italian immigration to the United States and Argentina. A sketch of Chinese immigration to the United States described how economics and deep racial biases might combine to restrict and even halt the flow from some parts of the world. Part 2 concluded with observations about the initial, formative reactions of Americans to massive migration before the Ellis Island era.

Document 13

Explain the great stream from Ireland to the United States. What political event in Germany set off migrations in 1848? Which of the streams shown on the map consisted of free laborers and which of slave?

Compare this map with **Document 1**, "Major World Migrations, 1700-1810." What are the differences in migration patterns in these two periods? What explains the cessation of African migration to the United States in the 1830 to 1855 era and the continuing of African migration to Brazil and the Caribbean?

Document 14

Using the chart, determine which countries of the world received the most immigrants. Next, coordinate the information from this chart with the data provided by **Document 23**, "Major World Migrations, 1890-1915." Was the pattern of immigration the same in 1890-1915 as for 1820-1930? If not, how did it differ?

Document 15

Using the map, determine which countries of the world were sending immigrants to the receiving countries.

What changes in immigration patterns are evident by comparing this map with the one for 1890-1915, **Document 23**?

Viewed from the perspective of the sending countries of southern and eastern Europe, which were the most important receiving countries during the period 1890-1915? What events in the Southern Hemisphere explain the migration of Europeans to South Africa? Where else in the Southern Hemisphere were Europeans migrating, and what political and social consequences did these migrations have? What does this map indicate about migration from and within the British Empire?

Document 16

Could people be persuaded to leave their homeland today for the kinds of reasons suggested in this document? Why or why not?

Document 17

What advice does Edward Johnson give to Puritans leaving for America? Does today's world provide instances of religious belief exerting such a strong influence on major life decisions?

Document 18

How would you describe the attitude of the Congressional investigators toward the immigrant Antonio di Dierro? Compare this testimony to **Document 8**, which relates to early twenieth-century Puerto Rican contract laborers. What explains the differing receptions accorded Mr. Di Dierro and the Puerto Rican migrants? Do you respect Mr. Di Dierro's refusal to work for low wages?

Document 19

What are the sources of migration from Europe to the United States? Explain the high proportion of Irish immigrants in the period of the 1830s and 1840s. When do the sources of European migration begin to change significantly? Why?

Document 20

Does your community, city, or town appear on this map? Can you determine which immigrant groups had settled in your area by 1830? Are these groups still important in your community?

Document 21

Locate your town or city on this map. Was it an urban area in 1910? By talking to members of your community can you determine which immigrant groups, if any, had settled in your area by 1910? How has the local population changed since then?

Use the world maps in this guide—**Documents 1, 13, 15, 23, 40, 46**—to explain the ethnic characteristics of people living in your part of the United States. Describe the ethnic neighborhoods in your town or city. What does immigration have to do with this ethnic profile?

Document 22

How is Sarah Rice's life like and unlike yours? What was her attitude toward her father? Toward her religious background? Is it necessary to leave home in order to grow up?

Document 23

What were the major destinations for immigrants other than the United States? How and where did the influx of Europeans contribute to the development of multicultural societies throughout the world?

Document 24 demonstrates that other multinational societies were forming during this period. What multi-national societies did Chinese immigrants help form?

Use **Document 23** in conjunction with the pie charts in **Documents 24** and **25** to discuss the impact of U.S. restrictionist policy on Chinese immigration. Do these documents demonstrate that federal immigration policy influences the flow of immigrants to the United States and even elsewhere?

Document 26

Is it possible to predict from this account what the American reception to Germans might be? How would it compare to the reception of the Irish? How did the states described above formally respond to the new German immigrants?

Document 27

Using the chart and the map, **Document 15**, "Major World Migrations, 1860-85," explain differences between the two major receiving nations, Argentina and the United States. Did these differences persist from the 1860-85 period to the 1960s?

Describe the ethnic neighborhoods in your town or city. What does immigration have to do with this ethnic profile?

Document 28

Which groups are portrayed? What does the cartoon imply about each group? What ethnic stereotypes do you see? Whose point of view does the cartoon represent, the resident American's or the newcomer's? What does it say about each group's potential for assimilation into American life?

Document 29

How does this immigrant working man see himself and his situation? How do his self-portrait and portrait of the United States differ from those of long-term resident observers? Is he likely to return home?

Compare this document to **Document 30**, song lyrics written by workers against Chinese immigrants. Read your local newspaper and look for articles by and about immigrants. Do these articles reveal the same concerns as the documents from the nineteenth century? Who is writing them? Whose point of view is represented?

Document 30

Who is the "Sam" referred to in the song's first line? What fears and resentments does the song reveal? Who are the resented persons? How do these attitudes compare to today's anti-immigrant attitudes? Are the Chinese thought of differently today?

Document 31

What does this document reveal about American attitudes toward the Chinese? Does this portrait of the brilliant, destructive Fu-Manchu remind you of any adventure stories you read or see at the movies today? Do Americans today retain the early twentieth-century stereotypes of Asians? Of any other foreign people?

Document 32

Why did the immigration inspector ask witnesses to testify on Chu Hoy's behalf? Many of the inspector's questions have little to do with determining that Chu Hoy was a merchant, not a laborer, and therefore not subject to the exclusion laws concerning laborers. Why was the inspector asking questions about the personal affairs of Chinese immigrants? What stereotypes about the Chinese appear in the questions?

Document 33

Why did Chu Yuck Jan need this exit visa? What, in the judgment of American policymakers, qualified him to leave and then reenter the United States?

Part 3: Ellis Island and After

Document 34

What were some Progressive Era ideals expressed in this letter, and how did they relate to immigration? Do you think that these ideals apply today toward the Americanization process? If so, why?

Document 35

How did the social attitudes of the day influence the inspectors' concepts of health? Do you accept the health inspectors' assumptions about racial characteristics? How do you feel about mental or physical disease as a cause for excluding persons from entering the United States?

Document 36

Answer the questions yourself, assuming you are an entering immigrant. How do you react to these questions? Which ones, if any, seem strange? Do you think you could, and would, answer each of them truthfully? Why, or why not?

Document 37

This document suggests that the immigration experience differed for men and for women. Discuss what you imagine some of these differences might be. Discuss the major concerns that an immigrant man or woman might have on arriving in a new country.

Document 38

What do you think of the Harvard students described in this article? How would you react if your chances of getting into college were influenced by your ethnic or racial heritage? By your sex?

Document 39

Discuss how the interpretation of immigration law in this document conflicted with human values regarding the protection of young children.

See **Document 7**, the Universal Declaration of Human Rights, for a different perspective. With which perspective do you agree?

Document 40

If this map is compared with the map of the 1890–1915 period, **Document 23**, what dramatic differences in migration appear? What political events explain these changes in the world's migration patterns? What explains French migration to Algeria? East European migrations within and outside Europe? What multinational societies were developing during this era?

Explain the population movement out of Palestine to Jordan. Look at Asia, where, as the map suggests, millions of people were displaced. What events in India brought this about?

Document 41

The Rubin family's history reveals the complexity of voluntary migration. Did they have a real choice? Were they political or religious refugees? What role did chance play in their successful journey to the United States?

Document 42

Using the chart, describe how the sources of immigration to the United States have changed since 1880. What political and economic events influenced the migration flow? How did legislation influence the migration flow?

Document 43

Using the chart, describe the changes between 1950 and 1980 in immigration to the United States. What are the sources of recent immigration to the United States? Compare this chart to **Document 42,** "Yearly Immigration to the United States, 1880-1940." How do the sources of immigration in the two periods differ?

Document 44

On what bases did Judge Pfaelzer rule against Proposition 187? Do you think that persons entering the United States illegally are entitled to educational, health, and other benefits? Relate your response to **Document 7,** the Universal Declaration of Human Rights.

Document 45

How has the proportion of women and men, which experts call the sex ratio, changed over time? Certain events, such as war or changes in U.S. immigration policy, have altered the sex ratio. For example, after the world wars, many women entered the United States as the "war brides" of soldiers. How have recent changes in the labor market influenced female migration patterns?

Document 46

If you were to compare immigration to the United States during the colonial era, the nineteenth through early twentieth centuries, and now, how would you describe the differences in peoples migrating during these three eras? Use the world maps provided in this guide to answer this question. See **Documents 1,13,15,23,40.**

How have recent migrations affected the ethnic character of your community? What patterns do you discern concerning migration to and throughout Europe? Is Europe likely to become another United States, a major receiving area of immigrants from the developing world? What other parts of the world show major migrations? What explains these movements?

Read local newspapers for news of recent immigrants and refugees from troubled parts of the world. What do the articles reveal about public attitudes to immigration? Have Americans changed their attitudes toward immigrants?

5. Resources

5.1 COLLECTIONS AND STUDIES

5.1.1 Beginning Points

An indispensable work as a reference tool and for articles on immigration is Stephan Thernstrom et al., *Harvard Encyclopedia of American Ethnic Groups* (Cambridge: Belknap Press of Harvard University, 1980). Its more than one thousand pages contain articles on individual ethnic groups from Acadians to Zoroastrians and thematic essays on such subjects as naturalization and prejudice.

One of the best anthologies of articles in immigration history is George E. Pozzetta's twenty-volume *American Immigration and Ethnicity* series published by Garland Press (New York, 1991). Each volume covers a different topic including unions, work, politics, education, ethnic communities and institutions, law, family, crime, and Americanization.

Another good anthology is Ronald Takaki, *From Different Shores: Perspectives on Race and Ethnicity in America* (New York: Oxford University Press, 1987). Rudolph J. Vecoli

and Susan Sinke, eds., *A Century of European Migrations, 1830-1930* (Urbana: University of Illinois Press, 1991), treat the great European migrations from a transnational perspective. Virginia Yans-McLaughlin, ed., *Immigration Reconsidered: History, Sociology, Politics* (New York: Oxford University Press, 1990), a book of essays that summarizes much of the recent scholarship, should also be consulted on a number of topics including immigration policy, the immigration process, Latin American immigration, and the oral history of immigration.

5.1.2 Bibliographies

Among the most useful bibliographies are the *Balch Institute Historical Reading Lists*, twenty pamphlets, each with an essay and annotated bibliography, by grade level, on a different ethnic group (Philadelphia: Balch Institute, 1975–76). See also *Immigration and Ethnicity: A Guide to Information Sources*, compiled by John D. Buenker and Nicholas Burkel and published in 1977 by the Gale Research Company of Detroit. It has sections on old, new, and post-1920s immigration, essays on assimilation and legislation, and

listings of government publications. Jack F. Kinton, *American Ethnic Groups and the Revival of Cultural Pluralism: An Evaluation Source Book for the 1970s* (Aurora, Ill.: Social Science and Sociological Resources, 1979), lists major texts, journals, films, research centers, and publishers of ethnic studies. *European Immigration and Ethnicity in the United States and Canada*, edited by Donald Byre (Santa Barbara, 1977), contains more than 4,000 abstracts of articles.

Some bibliographies of particular groups include Don Heinrich Tolzman, *German-Americana* (Metuchen, N.J.: Scarecrow Press, 1975); Francisco Cordasco, *The Italian-Americans* (Detroit: Gale Research Co., 1978); Leo Pap, *The Portuguese in the United States* (1970), and Michael Cutsumbis, *A Bibliographic Guide to Greeks in the United States* (1976), both published by the Staten Island Center for Migration Studies.

Aids to the study of various East European groups are Adam S. Eterovich, *A Guide and Bibliography to Research on Yugoslavs in the United States and Canada* (San Francisco: R. & E. Research Associates, 1975); Ester Jurabek, *Czechs and Slovaks in North America* (New York: Czechoslovak

Society of Arts and Sciences in America, 1976); Joseph Szeplaki, *Hungarians in the United States and Canada* (St. Paul: Immigration History and Research Center, 1977); Joseph W. Zuraski, *Polish American History and Culture* (Chicago: Polish Museum of America, 1976); Roman Weres, *Ukraine: Selected References in the English Language* (Chicago: Ukrainian Research and Information Institute, 1974); William W. Brickman, *The Jewish Community in America* (New York: B. Franklin, 1977).

Philip Kayal has compiled "An Arab-American Bibliography" for Barbara Aswad's *Arabic-Speaking Communities in American Cities* (Staten Island: Center for Migration Studies, 1974).

Bibliographies on Filipinos, Koreans, and East Indians are appended to H. Brett Melendy's *Asians in America* (Boston: Twayne Publishers, 1977); Chinese and Japanese are included in Isao Fugimoto, *Asians in America* (Davis: University of California, 1971).

Recent bibliographies on immigration from the Western Hemisphere include Lambros Comitas, *The Complete Caribbeans, Vol. I: 1900–1975* (Millwood, N.Y.: KTO Press, 1977); the United States Department of Housing and Urban Development's *Hispanic Americans in the United States* (1975); Frank Pino, *Mexican Americans* (East Lansing: Latin American Studies Center, Michigan State University, 1974); and Francisco Cordasco, *Puerto Ricans on the United States Mainland* (Totowa, N.J.: Roman & Littlefield, 1972).

The *Journal of American Ethnic History*, Transaction Periodical Consortium, Rutgers University, New Brunswick, N.J. contains reviews of recent books.

5.1.3 Accessible Synthetic Works

John Bodnar's *The Transplanted: A History of Immigrants in Urban America* (Bloomington: University of Indiana Press, 1985) remains the best synthetic study of the history of immigration to North America presented within a global perspective. Philip Curtin's *The Atlantic Slave Trade: A Census* (Madison: University of Wisconsin Press, 1969) portrays slavery as part of a global economy and global labor market. Walter Nugent, *Crossings: The Great Transatlantic Migrations, 1870–1914* (Bloomington: Indiana University Press, 1992), places immigration to the United States in the broader context of Atlantic migrations. Reed Ueda, *Postwar Immigrant America: A Social History* (Boston: Bedford Books of St. Martin's Press, 1994), is an excellent, up-to-date treatment of U.S. migration from a global perspective. See also Robin Cohen, ed., *The Cambridge Survey of World Migration* (Cambridge: Cambridge University Press, 1995).

Some popular recent books on immigration are: Thomas Archdeacon, *Becoming American: An Ethnic History* (New York: Free Press, 1983); Bernard Bailyn, *The Peopling of British North America* (New York: Knopf, 1986); Roger Daniels, *Coming to America: A History of Immigration and Ethnicity in American Life* (New York: HarperCollins, 1990); Lawrence Fuchs, *The American Kaleidoscope: Race, Ethnicity, and the Civic Culture* (Hanover, N.H.: University Press of New England, 1990); Alan M. Kraut, *The Huddled Masses: The Immigrant in American Society, 1880-1921* (Arlington Heights, Ill.: Harlan Davidson, Inc. 1982).

For nativism and anti-Semitism see David H. Bennett, *The Party of Fear: From Nativist Movements to the New Right in American History* (Chapel Hill: University of North Carolina Press, 1988); David Gerber, ed., *Anti-Semitism in American History* (Urbana: University of Illinois Press, 1986). John Higham, *Strangers in the Land: Patterns of American Nativism, 1860-1925* (New York: Atheneum, 1963), remains a definitive study; see also Ronald Takaki, *Iron Cages: Race and Culture in Nineteenth-Century America* (New York: Knopf, 1979; reprint, Oxford University Press, 1990).

Several fine books address recent immigration, including David W. Reimers, *Still the Golden Door: The Third World Comes to America* (New York: Columbia University Press, 1992); Nancy Foner, ed., *New Immigrants in New York* (New York: Columbia University Press, 1987); Alejandro Portes and Ruben G. Rumbaut, *Immigrant America: A Portrait* (Berkeley, University of California Press, 1992, 2d ed.). On the phenomenon of return migration see Mark Wyman, *Round-Trip to America: The Immigrants Return to Europe, 1880–1930* (Ithaca: Cornell University Press, 1993).

Important books about the exclusion of immigrants include: Sucheng Chan, ed., *Entry Denied, Exclusion and the Chinese Community in America, 1882-1943* (Philadelphia: Temple University Press, 1991), and Alan Kraut, *Silent Travelers: Germs, Genes, and the "Immigrant Menace"* (New York: Basic Books, 1994), which examines the idea that newcomers brought diseases to America and throws an interesting perspective on the Ellis Island health inspection.

David Ward, *Cities and Immigrants: A Geography of Change in Nineteenth*

Century America (New York: Oxford University Press, 1971), remains the classic study on settlement patterns of immigrants. The Tenement Museum has compiled *Lower East Side Heritage Trails* (New York: New York University Press, forthcoming), which provides six self-guided walking tours of the Lower East Side and examines the history of the groups that have lived in the neighborhoods: Africans, Chinese, Germans, Irish, Italians, and Jews.

On the issue of refugees in recent times see Carole Kismaric, *Forced Out: The Agony of the Refugee in Our Time* (New York: Random House, 1989). Guy S. Goodwin-Gill, *The Refugee in International Law* (Oxford: Clarendon Press, 1983; 2d. ed., 1996), treats refugees within a global context.

5.1.4 Family History

Ira Wolfman, *Do People Grow on Family Trees: Genealogy for Kids and Other Beginners* (New York: Workman Publishing, 1991), is the official Ellis Island handbook of family history. Other good aids for doing family history are: *Family Folklife: Interviewing Guide and Questionnaire* (Washington, D.C.: Folklife Program, Office of American and Folklore Studies, Smithsonian Institution). Dominic Candeloro, *Making History: A Handbook for Italian American Social History Projects* (Washington, D.C.: National Italian American Foundation, 1990); Thad Silton, George L. Mehafey, and O.L. Davis, *Oral History: A Guide for Teachers (and Others)* (Austin: University of Texas Press, 1983), *The Oral History Review*, the journal of the Oral History Association is published twice a year by the Association in Alburquerque, N.M. 87190-3968; David E. Kyvig and

Martin A. Marty, *Your Family History: A Handbook for Research and Writing* (Arlington Heights, Ill.: Harlan Davidson, Inc., 1978). Individuals interested in tracing their family immigration history should contact the National Archives and Records Administration, 7th and Pennsylvania Ave. NW, Washington, D.C., (202)-501-5403 or the National Archives and Records Administration, North East Region, New York Office, 201 Varick St., N.Y., N.Y., 10014 (212) 337-1300.

5.1.5 Ellis and Angel Islands

For the history of Ellis Island and Angel Island see: Judy Yung, *Island, Poetry and History of Chinese Immigrants on Angel Island, 1910–1940* (San Francisco: Chinese Culture Foundation, 1980); Barbara Benton, *Ellis Island: A Pictorial History* (New York: Facts on File, 1985); David Brownstone, et al., *Island of Hope, Island of Tears* (New York: Rawson, Wade, 1979); Norman Kotker, *et al., Ellis Island: Echoes from a Nation's Past* (New York: Aperture Foundation, 1989); Geroges Perec with Robert Bober, *Ellis Island* (New York: New Press, 1995) is a collage of historic and contemporary photos, prose, and interviews with immigrants who came through Ellis Island. Thomas Pitkin, *Keepers of the Gate: A History of Ellis Island* (New York: New York University Press, 1975); Pamela Reeves, *Ellis Island: Gateway to the American Dream* (New York: Dorset Press, 1991); Bernice Siegal and DyAnne DiSalvo-Ryan, *Sam Ellis's Island* (New York: Four Winds, 1985). Wilton Tifft, *Ellis Island* (New York: Norton, 1979), provides wonderful historic photos. M. Mark Stolarik, ed., *Forgotten Doors: The Other Ports of Entry to*

the United States (Philadelphia and London: Balch Institute and Associated University Press, 1988), documents ports of entry other than Ellis and Angel Islands.

5.1.6 Immigrant Women

See: Donna Gabaccia, *From the Other Side: Women, Gender, and Immigrant Life In the U.S., 1820–1990* (Bloomington: Indiana University Press, 1994); see also her *Immigrant Women in the United States, A Selectively Annotated Multidisciplinary Bibliography* (New York: Greenwood Press, 1989); Elizabeth Ewen, *Immigrant Women in the Land of Dollars: Life and Culture on the Lower East Side, 1890–1925* (New York: Monthly Review Press, 1985). Kathie Friedman-Kasaba, *Memories of Migration: Gender, Ethnicity, and Work in the Lives of Jewish and Italian Women in New York, 1870–1924* (Albany: State University of New York Press, 1996), approaches women's migrations from a world perspective. Maxine Seller, ed., *Immigrant Women* (Albany: State University of New York, 2d ed., rev., 1981), is a good anthology of essays and excerpts from immigrant women's writings; Cecyle Neidle, *America's Immigrant Women: Their Contribution to the Development of a Nation from 1609 to the Present* (New York: Hippocrene Books, 1975), and Doris Weatherford, *Foreign and Female: Immigrant Women in America, 1840–1938* (New York: Schocken Books, 1986), provide chronological treatments of this aspect of women's history.

The following books treat contemporary female immigrants: Rita J. Simon and Caroline Brettell, eds., *International Migration: The Female Experience* (Totowa,

N.J.: Rowman & Allanheld, 1986); Delores Mortimer and Roy Bryce-Laporte, eds., *Female Immigrants to the United States: Caribbean, Latin American, and African Experiences* (Washington D.C.: Research Institute on Immigration and Ethnic Studies, Smithsonian Institution, 1981).

5.1.7 Statistics on Immigration

The most accessible source for finding the number of immigrants to the U.S. is an almanac like *Information Please* or *The World Almanac and Book of Facts*. Most of them have a section on immigration and give the numbers by country or continent by decade since 1820. *The World Almanac and Book of Facts*, published annually by the Newspaper Enterprise Association, Inc., New York, includes a summary of the current immigration law.

The *Harvard Encyclopedia of American Ethnic Groups* has three thematic essays that focus on the immigration process: economic and social characteristics; history of United States policy; settlement patterns and spatial distribution. Because the encyclopedia encompasses more than the study of immigration and the essays vary considerably, not all immigrant groups can be traced decade by decade.

William J. Bromwell, *History of Immigration to the United States* (New York: Arno Press, 1969); Basic Books (New York, 1976) issued the same material under the title *The Statistical History of the United States from Colonial Times to the Present*. These two works, practically identical, are available at the reference desk of most libraries. An earlier version, covering the years up to 1957, is often available if the new edition is not.

A slightly more complete account of immigration to America during the years before 1924 is available in Walter F. Willcox, ed., *International Migrations*, 2 vols. (New York: Gordon and Preach Science Publishers, Inc.: 1929–31, rpt., 1969). Volume I includes statistics for most of the world; the section on the United States (pp. 374–500) contains some typographical errors, particularly transposed columns, but this is a valuable source, nevertheless, since it brings together fairly specific data for more countries than does the census monograph. The Immigration and Naturalization Service publishes useful *Statistical Yearbooks* which often contain historical as well as contemporary statistics.

5.1.8 Slavery, Indenture, and Settlement of early America

See: Barbara L. Solow, *Slavery and the Rise of the Atlantic Slave System* (Cambridge: W. E. B. Du Bois Institute for Afro-American Research, Harvard University, 1991); James A. Rawley, *The Transatlantic Slave Trade: A History* (New York: Norton, 1981); Ida Altman and James Horn, eds., *"To Make America," European Emigration in the Early Modern Period* (Berkeley: University of California Press, 1991); Virginia DeJohn Anderson, *New England's Generation: The Great Migration and the Formation of Society and Culture in the Seventeenth Century* (Cambridge and New York: Cambridge University Press, 1991); J. H. Elliott, *Spain and Its World: 1500-1700* (New Haven: Yale University Press, 1989); Bernard Bailyn, *The Peopling of British North America* (New York: Knopf, 1986); Wilfred Oldham, *Britain's Convicts to the Colonies* (Sydney: Library of Australian History, 1990); John

Van der Zee, *Bound Over: Indentured Servitude and American Conscience* (New York: Simon & Schuster, 1985); David W. Galenson, *White Servitude in Colonial America: An Economic Analysis* (Cambridge and New York: Cambridge University Press, 1981).

5.1.9 Immigration Policy

Recent books on this subject include: Roy Beck, *The Case against Immigration: The Moral, Economic, Social, and Environmental Reasons for Reducing U.S. Immigration Back to Traditional Levels* (New York: W.W. Norton & Co., 1996); Charles B. Keely, *U.S. Immigration: A Policy Analysis* (New York: The Population Council, 1979); Michael C. LeMay; *From Open Door to Dutch Door: An Analysis of U.S. Immigration Policy Since 1820* (New York: Praeger, 1987); Michael Teitelbaum and Myrna Weiner, eds., *Threatened Peoples and Threatened Borders: World Migrations and U.S. Policy* (New York: W.W. Norton & Co., 1995); and Chilton Williamson Jr., *The Immigration Mystique: America's False Conscience* (New York: Basic Books, 1996).

5.2 STUDIES, BIOGRAPHIES, AND FICTION ABOUT IMMIGRANT GROUPS

This section lists some of the many works of nonfiction, autobiography, and fiction available about ethnic and national groups that have been significant in immigration to the United States. The nonfiction works include scholarly books and articles.

Autobiographies are invaluable for providing an authentic "inside" view of the immigrant experience and of the sending culture. Fictional works have to be treated more carefully, for authors who do not see themselves as historians may distort the past. Moreover, it is often difficult for novelists to portray accurately a culture not their own.

5.2.1 Recent Immigrants — General Works, Collections of Essays, and Oral Histories

Nonfiction

FONER, NANCY, ed. *New Immigrants in New York*. New York: Columbia University Press, 1987.

MANGIAFICO, LUCIANO. *Contemporary American Immigrants: Patterns of Filipino, Korean, and Chinese Settlement in the United States*. New York: Praeger, 1988.

SANTOLI, AL. *New Communities, An Oral History: Immigrants and Refugees in the U.S. Today*. New York: Viking Press, 1988.

SIEMS, LARRY. *Between the Lines: Letters Between Undocumented Mexican and Central American Immigrants and Their Families*. Hopewell, N.J.: Ecco Press, 1992.

WALDINGER, ROGER AND BOZORGMEHR, ed. *Ethnic Los Angeles*. New York: Russel Sage Foundation, 1996.

5.2.2 African Americans

Nonfiction

GROSSMAN, JAMES. *Land of Hope: Chicago, Black Southerners and the Great Migration*. Chicago: University of Chicago Press, 1989.

HENRI, FLORETTE. *Black Migration: Movement North, 1900–1920*. Garden City: Anchor Press, 1975.

LEMANN, NICHOLAS. *The Promised Land: The Great Black Migration and How It Changed America*. New York: Albert A. Knopf, 1991.

Autobiography and Fiction

ANGELOU, MAYA. *I Know Why the Caged Bird Sings*. New York: Random House, 1967.

BROWN, CLAUDE. *Manchild in the Promised Land*. New York: Signet, 1965.

MALCOLM X. *The Autobiography of Malcolm X*. New York: Ballantine, 1973.

5.2.3 Arabs

Nonfiction

ASWAD, BARBARA. *Arabic Speaking Communities in American Cities*. Staten Island: New York Center for Migration Studies, 1974.

5.2.4 Armenians

Nonfiction

MINASIAN, EDWARD, ed. *Recent Studies in Modern Armenian History*. Cambridge: Armenian Heritage Press, 1972.

MIRAH, ROBERT. *Torn between Two Lands: Armenians in American, 1890 to World War I*. Cambridge: Harvard University Press, 1983.

Autobiography and Fiction

BABA, HARRY. *For the Grape Season*. New York, 1960.

HAGOPIAN, RICHARD. *The Dove Brings Peace*. New York: Farrar and Rinehart Inc, 1944. Saroyan, William. *My Name Is Aram*. New York: Harcourt, Brace and Co., 1940.

5.2.5 Asians

(See also Chinese, Filipinos, Japanese, Indians, Koreans, Vietnamese)

Nonfiction

BARRINGER, HERBERT *et al., Asians and Pacific Islanders in the United States*. New York: Russel Sage Foundation, 1995.

CHAN, SUCHENG. *Asian Americans: An Interpretive History*. Boston: Twayne, 1991.

DANIELS, ROGER. *Asian America: Chinese and Japanese in the United States since 1850*. Seattle: University of Washington Press, 1988.

LEE, JOANN FAUNG JEAN. *Asian Americans*. New York: New Press, 1992. (See 5.2.13).

MANGIAFICIO, LUCIANO. *Contemporary American Immigrants: Patterns of Filipino, Korean, and Chinese Settlement in the United States*. New York: Praeger, 1988.

TAKAKI, RONALD. *Strangers from a Different Shore: A History of Asian Americans*. Boston: Little, Brown and Co., 1989.

5.2.6 Austrians

Autobiography and Fiction
BECK, JOSEPH CLARK. *Fifty Years in Medicine*. Chicago: McDonough & Co., 1940.

STEINER, EDWARD A. *From Alien to Citizen*. New York: F.H. Revell, 1931 (rpt, New York: Arno Press, 1975).

5.2.7 Bohemians

Autobiography and Fiction
CATHER, WILLA. *My Antonia*. Boston: Houghton Mifflin, 1918.

5.2.8 British

Nonfiction
BERTHOFF, ROWLAND. *British Immigrants in Industrial America, 1790-1950*. Cambridge: Harvard University Press, 1953.

5.2.9 Bulgarians

Autobiography and Fiction
CHRISTOWE, STOYAN. *This Is My Country*. New York: Lippincott, 1938.

YANKOFF, PETER DEMETROFF. *Headlights to Success: Or, the Story of a Bulgarian Boy*. Ft. Smith, Ark.: Calvert-McBride, 1920.

5.2.10 Caribbean

Nonfiction
PALMER, RANSFORD W. *In Search of a Better Life: Perspectives on Migration from the Caribbean*. New York: Praeger, 1990.

5.2.11 Central Americans

Nonfiction
DORAN, TERRY ET AL. *A Road Well Traveled: Three Generations of Cuban American Women*. Newton, Mass.: Education Development Center, Women's Educational Equity Act Publishing Center, 1988.

POITRAS, G. *International Migration to the U.S. from Costa Rica and El Salvador*. San Antonio: Border Research Institute, 1980.

5.2.13 Chinese

Nonfiction
TSAI, SHIH-SHAN HENRY. *The Chinese Experience in America*. Bloomington: Indiana University Press, 1975.

YUNG, JUDY. *Chinese Women of America: A Pictorial History*. Seattle: University of Washington Press, 1986.

Autobiography and Fiction
CHIN, FRANK. *The Chickencoop Chinaman and the Year of the Dragon*. Seattle: University of Washington Press, 1981.

KANG, YOUNGHILL. *East Goes West: The Making of an Oriental Yankee*. New York: C. Scribner's Sons, 1937.

KINGSTON, MAXINE HONG. *Chinamen*. New York: Albert A. Knopf, 1977.
———. *The Woman Warrior: Memoirs of a Girlhood among Ghosts*. New York: Albert A. Knopf, 1977.

LEE, JOANN FAUNG. *Asian Americans: Oral Histories of First to Fourth Generation Americans from China, the Philippines, Japan, India, the Pacific Islands, Vietnam and Cambodia*. New York: New Press, 1992.

LOWE, PARDEE. *Father and Glorious Descendant*. Boston: Little, Brown, and Co., 1943.

5.2.14 Cubans

Nonfiction
BOSWELL, T. D., AND J. R. CURTIS. *The Cuban-American Experience*. Totowa, N. J.: Rowman and Allanheld, 1984.

PORTES, ALEJANDRO, AND ROBERT BACH. *Latin Journey: Cuban and Mexican Immigrants in the United States*. Berkeley: University of California Press, 1985.

5.2.15 Dominicans

Nonfiction
GEORGES, EUGENIA. *The Making of a Transnational Community: Migration, Development, and Cultural Change in the Dominican Republic*. New York: Columbia University Press, 1990.

HENDRICKS, D. L. *The Dominican Diaspora: From the Dominican Republic to New York City*. New York: Teacher's College Press of Columbia University, 1974.

5.2.12 Dutch

Nonfiction
LUCAS, HENRY S. *Netherlanders in America*. Ann Arbor: University of Michigan Press, 1955, 1981.

5.2.16 Filipinos

Nonfiction

VALLANGCA, CAUDAD CONCEPCION. *The Second Wave: Pinay and Pinoy, 1945–1960*. San Francisco: Strawberry Hill Press, 1987.

Autobiography and Fiction

BUAKEN, MANUEL. *I Have Lived with the American People*. Caldwell, Id.: Caxton Printers, 1948.

BULOSAN, CARLOS. *America Is in the Heart: A Personal History*. Seattle: University of Washington Press, 1973, 1946.

5.2.17 Finns

Nonfiction

KARNI, MICHAEL, ED. *The Finnish Experience in the Western Great Lakes Region: New Perspectives*. Vammala: Institute for Migration of Turku, Finland, 1975.

ROSS, CARL, AND K. MARIANNE WARGELIN BROWN, *Women Who Dared: The History of Finnish American Women*. St. Paul, MN: Immigration History Research Center, 1986.

5.2.18 French-Canadians

Nonfiction

BRAULT, GERALD J. *The French-Canadian Heritage in New England*. Hanover, NH: University Press of New England, 1986.

5.2.19 Germans

Nonfiction

RIPLEY, LAVERN J. *The German-Americans*. Boston: Twayne, 1976.

Autobiography and Fiction

ALDRICH, BESS STREETER. *Spring Came on Forever*. New York: Grosset and Dunlap, 1935.

DREISER, THEODORE. *Jennie Gerhardt*. New York: Harper, 1911.

JORDAN, MILDRED. *One Red Rose Forever*. New York: Grosset and Dunlap, 1941.

SUCKOW, RUTH. *Country People*. New York: Alfred A. Knopf, 1924.

5.2.20 Greeks

Nonfiction

SALOUTOS, THEODORE. *The Greeks in the United States*. Cambridge: Harvard University Press, 1964.

SCOURBY, ALICE. SALOUTOS, THEODORE. *The Greek Americans*. Boston: Twayne, 1984.

Autobiography and Fiction

COTSAKIS, ROXANE F. *Wing and the Thorn*. Atlanta: Tupper and Love, 1952.

KAZAN, ELIA. *America, America*. New York: Stein and Day, 1962.

PETRAKIS, HARRY MARK. *The Odyssey of Kostas Volakis*. New York: D. McKay Co, 1963.

VARDOULAKIS, MARY. *Gold in the Streets*. New York: Dodd, Mead & Co., 1945.

5.2.21 Haitians

Nonfiction

LAGUERRE, MICHAEL S. *American Odyssey: Haitians in New York City*. Ithaca: Cornell University Press, 1984.

MILLER, JAKE. *The Plight of Haitian Refugees*. New York: Praeger, 1984.

5.2.22 Hawaiians

Nonfiction

KIKUMURA, AKEMI. *Issei Pioneers: Hawaii and the Mainland, 1855–1924*. Los Angeles: Japanese American National Museum, 1992.

5.2.23 Hispanics

Nonfiction

BEAN, FRANK D., AND MARTA TIENDA. *The Hispanic Population of the United States*. New York: Russel Sage Foundation, 1987.

MOORE, J. AND H. PACHON. *Hispanics in the United States*. Englewood Cliffs, N.J.: Prentice-Hall, 1985.

5.2.24 Hungarians

Nonfiction

VARDY, STEVEN BELA. *The Hungarian Americans*. Boston: Twayne, 1985.

Autobiography and Fiction

ROMBAUER, RODERICK EMILE. *The History of A Life*. St. Louis: 1903.

SULEIMAN, SUSAN RUBIN, *Budapest Diary: In Search of the Motherbook*. Lincoln: University of Nebraska Press, 1996.

THOREK, MAX. *A Surgeon's World: An Autobiography*. Philadelphia: J.B. Lippincott Co., 1943.

5.2.25 Indians

Autobiography and Fiction

MUKERJI, DHAN GOPAL. *Caste and Outcaste*. New York: E.P. Dutton and Co., 1923.

5.2.26 Irish

Nonfiction

DINER, HASIA. *Erin's Daughter's in America: Irish Immigrant Women in the Nineteenth Century*. Baltimore: Johns Hopkins University Press, 1983.

MILLER, KERBY A. *Emigrants and Exiles: Ireland and the Irish Exodus to North America*. New York: Oxford University Press, 1985.

Autobiography and Fiction

CULLINAN, ELIZABETH. *House of Gold*. Boston: Houghton Mifflin, 1970.

CURRAN, MARY DOYLE. *The Parish and the Hill*. Boston: Houghton Mifflin, 1948.

DEASY, MARY. *The Hour of Spring*. Boston: Little, Brown and Co., 1948.

DINEEN, JOSEPH. *Ward Eight*. Boston: Waverly House, 1936.

DOOLEY, ROGER. *Days Beyond Recall*. Milwaukee: Bruce Pub. Co., 1949.

DUNPHY, JACK: *John Fury. A Novel in Four Parts*. New York: Harper & Bros., 1946.

FARRELL, JAMES T. *Studs Lonigan*. (3 vols.). New York: The Modern Library, 1938.

MCHALE, TOM. *Farragan's Retreat*. New York: Viking, 1971.

MCSORLEY, EDWARD. *Our Own Kind*. New York: Harper & Bros., 1946.

O'CONNOR, EDWIN. *The Last Hurrah*. Boston: Little, Brown and Co., 1956.

POWERS, J. F. *The Presence of Grace*. Garden City: Doubleday, 1956.

SMITH, BETTY. *A Tree Grows in Brooklyn*. New York: Harper & Bros., 1943.

TULLY, JIM. *Shanty Irish*. New York: A. & C. Boni, 1928.

5.2.27 Italians

Nonfiction

CAROLI, BETTY B., ET AL. *The Italian Immigrant Woman in North America*. Toronto: The Multicultural History Society of Ontario, 1978.

FOERSTER, ROBERT. *Italian Emigration of Our Time*. New York: Russell & Russell, 1968; originally published in 1919.

MANGIONE, JERRE, AND BEN MORREALE. *La Storia: Five Centuries of the Italian American Experience*. New York: HarperCollins, 1991.

MORMINO, GARY R. *Immigrants on the Hill: Italian Americans in St. Louis, 1882–1982*. Champaign: University of Illinois Press, 1986.

YANS-MCLAUGHLIN, VIRGINIA. *Family and Community: Italian Immigrants in Buffalo, 1880–1930*. Ithaca: Cornell University Press, 1977. Urbana: University of Illinois Press, 1977, paperback ed.

Autobiography and Fiction

ANGELO, VALENTI. *The Golden Gate*. 1939; New York: Arno Press, 1975.

CAUTELA, GIUSEPPE. *Moon Harvest*. New York: Dial Press, 1925.

D'AGOSTINO, GUIDO. *Olives on the Apple Tree*. New York: Arno Press, 1940.

D'ANGELO, PASCAL. *Son of Italy*. New York: Arno Press, 1924.

DIDONATO, PIETRO. *Christ in Concrete*. Indianapolis: Bobbs-Merrill Co., 1939.

———. *This Woman*. New York: Ballantine, 1958.

———. *Three Circles of Light*. New York: Julien Messer, 1960.

ETS, MARIE H. *Rosa, The Life of an Italian Immigrant*. Minneapolis: University of Minnesota Press, 1970.

FANTE, JOHN. *Wait Until Spring, Bandini*. New York: Stackpole, 1938.

FORGIONE, LOUIS. *The River Between*. New York: E.P. Dutton, 1928.

LAPOLLA, GARIBALDI. *The Fire in the Flesh*. New York: Vanguard Press, 1931.

———. *The Grand Gennaro*. New York: Vanguard Press, 1935.

MANGIONE, JERRE. *Mount Allegro*. Boston: Houghton Mifflin, 1943.

PANUNZIO, CONSTANTINE. *The Soul of an Immigrant*. New York: Macmillan, 1924.

PUZO, MARIO. *The Fortunate Pilgrim*. New York: Atheneum, 1965.

5.2.28 Jamaicans

Nonfiction

PETRAS, ELIZABETH MCLEAN. *Jamaican Labor Migration: White Capital and Black Labor, 1850–1930*. Boulder, CO: Westview Press, 1988.

5.2.29 Japanese

Nonfiction

CONROY, HILARY, AND T. SCOTT MIYAKAKA. *East Across the Pacific: Historical and Sociological Studies of Japanese: Immigration and Assimilation*. Santa Barbara: Clio Press, 1972.

GLENN, EVELYN NAKANO. *Issei, Nisei, War Bride: Three Generations of Japanese American Women in Domestic Service*. Philadelphia: Temple University Press, 1986.

ICHIOKA, YUJI. *The Issei: The World of the First Generation Japanese Immigrants, 1885–1924*. New York: Free Press, 1988.

WILSON, ROBERT, AND BILL HOSOKAWA. *East to America: A History of the Japanese in the United States*. New York: Morrow, 1980.

Autobiography and Fiction

SUGIMOTO, ETSU INAGAKI. *A Daughter of the Samurai*. Garden City: Doubleday, 1925.

SONE, MONICA (ITO). *Nisei Daughter*. Boston: Little, Brown and Co., 1953.

5.2.30 Jews

Nonfiction

GLENN, SUSAN. *Daughters of the Shtetl, Life and Labor in the Immigrant Generation*. Ithaca: Cornell University Press, 1991.

GOREN, ARTHUR. *The American Jews*. Cambridge: Belknap Press of Harvard University Press, 1982.

HOWE, IRVING. *World of Our Fathers*. New York: Harcourt, Brace, Jovanovich, 1976.

WEINBERG, SYDNEY S. *The World of Our Mothers: Lives of Jewish Immigrant Women*. Chapel Hill: University of North Carolina Press, 1988.

Autobiography and Fiction

ANTIN, MARY. *The Promised Land*. New York: Houghton Mifflin, 1912.

ASCH, SHOLEM. *America*. New York: Alpha Omega, 1918.

_____. *The Mother*. New York: H. Liveright, 1930.

CAHAN, ABRAHAM. *The Imported Bridegroom and Other Stories*. 1898; New York: Houghton Mifflin, 1968.

_____. *The Rise of David Levinsky*. New York: Harper & Bros., 1917.

GOLD, MICHAEL. *Jews without Money*. 1935; New York: Avon Books, 1965.

KAZIN, ALFRED. *A Walker in the City*. New York: Harcourt Brace Jovanovich, 1951.

ROTH, HENRY. *Call It Sleep*. New York: Avon, 1934.

YEZIERSKA, ANZIA. *Bread Givers*. 1925; New York: Perseo Books, 1975.

_____. *Hungry Hearts*. Boston: Houghton Mifflin, 1920.

_____. *Red Ribbon on a White Horse*. New York: Scribner, 1950.

5.2.31 Koreans

Nonfiction

KIM, ELAINE H. *East to America*. New York: New Press, 1996.

KIM, ILSOO. *New Urban Immigrants: The Korean Community in New York*. Princeton: Princeton University Press, 1981.

YU, EUI-YOUNG, AND EARL H. PHILLIPS, EDS. *Korean Women in Transition: At Home and Abroad*. Los Angeles: Center for Korean-American and Korean Studies, California State University, 1987.

Autobiography and Fiction

KANG, YOUNGHILL. *East Goes West*. New York: C. Scribner's Sons, 1937.

LEE, MARY PAIK. *Quiet Odyssey: A Pioneer Korean Woman in America*. Sucheng Chan, ed. Seattle: University of Washington Press, 1990.

5.2.32 Latinos

Nonfiction

COTERA, MARTHA. *Latina Sourcebook: Bibliography of Mexican American, Cuban, Puerto Rican, and Other Hispanic Women*. Materials in the U.S. Austin, TX: Information Systems Development, 1982.

HEYCK, DENIS LYNN DALY, ED. *Barrios and Borderlands: Cultures of Latinos and Latinas in the United States*. New York: Routledge, 1994.

5.2.33 Lithuanians

Nonfiction

ALILUNAS, LEO, ED. *Lithuanians in the United States*. San Francisco: R&E Research Associates, 1978.

Autobiography and Fiction

SINCLAIR, UPTON. *The Jungle*. New York: Doubleday, Page and Co., 1906.

VITKAUSKAS, AREJAS. *An Immigrant's Story*. New York: Philosophical Library, 1956.

5.2.34 Mexicans

Nonfiction

DAVIS, MARILYN P. *Mexican Voices, American Dreams: An Oral History of Mexican Immigration to the United States*. New York: Henry Holt, 1990.

MCWILLIAMS, CAREY. *North from Mexico*. New York: Greenwood Press, 1968.

MIRANDE, ALFREDO, AND EVANGELINA ENRIQUEZ. *La Chicana, The Mexican-American Woman*. Chicago: University of Chicago Press, 1979.

SIEMS, LARRY, ED. *Between the Lines: Letters between Undocumented Mexican and Central American Immigrants and Their Families*. Hopewell, N.J.: Ecco Press, 1992.

Autobiography and Fiction

CISNEROS, SANDRA. *The House on Mango Street*. Houston, TX: Arte Publico Press, 1983.

GALARZA, ERNESTO. *Barrio Boy*. Notre Dame: Notre Dame University Press, 1971.

GAMIO, MANUEL. *The Mexican Immigrant: His Life-Story: Autobiographic Documents Collected by Manuel Gamio*. Chicago, 1931; rpt, New York: Dover Press, 1971.

VILLARREAL, JOSE ANTONIO. *The Fifth Horseman*. Garden City: Doubleday, 1974.

_____. *Pocho*. Garden City: Doubleday, 1959.

5.2.35 Native Americans

Nonfiction

HOROWITZ, DAVID. *The First Frontier: The Indian Wars and America's Origins*. New York: Simon & Schuster, 1978.

JAHODA, GLORIA. *The Trail of Tears*. New York: Holt, Rinehart and Winston, 1975.

UTLEY, ROBERT M., AND WILCOMB E. WASHBURN. *The American Heritage History of the Indian Wars*. New York: Simon & Schuster, 1978.

Autobiography and Fiction

MOMADAY, N. SCOTT, *House Made of Dawn*. New York: Harper & Row, 1968.

_____. *The Names*. New York: Harper & Row, 1976

_____. *The Way to Rainy Mountain*. Albuquerque: University of New Mexico Press, 1969.

SILKO, LESLIE MARMON. *Ceremony*. New York: Viking, 1977.

VIZENOR, GERALD. *Darkness in St. Louis Bearheart*. St. Paul: Truck Press, 1978.

_____. *Wordarrows*. Minneapolis: University of Minnesota Press, 1978.

WELCH, JAMES. *Winter in the Blood*. New York: Harper & Row, 1974.

5.2.36 Poles

Nonfiction

BUKOWCZYK, JOHN J. *And My Children Did Not Know Me: A History of Polish Americans*. Bloomington: Indiana University Press, 1986.

GREENE, VICTOR R. *For God and Country: The Rise of Polish and Lithuanian Ethnic Consciousness in America, 1860–1910*. Madison: State Historical Society of Wisconsin, 1975.

MORAWSKA, EWA. *For Bread with Butter: The Life-World of East Central Europeans in Johnston, Pennsylvania, 1890–1940*. New York: Cambridge University Press, 1985.

Autobiography and Fiction

BANKOWSKY, RICHARD. *A Glass Rose*. New York: Random House, 1958.

SIENKIEWICZ, HENRYK. *After Bread*. New York: R.F. Fenno & Co., 1897.

_____. *In the New Promised Land*. London: Jarrold, 1900.

5.2.37 Puerto Ricans

Nonfiction

FITZPATRICK, JOSEPH. *Puerto Rican Americans: The Meaning of Migration to the Mainland*, 2d ed.; Englewood Cliffs, N.J.: Prentice-Hall, 1987.

MORALES, JULIO. *Puerto Rican Poverty and Migration: We Just Had to Try Elsewhere*. New York: Praeger, 1986.

Autobiography and Fiction

THOMAS, PIRI. *Down These Mean Streets*. New York: Albert A. Knopf, 1967.

5.2.38 Rumanians

Autobiography and Fiction
BERCOVICI, KONRAD. *It's the Gypsy in Me*. New York: Prentice-Hall, 1941.

5.2.39 Scandinavians

Nonfiction
BLEGEN, THEODORE, ED. *Land of Their Choice: The Immigrants Write Home*. Minneapolis: University of Minnesota Press, 1955.

HVIDT, KRISTIAN. *Flight to America: The Social Background of 300,000 Danish Emigrants*. New York: Academic Press, 1975.

RUNBLOM, HARALD, AND HANS NORMAN, EDS. *From Sweden to America: A History of the Migration*. Minneapolis: University of Minnesota Press, 1976.

SEMMINGSEN, INGRID. *Norway to America: A History of the Migration*. Minneapolis: University of Minnesota Press, 1978.

Autobiography and Fiction
BOJER, JOHAN. *The Emigrants*. New York: Grosset & Dunlap, 1925.

CATHER, WILLA. *O Pioneers*. Boston: Houghton Mifflin, 1913.

MOBERG, VILHELM. *The Emigrants*. Stockholm: Albert Bonniers Forlag, 1950.

————. *Unto a Good Land*. New York: Simon & Schuster, 1954.

ROLVAAG, OLE. *Giants in the Earth*. New York: Harper & Row, 1927.

5.2.40 Scots

Nonfiction
DONALDSON, GORDON. *The Scots Overseas*. London: R. Hale, 1966.

5.2.41 Slavs

Autobiography and Fiction
ADAMIC, LOUIS. *Laughing in the Jungle*. New York: Harper & Bros., 1932.

PUPIN, MICHAEL. *From Immigrant to Inventor*. New York: Scribner, 1930.

SANJEK, LOUIS. *In Silence*. New York: Fortuny, 1938.

VECKI, VICTOR. *Threatening Shadows*. Boston: Stratford, 1931.

WAKSMAN, SELMAN A. *My Life with the Microbes*. New York: Simon & Schuster, 1954.

5.2.42 Syrians

Autobiography and Fiction
HADDAD, GEORGE. *Mt Lebanon to Vermont: Autobiography of George Haddad*. Rutland, VT: The Tuttle Co., 1916.

HAWIE, ASHAD G. *The Rainbow Ends*. New York: Theodore Gaus, 1942.

SHADID, MICHAEL A. *A Doctor for the People: The Autobiography of the Founder of America's First Co-operative Hospital*. New York: Vanguard Press, 1939.

5.2.43 Turks

Autobiography and Fiction
NAKASHIAN, AVEDIS. *A Man Who Found a Country*. New York: T.Y. Crowell, 1940.

5.2.44 Vietnamese

Nonfiction
KELLY, G. P. *From Vietnam to America: A Chronicle of Vietnamese Immigration to the United States*. Boulder, CO: Westview Press, 1977.

5.3 TEACHING RESOURCES

5.3.1 Overview

This guide enables teachers to integrate the immigration experience, a central theme of American and world history, as well as visits to the Ellis Island Museum, into the high school and junior high school curricula. College teachers will also find it useful. The guide was developed in consultation with teachers, many of whom told us that in the school year's carefully programmed curricula they do not have much time to spend on immigration, a subject usually confined to American history courses for the period from 1890 to 1924. Nor do they have enough time to draw up lessons and exercises for global history courses, in which immigration throughout the world could be understood as a significant, continuing theme. Finally, as teachers correctly reminded us, since not all of their students are descended from immigrants who passed through Ellis Island, some way has to be found to relate the immigration theme to the family experiences of everyone. This guide offers approaches to addressing these and other pedagogical problems.

The guide discusses Ellis Island in the context of worldwide patterns of migration and immigration since the fifteenth century. Instead of focusing on specific ethnic/immigrant groups—a standard approach—it analyzes the immigration process. The first three parts are intended for teacher's reading and preparation, and documents, questions and activities (Part 4) are for classroom use. Each part presents thematic approaches for thinking about immigration within the context of U.S. history and world

history from the fifteenth century to the present. We expect, however, that teachers of languages, literature, and ethnic studies, along with social studies and history teachers, will find the guide useful. Teachers working in a chronological, global, or American framework can draw from the guide to insert the story of migration into several periods of history. Teachers will find, for example, how the migration process relates to colonial settlement, slavery, industrialization, geography, labor economics, gender, immigration law and policy, and racial attitudes. Teachers preparing for a visit to the Ellis Island Museum will especially benefit from the section in Part 3 on Ellis Island.

The guide's three-part story approaches migration from different perspectives. Part 1 defines basic terms and concepts, explains how scholars understand the migration process, and provides a worldwide historical background that will help in understanding the materials presented in the next two parts. A series of family histories gathered from a fictional classroom to illustrate these concepts, suggest ways of engaging students with their own and other students' migration histories. Part 2 examines the migration history of the Western Hemisphere from the fifteenth century to the present, with an emphasis on the vast movements of people from Europe, Asia, and Africa. It also discusses American perceptions of immigrants. Part 3 concentrates on immigration policy and on Ellis Island itself as an immigrant-processing station, including a description of the island's busiest period, from 1892 through 1924. A final section of Part 3 discusses recent trends in world and U.S. migration. Following completion of the

migration and immigration story in Part 3, the guide presents in Part 4 selected documents cross-referenced to sections in the text. Part 4 also contains exercises and questions cross-referenced to the text and to documents. Teachers reading the text can quickly find illustrative materials in the documents and exercise sections; those who begin with the documents can quickly locate relevant background to the documents in the text and exercises. Maps and tables in the documents section provide additional information and possibilities for student exercises.

The guide is also a sourcebook. Its bibliographies (**Part 5**) and filmography (**Part 6**) list many standard works on immigration and works by writers, historians, other scholars, and filmmakers who have presented stories of different immigrant groups as well as general immigration themes. The bibliography of novels and autobiographies (**5.2**) will be useful to those seeking literary documentation of the immigrant and ethnic experience. A list of published teaching aids (**5.10**) can supplement the documents and exercises.

5.3.2 The Ellis Island Immigration Museum Activities for School Groups

The following information concerning educational programs at the Ellis Island Museum is gleaned from an official publication of The Statue of Liberty Ellis Island National Monument. For visiting school groups: There must be one teacher or adult chaperone for every ten students. Students must remain with their chaperones at all times.

Student Orientation Film: In conjunction with reserved programs at the Ellis

Island Immigration Museum, school groups must view the student orientation film. This ten-minute film, narrated by James Earl Jones, is shown in the Student Orientation Center at Ellis Island.

All groups who reserve the NYNEX Learning Center or the documentary film *"Island of Hope, Island of Tears" are required* to see the orientation film before their program. Groups who do not check in on time at the Ellis Island Information Desk willl not be permitted to attend their reserved activity.

5.3.3 NYNEX Learning Center

A thirty-minute interactive video program, ideal for students learning about immigration in class. The NYNEX program is led by a National Park ranger and students answer questions about immigration from electronic panels at their seats. The center can accommodate up to 50 people. This program is recommended for students in grades 3 through 9. The NYNEX Learning Center can be reserved on weekdays only. Contact the reservations coordinator at (212) 363-7620.

5.3.4 Junior Rangers Programs

Designed for younger students (grades 3 through 7), this ranger-guided program lasts approximately one hour. Join a park ranger for an introduction to the National Park Service and learn about its mission of resource preservation and protection. With the ranger, students experience what it was like to undergo inspection at Ellis Island. Topics of discussion include world events that prompted immigration to America, moving to a new home in a new land, and the role and development of Ellis Island. They will learn the importance of this site

by completing an activity booklet about immigration. Students can earn an Ellis Island Junior Ranger Badge and Certificate upon successful completion of the program.

5.3.5 Documentary Film

See the section "About the Ellis Island Museum" in the back of this guide for a description of the film and its schedule. Certain shows are reserved for student groups on weekdays only. Contact the reservations coordinator at (212) 363-7620 for more information.

5.3.6 Board of Special Inquiry Programs

See the section "About the Ellis Island Museum" in the back of this guide for a description of this activity. Check at the information desk for program times.

5.3.7 Teaching Guide

For educators teaching grades 5 through 8, the guide was developed for teachers and students to heighten their understanding of immigration and to provide information about the Ellis Island Immigration Museum. To receive a free copy, call (212) 363-7620.

5.3.8 Activity Sheets

For children who are touring the Museum, these are available at the Ellis Island Information Desk. Completion of activity sheets will enhance an on-site trip by reinforcing information learned from the exhibits. Teachers can also use these worksheets as post-site visit materials.

5.3.9 Classroom Materials and Activities

The following list describes teaching tools, guides, and materials as well as information about how to do oral history.

Two resources for identifying available materials are: *Human Relations Materials for the School from the Anti-Defamation League*, published by B'nai B'rith, 823 United Nations Plaza, New York, NY 10017; phone 212/490-2525. The league has branches in many cities. See also the *Social Studies School Service* catalogues, 10200 Jefferson Blvd., Room 1311, P.O.B. 802, Culver City, CA 90232-0802; phone 310/839-2436 or 1-800-421-4246.

Americans All: A National Education Program has teacher resources, student materials, teacher guides, audio and visual materials. For grades 3-4, 7-9. Write: 5760 Sunnyside Ave., Beltsville, MD 20705. Phone: 301/982-5622; fax: 301/982-5628.

CHARLOTTE C. ANDERSON (ed.), *Beyond Boundaries: Law in a Global Age* (New York: Global Perspectives in Education, 1983), contains material on migration and immigration. Global Perspectives in Education, Inc., 218 East 18th Street, New York, NY 10003. 212/228-2470.

JAY ANDERSON, *The Living History Sourcebook* (Nashville: American Association for State and Local History, 1985), contains hundreds of entries of museums, books, suppliers, films, and other sources, and also many photographs. American Association for State and Local History, 530 Church Street, Nashville, TN 37219-2325. 615/255-2971.

The Balch Institute for Ethnic Studies and the Anti-Defamation League, *Ethnic Images in Advertising* is an excellent catalogue of labels and trade cards that shows how advertisers used ethnic images to sell products. The Balch Institute for Ethnic Studies, 18 S. 7th Street, Philadelphia, PA 19106. 215/925-8090 ext. 241.

WILLA K. BAUM, *Oral History for the Local Historical Society* (Nashville: American Association for State and Local History, 1987), a revised edition of a now-standard work, includes basic information about doing oral history. American Association for State and Local History, 530 Church Street, Nashville, TN 37219-2325. 615/255-2971.

JEREMY BRECHER, *History from Below. How to Uncover and Tell the Story of Your Community, Association, or Union* (New Haven: Advocate Press/Commonwork Pamphlets, 1988), is a good starting point for assembling the history of a local organization, group, or place. It includes basic information about how to do research and conduct interviews, and also includes sample project designs.

CYNTHIA STOKES BROWN, *Like It Was: A Complete Guide to Writing Oral History*, is available from Teachers and Writers Collaborative, 5 Union Square West, NY, NY, 10013.

TODD CLARK, ed., *The Bill of Rights in Action: Immigration* (Los Angeles: Constitutional Rights Foundation, 1981), covers the history of U.S. immigration laws through discussion questions, photographs, and a simulation of the Presidential Commission on Illegal Aliens. Grades 7-12. $.50 for one, $10.00 for 35. Constitutional Rights Foundation, 1510 Cotner Avenue, Los Angeles, CA 90025. 213/487-5590.

Coming to America: American Immigrants Series (New York: Dell, 1981) contains five books on the Far East, British Isles, northern Europe, southern Europe, Mexico/Puerto Rico/Cuba, respectively. Each book describes the old-country milieu, the crossing, arrival, and reaction to the new land by means of diaries, letters, photographs, and interviews. Five books and guide, $14.00. Grades 9-12. Dell, Division of Bantam Doubleday, 1540 Broadway, New York, NY. 10036 212/354-6500.

CARLOS CORTES, *Teaching about Human Migration in Global Perspective*, Occasional Paper No. 4 (New York: Global Perspectives in Education, 1983), is an eleven-page booklet that discusses ways of placing migration studies into the classroom. Global Perspectives in Education, Inc., 218 East 18th Street, New York, NY 10003. 212/228-2470.

GERALD A. DANZER, *Public Places: Exploring Their History* (Nashville: American Association for State and Local History, 1988), is a useful book for planning how to research the history of public places. The author relates history to function in discussing parks, government and commercial places and buildings, and the like. American Association for State and Local History, 530 Church Street, Nashville, TN 37219-2325. 615/255-2971.

JAMES WEST DAVIDSON AND MARK HAMILTON LYTLE, "The Mirror with a Memory: Photographic Evidence and the Urban Scene," in their book *After the Fact: The Art of Historical Detection* (New York: Alfred A. Knopf, 1986) explain the use of historical photographs by analyzing those of former immigrant Jacob Riis, renowned photographer of Ellis Island-era immigrant life. Reproductions of Ellis Island photographs can be obtained from the National Park Service. A list of subjects and reproduction fees can be ordered from them from Photo Librarian, Liberty Island, New York, New York 10004. Grades 9-12.

THOMAS DUBLIN, ed., *Becoming American, Becoming Ethnic: College Students Explore Their Roots*. (Philadelphia: Temple University Press, 1996) is an excellent collection of student family history writing. Useful for high school and college.

DAVID K. DUNAWAY AND WILLA K. BAUM, eds., *Oral History: An Interdisciplinary Anthology* (Nashville: American Association for State and Local History) is an anthology intended for advanced studies in oral history. The book contains essays about the development of the field and its current direction. American Association for State and Local History, 530 Church Street, Nashville, TN 37219-2325. 615/255-2971.

SARAH EGAN AND LYNN PARISI, "Resource List on Immigration," *Social Education* (March 1986), pp. 195-98, includes suggested readings, classroom activities, simulations, bibliographies, films, and film strips.

WILLIAM FLETCHER, *Recording Your Family History* (Berkeley: Ten Speed Press, 1989), discusses video and audio tapes as methods of capturing history. This is a revised edition of what was formerly entitled *Talking Your Roots*. Ten Speed Press, P.O. Box 7123, Berkeley, CA 94707. 510/559-1600; 1-800-841-2665.

BILL FRELICK, "Who Are the Refugees?" *Social Education* (March 1986), p. 194, uses a 1984 public opinion survey of attitudes toward refugees for a student exercise. Students evaluate the attitudes and criteria.

Gateway: A Simulation of Immigration Issues in Past and Present. (Lakeside, CA: Interact) offers a simulation of immigrant concerns and governmental reactions. Grades: 6-12. 35 student guides, teacher's guide. $16.00. Interact, P.O. Box 977B, Lakeside, CA 92040.

HEIDI HURSH AND MICHAEL PREVEDEL, *Activities Using the "State of the World Atlas"* (Denver: Center for Teaching International Relations, University of Denver, 1983), make the *State of the World Atlas,* Michael Kidron and Ronald Segal, eds. (New York: Simon and Schuster, 1981) available to classroom use through this 151-page guide. Center for Teaching International Relations, University of Denver, Denver CO 80208. 303/753-2426.

SOCIAL STUDIES SCHOOL SERVICE, *Immigration Graph Skills and Photo Aids*, presents immigration to the United States, 1820-1975, through graph reading and research assignments, using charts, activity cards, and photographs. Teacher's guide included. $38.95. Grades 9-12. Social Studies School Service, 10200 Jefferson Boulevard, P.O. Box 802, Culver City, CA 90232-0802. 310/839-2436; 1-800-421-4246.

"Immigration: Growth of a Nation," is a two-part audiovisual presentation which explores the important movements in the patterns of immigration. Part I, 1820-1920, and Part II, the more recent decades; two filmstrips; two cassettes and a teacher's guide. Opportunities for Learning Inc., 100 Paragon Parkway, Munsfield, OH 44903. 1-800-777-7116.

KEITH MELVILLE, ed., *Admission Decisions* (Dayton: National Issues Forums Institute, 1994), is a booklet that illustrates the immigration debate with pictures, cartoons, charts. Reading quizzes on opinions of immigration. Adult and grades 9-12 or abridged edition for 6th grade $3.25, videocassette: $35.00 (also includes kids and crime and "tug of war in the school yard." National Issues Forums Institute, 100 Commons Road, Dayton, OH 45459. 1-800-433-7834.

GAYLE MERTZ. *Immigration: Law, Customs, History: 5th Grade Curriculum.* (Bloomington: ERIC, 1984); also authors: Safeguard Law Related Education Program (Boulder CO.); St. Vrain Valley School District (Longmont, CO.); U.S. Department of Education, discusses the history of immigration laws through a chart, graphs, bibliography, vocabulary quizzes.

JOAN MORRISON AND CHARLOTTE FOX ZABUSKY, *American Mosaic: The Immigration Experience in the Words of Those Who Lived It* (New York: E.P. Dutton, 1980), provide immigrants' descriptions of their reasons for migrating to the United States and their experiences during the trip. Illustrated. Grades 9-12.

NEW YORK STATE EDUCATION DEPARTMENT, *Italian Americans: Looking Back—Moving Forward* (Albany: University of the State of New York, 1994), is an excellent guide with reproducible archival materials and essays. It focuses on Italian Americans but is designed for use in discussing other groups and also general issues concerning race and ethnicity. Publication Sales Desk, Room 212, Education Building Annex, Albany, NY 12234.

THEODORE SALOUTOS has written *The Greeks in the United States: A Student's Guide to Localized History* (New York: Teacher's College Press of Columbia University, 1977).

THOMAS J. SCHLERETH, *Artifacts and the American Past* (Nashville: American Association for State and Local History, 1980), defines "artifact" broadly to include any "cultural statement," and then applies that definition to help teachers find ways of taking classes into the field for the study of history. American Association for State and Local History, 530 Church Street, Nashville, TN 37219-2325. 615/255-2971.

LINDA SIMMONS, Wynell Burroughs, and Jean Mueller, eds., "Teaching with Documents: Chinese Exclusion Forms," *Social Education* (March 1986), pp. 212-13, describes the history of U.S. policies and attitudes toward Chinese immigrants, with teaching suggestions for using the forms or examining other ethnic groups in relation to the laws. Grades 9-12.
Social Issues Resources Series, Inc. (Box 2507, Boca Raton, FL 33427; 800-327-0513) culls articles from current magazines and newspapers on selected themes. One, "Ethnic Groups," has articles on the immigration process, as in "The Move to America: Our Family's Odyssey," *Newsday*, April 27, 1986, tracing the saga of immigrants from the Dominican Republic to New York City. Grades 9-12.

JAMES WATTS AND ALLEN F. DAVIS, *Generations: Your Family in Modern American History* (New York: Alfred A. Knopf, 1978), offers first-person narratives, many by immigrants, and suggestions on helping students write their own family history.

5.3.10 Bibliography on Teaching Strategies

The teaching of immigration studies relates to discussions concerning multicultural education. The articles and books below refer to controversies surrounding this issue as well as to teaching methodologies.

AACTE Commission on Multicultural Education. "No One Model America: A Statement on Multicultural Education," *Journal of Teacher Education*, 24 (Winter 1973), 264-65.

BANKS, JAMES A. *Multicultural Education in Western Societies*. New York: Praeger, 1986.

_____. "Cultural Pluralism and the Schools," *Educational Leadership*, 32 (Dec. 1974), 163-66.

_____. "Ethnic Studies as a Process of Curriculum Reform," *Social Education*, 40 (Feb. 1986), 76-80.

_____. *Multiethnic Education: Practices and Promises*. Bloomington: Phi Delta Kappa Educational Foundation, 1977.

_____. With Ambrose A. Clegg, Jr. *Teaching Strategies for the Social Studies: Inquiry, Valuing, and Decision-Making*. Reading, Mass.: Addison-Wesley Publishing Co., 1977.

_____. *Teaching Strategies for Ethnic Studies*, 2d ed., Boston: Allyn and Bacon, 1979.

_____. With Cherry McGee Banks, *Multiculturalism and Education: Issues and Perspectives*. Boston: Allyn and Bacon, 1989.

BENOIT, BOB. "'They Are Not Like Us': Teaching about Immigrants in Rural Schools," *Social Education* (Oct. 1991), 396-97.

DEDRICK, MARION R. "A Study of Immigrant Experience," *Social Education* (Jan. 1993), 45-47.

GIFFORD, BERNARD R., AND PAULA GILLETT. "Teaching in a Great Age of Immigration," *Social Education* (March 1986), 184-85.

GLAZER, NATHAN. "Additional Comments," New York State Social Studies Review and Development Committee, *One Nation, Many Peoples: A Declaration of Cultural Interdependence*. Albany, 1991.

_____. "In Defense of Multiculturalism," *The New Republic* (Sept. 2, 1991), 18-22.

HAVERKAMP, BETH, AND WYNELL SCHAMEL. "Photographs of Ellis Island: The High Tide of Immigration," *Social Education* (Sept. 1994), 303-07.

JANZEN, ROD. "Five Paradigms of Ethnic Relations," *Social Education* (Oct. 1994), 349-53.

JOYCE, WILLIAM W. "Minority Groups in American Society: Imperatives for Educators and Publishers," in Jonathan C. McLendon, William Joyce, and John R. Lee, eds., *Readings in Elementary School Studies: Emerging Changes*. 2d ed. Boston: Allyn and Bacon, 1970, 289-90.

LOEWEN, JAMES. *Lies My Teacher Told Me: Everything Your American History Textbook Got Wrong*. New York: New Press, 1995.

MATTE, JACQUELINE. "Southeastern Indian, Precontact to the Present: Introductory Essay," *Social Education* (Oct. 1993), 292-314.

PATRICK, JOHN J. "Immigration in the Curriculum," *Social Education* (March 1986), 172-76.

RAVITCH, DIANE. "Multiculturalism: E Pluribus Plures," *American Scholar*, 59 (1990), 337-54.

_____. "Multiculturalism: E Pluribus Plures [part 2]," *American Scholar*, 60 (1991), 267-76.

SCHAMEL, WYRELL BURROUGH, AND RICHARD A. BLONDO. "The Statue of Liberty Deed of Presentation," *Social Education* (Sept. 1992), 299-302.

SCHLESINGER, ARTHUR JR. *The Disuniting of America: Reflections on a Multicultural Society.* Knoxville: Whittel Direct Books, 1991.

THERNSTROM, STEPHAN. "The Humanities and Our Cultural Heritage," in Chester Finn, Jr., Diane Ravitch, and P. Holley Roberts, eds., *Challenges to the Humanities.* New York: Holmes and Meier, 1985.

WILSON, ANGENE. "The Immigrant Student Challenge," *Social Education* (March 1986), 189-93.

6. Films, Videos, and Filmstrips

To purchase or rent any of the films and videos in the listing below, call or write the distributor listed in each entry. A list of distributors, with addresses and phone numbers, is provided in 6.6. The descriptions provided here come from library reference works and distributors' catalogues. Filmstrips and slide shows are marked with an asterisk (*).

6.1 FINDING AIDS

For a guide to videos see *The Video Sourcebook*, 2 vols., David J. Weiner, ed., which is regularly updated. Other recent film and video listings are available in *Human Relations Materials for the Schools*, published by the Anti-Defamation League of B'nai B'rith, 823 United Nations Plaza, New York, NY 10017; (212) 490-2525. The league has branches in major cities. The American Historical Association publishes a pamphlet by John E. O'Connor, *Teaching History with Film and Television* (Washington D.C., 1987).

6.2 IMMIGRATION POLICY

Immigration Reform, Part 2
"The Constitution: That Delicate Balance" series
60 min., 1/2"VHS, color, 1984.

Covers legal criteria for admitting immigrants; describes rights of immigrants, social services, and employment.
UNIVERSITY FILM & VIDEO

Radio, Racism, and Foreign Policy
"Between the Wars" series
22 min., 16mm, color, ca. 1978.

Describes U.S. restrictions on immigration after World War I and examines the interwar period of racial and ethnic discrimination. Radio projected a standard image of the "good" American.
UNIVERSITY FILM & VIDEO

6.3 THE "NEW" IMMIGRATION

Bittersweet: The Asian-Indian Experience in the U.S.A.
42 min., color video, 1995.

Focuses on Asian Indian immigrants to the United States who discuss the complex social and personal issues of their dual cultural influences. Illuminates issues of cultural identity and the problems of defining community in an adopted land.
CINEMA GUILD

Immigration Backlash
28 min., VHS format, 1994.

A specially adapted Phil Donahue program sets out the dilemma: How can Americans, most of whom are themselves descended from immigrants, argue against immigration?
FILMS FOR THE HUMANITIES AND SCIENCES

In the Shadow of the Law
58 min., color, VHS format, 1991.

Explores the daily lives of four families who have lived illegally in the United States for many years. New immigration laws elicit both hope and apprehension.
UNIVERSITY OF CALIFORNIA EXTENSION

Multicultural Peoples of North America Series

Fifteen 1/2-hour VHS cassettes, available separately.

Each episode focuses on a different immigrant group and tells a story through interviews with three generations of family members. Includes African Americans, Amish, Arabs, Central Americans, Chinese, Germans, Greeks, Irish, Jews, Koreans, Mexicans, Poles, and Puerto Ricans.
FILMIC ARCHIVES

The New Immigrants

60 min., VHS, 1993, free learning guide.

Examines the "new immigrants" and asks who they are, where they come from, and how their American communities have evolved.
FILMIC ARCHIVES

The New Pilgrims

25 min., 1/2" VHS, color, 1984.

A news report examines the origins of the latest wave of immigrants to the United States through interviews with new arrivals from Central America, Mexico, Vietnam, Korea, and the Philippines. Reveals how the "new pilgrims" are adjusting to life in the United States and their effect on the nation's labor force.
UNIVERSITY FILM & VIDEO

Whose America Is It?

46 min., 1/2" video, 1985

Produced by CBS News, the program examines problems associated with immigration, including issues of acculturation and competition for jobs.
CAROUSEL FILMS

6.4 STATUE OF LIBERTY AND ELLIS ISLAND

Astray from Steerage

22 min., 16mm, B&W, silent, 1920.

U.S. immigration procedures become springboard for surreal humor.
MUSEUM OF MODERN ART

Ellis Island

("Nation of Immigrants" series)
12 min., 16mm & 1/2" or 3/4" video, 1971.

Focuses on Ellis Island during the decade 1900–10.
FILMS, INC.

Ellis Island

30 min., 16mm, color, 1985.

Reflects on the immigrant experience using the abandoned structures at the island to connect past and present.
Actors reconstruct the entry process.
ART INSTITUTE OF CHICAGO

Ellis Island

9 min., 16mm, color, 1974.

Young filmmakers explore the ruined Ellis Island and interview immigrants who passed through the station.
YOUTH FILMS, INC.

Ellis Island

3 hours, VHS format, color and B&W, 1997

A comprehensive history of the island and an attempt to place it in historical context.
THE HISTORY CHANNEL

Ellis Island: Every Man's Monument

60 min., VHS, color, ca. 1991.

A history of Ellis Island, a tour of the exhibits, and reflections upon immigration.
PANORAMA PRODUCTIONS

Gateway

70 min., feature film, B&W, ca. 1938.

An Irish woman immigrant meets a returning war correspondent on a liner bound for New York and is detained at Ellis Island. Partly filmed at Ellis Island.
TWENTIETH CENTURY FOX

The Huddled Masses, Number 9

("Destination America" series)
52 min., 16mm & 1/2" VHS, color, ca. 1973

Alistair Cooke visits ships' holds, Ellis Island, the Lower East Side, and other places evoking turn-of-the-century immigration. Contemporary scenes show Chinese, Puerto Rican, and Black children saluting the U.S. flag.
UNIVERSITY FILM & VIDEO

Island of Hope, Island of Tears
29 min., VHS, 1990

Inspired by the celebration and renovation of Ellis Island, and displayed at the museum, this documentary traces the origins of the European migration in the late 1880s, the meaning that America had for so many of the ancestors who entered this land, and the rich and culturally diverse populations that make up the United States.
NEW DIMENSION MEDIA

The Statue of Liberty
58 min., 1/2" video, color, 1984.

Documentary by Ken Burns traces the monument's history and its role as symbol and cultural beacon.
DIRECT CINEMA

The Statue of Liberty
14 min., 16mm & 1/2" or 3/4" video, 1966.

A history teacher and his son visit the statue and learn its history and the story of immigration.
HANDEL FILM CORP.

Witness to History: Turn-of-the-Century America
16 min., 1/2" or 3/4" video, 1987.

Eye witness dramatization of the immigration experience at Ellis Island in its heyday.
GUIDANCE ASSOCIATES

6.5 IMMIGRANTS IN THE UNITED STATES

America and Louis Hine
56 min., 1/2" VHS, color, ca. 1986.

Portrays life and times of Louis Hine (1874–1940), whose photographs captured the living conditions and aspirations of immigrants.
UNIVERSITY FILM & VIDEO

The Distorted Image: Stereotype and Caricature in American Popular Graphics, 1850–1922*
28 min., color filmstrip (60 frames), discussion guide.

Cartoons and illustrations from major magazines reveal the stereotyping that has affected all minority groups. Presentation designed for students of history, sociology, and psychology.
ANTI-DEFAMATION LEAGUE OF B'NAI B'RITH

The Immigrant
16 min., 16mm B&W, silent.

Misadventures of Charlie Chaplin as an immigrant in steerage.
NATIONAL CENTER FOR JEWISH FILMS

The Immigrant Experience: The Long, Long Journey
28 min., 16mm color, 1973.

Depicts an uprooted Polish family as a way of examining the problems and dreams of new immigrants. Includes interviews with the grandfather today as he describes his satisfaction with the opportunities his grandchildren enjoy.
UNIVERSITY FILM & VIDEO

Immigration in America's History
30 min., 3/4" or 1/2" video, 1960.

A dramatic reenactment of the major immigration waves to the United States.
CORONET INSTRUCTIONAL FILMS

Immigration in the Nineteenth Century
"Americans: A Nation of Immigrants" series
13 min., 16mm B&W, 1972.

Discusses mid-nineteenth-century European social and political unrest and describes the appeal of the New World to various peoples, including the Irish, Germans, Scandinavians, and Czechs.
UNIVERSITY FILM & VIDEO

Journey to Freedom
13 min., 16mm and video, color and B&W, with discussion guide.

Newsreel footage, photographs, and art tell the story of immigration to the United States.
ANTI-DEFAMATION LEAGUE OF B'NAI B'RITH

Land of Immigrants (*Rev. ed.*)
16 min., 16mm, color, 1981.

A boy and his family who set out to see the United States find "foreigners" everywhere. The film traces the waves of immigration and the forces behind them, such as religious persecution and the search for a better life.
UNIVERSITY FILM & VIDEO

A Nation of Immigrants *
16 min., filmstrip on video, 1990.

Traces the history of immigration from colonial times to the federal Immigration Act of 1965, emphasizing the contributions to American culture and society.
GUIDANCE ASSOCIATES

Old World, New World
"Destination America" series
58 min., 16mm, 1975.

Provides an overview of European immigration through a mix of historical film footage and interviews with descendants of the groups studied. The interviews include a man who arrived at age eighteen and later became an Ellis Island inspector.
MEDIA GUILD

Our Immigrant Heritage
32 min., 16mm, color, ca. 1968.

Explores reasons for immigration, areas of settlement, most common ways of making a living, contributions to American life and culture, and the reactions of native-born residents, including the activities of anti-immigrant societies. Includes African Americans.
ANTI-DEFAMATION LEAGUE OF B'NAI B'RITH

People
"American Enterprise" series
30 min., 16mm, color, ca. 1976.

Part of a series that explores the U.S. economic heritage, the film explores how immigrants helped create the world's largest economy.
UNIVERSITY FILM & VIDEO

The Untold Story *
18 min., color filmstrip. Part 1 of the series "Italians in America" (see **6.5.8.**)

Describes the European Age of Exploration, the European settlement of the Americas, industrialization, and Ellis Island-era immigration.
ANTI-DEFAMATION LEAGUE OF B'NAI B'RITH

The Urban Pioneers *
Slide show and accompanying audiotape recount the history of 97 Orchard Street, now part of the Lower East Side Tenement Museum, and the Lower East Side.
LOWER EAST SIDE TENEMENT MUSEUM

6.5.1 AFRICAN AMERICANS

Black Americans of Achievement
6 hours, 12 VHS cassettes, color.

Biographies of 12 influential African Americans include Frederick Douglass, Jackie Robinson, Sojourner Truth, Harriet Tubman, and Martin Luther King.
FILMIC ARCHIVES

Ethnic Notions
56 min., VHS, color.

Helps students locate ethnic stereotypes in the media and other cultural representations by tracing the origin of racial stereotypes from the 1820s to the Civil Rights era.
CALIFORNIA NEWSREEL

Eyes on the Prize
Six 60-min. cassettes, VHS, color, 1987.

Comprehensive TV series about the civil rights struggle of the 1950s and 60s.
FILMIC ARCHIVES

Family across the Sea
56 min., VHS, color, 1981.

Describes how scholars have found connections between South Carolina's Gullah people and the cultures of Sierra Leone.
CALIFORNIA NEWSREEL

Freedom Bags
32 min., VHS, ca. 1991.

Relates the story of African American women who migrated from the rural South during the early decades of the twentieth century.
FILMAKERS LIBRARY

Goin' to Chicago
58 min., VHS, 1991.

Personal stories trace the history of the African American migration from the rural South to northern and western cities.
CALIFORNIA NEWSREEL

I Remember Harlem
Three hours, 52 min., VHS, 1980.

Portrait of a major African American community.
FILMS FOR THE HUMANITIES AND SCIENCE

Immigrant from America

20 min., 16mm, 1970.

Explores the differences between white immigrants to the United States and black emigrants from the United States to show how prejudice and discrimination denied blacks opportunities given to other groups.

STERLING EDUCATIONAL FILMS

Immigrants in Chains

"Americans: A Nation of Immigrants" series
11 min., 16mm, 1972.

Slaves, abolitionists, and slave-owners comment on slavery as they experienced it.

UNIVERSITY FILM & VIDEO

Up South: African-American Migration in the Era of the Great War

"Who Built America?" series
30 min., 1/2" VHS, 1996

Through various sources shows how black culture helped sustain immigrants who were rejecting the oppression and indignity of the Jim Crow South. At the same time, however, the "promised land" of the urban North proved to be a difficult and contentious home.

AMERICAN SOCIAL HISTORY PRODUCTIONS, INC.

Where Did You Get That Woman?

28 min., video, 1983.

A portrait of a seventy-two-year-old African American washroom attendant stands as a piece of social history. With archival photographs and blues music, this documentary represents the shared experience of a generation of African American women during the Great Migration north.

FILMAKERS LIBRARY

6.5.2 ASIANS

A Dollar a Day, Ten Cents a Dance

29 min., color video, 1984.

Documents the history of more than 100,000 Pinoy men (Filipino American) who immigrated to American between 1924 and 1935. Prohibited from bringing their wives or marrying white women, they created bachelor societies.

CROSSCURRENT MEDIA

The Asianization of America

26 min., VHS, color.

Examines the fastest-growing immigrant group, fifty years after repeal of the Chinese Exclusion Act in 1944.

FILMS FOR THE HUMANITIES AND SCIENCES

Bittersweet Survival

30 min., color, 1982.

Looks at the resettlement of Southeast Asian refugees after the Vietnam War, at the mixed reception the refugees received, and at their attempts to maintain their identity.

THIRD WORLD NEWSREEL

Cambodian Doughnut Dreams

27 min., 16mm or video, 1990.

Cambodian immigrants work in doughnut shops in order to pursue the American dream while reconciling their horrific past with their difficult and hopeful future.

FIRST RUN/ICARUS

Carved in Silence

45 min., color video, 1988.

Tells the story of Angel Island, the "Ellis Island of the West." The Chinese Exclusion Act (1882) prevented most Chinese from entering the United States, and the few allowed in were detained and vigorously questioned. Contains scenes in the barracks and interviews with detainees.

CROSSCURRENT MEDIA

Eight Pound Livelihood

27 min., 1/2" video, 1984.

Family snapshots, archival photos, and music fill out this examination of Asian laundry workers. Many Asian immigrants found that because of government policy and widespread discrimination they could find work only in laundries.

CHINATOWN HISTORY MUSEUM

Farewell to Freedom

"Moore Report" series
55 min., 1/2" VHS, color, ca. 1981.

Portrays the efforts of Laotian Hmong people, U.S. allies during the Vietnam War, to emigrate to the United States.

UNIVERSITY FILM & VIDEO

The Golden Mountain on Mott Street
34 min., 3/4" or 1/2" video, B&W, 1968.

Made by WCBS-TV, the video discusses the problems that confront Chinese immigrants.
CAROUSEL FILMS

Home from the Eastern Sea
58 min., video, 1990.

Relates the story of Chinese, Japanese, and Filipino emigration to the United States by exploring the history of each nationality through personal stories. Each section can be shown alone.
FILMAKERS LIBRARY

Mah Jong Orphan
45 min., video, color. 1994.

Focuses on the chasm between a Chinese immigrant mother and her daughter.
FILMAKERS LIBRARY

Moving Mountains: The Story of the Yiu Mien
58 min., VHS or film, ca. 1990.

Looks at a group of Laotian refugees who settled in the Pacific Northwest.
FILMAKERS LIBRARY

My Mother Thought She Was Audrey Hepburn
17 min., video, color. 1991.

An amusing journey through and among San Francisco Chinatown's older and younger generations.
FILMAKERS LIBRARY

Postscript to a War: The Indochinese in America
45 min., 1/2" color video, 1981.

A group of refugees from war-torn Vietnam, resettled in Pennsylvania, suffer exploitation because of their ignorance of local ways and poor English. They work for poor wages and hope that their children will have a better life.
DOWNTOWN COMMUNITY TELEVISION, UNIVERSITY OF ILLINOIS

Remembrance
22 min., color video, 1991.

Shot in Philadelphia's Chinatown, the video documents the life of an elderly gentleman who had come to the United States in search of a better life and died, like so many others, poor and unmarried. Also explores changes in the nature of Asian immigration to the United States.
ANTI-DEFAMATION LEAGUE OF B'NAI B'RITH

Sewing Woman
14 min., 16mm and 1 and 1/2" and 3/4" video, 1983.

From a collection of oral histories, the film presents the life of an immigrant woman from China who worked in the U.S. garment industry for more than 30 years. As the yards of fabric pass through her machine, she describes her marriage in China at age 13, emigration to the United States as a war bride, and her life in San Francisco's Chinatown.
ANTI-DEFAMATION LEAGUE OF B'NAI B'RITH

So Far from India
49 min., VHS or film, ca. 1984.

Portrait of a family divided between two worlds.
FILMAKERS LIBRARY

Tapestry II
55 min., color, 1991.

Through archival photographs, oral histories, and folk song, this video weaves the history of 200 years of Asian American women's experiences, from the early immigration to the 1950s.
THIRD WORLD NEWS REEL

Through the Milky Way
19 min., color video, 1992.

Experimental video of a Korean woman's experience of emigrating to Hawaii at the turn of the century.
WOMEN MAKE MOVIES

6.5.3 BRITISH

Made in Britain
"Destination America" series
54 min., color video, 1975.

Interviews and historic photos portray the lives of English, Welsh, and Cornish immigrants, including many skilled workers.
MEDIA GUILD

6.5.4 GERMANS

Where Have All the Germans Gone?
"Destination America" series
52 min., video, 1975.

Examines Freistadt, Wisconsin, a typical center of German immigration, to explore issues of assimilation.
MEDIA GUILD

6.5.5 GREEKS

Pericles in America
70 min., 16mm, color, 1988; English and Greek with English subtitles.

Musical portrait of Pericles Halkias and the Epirote-Greek community of Astoria, Queens, N.Y. The film follows George, a young man working as a jeweler in New York City, who returns to Greece to be married in a traditional ceremony.
ICARUS FILMS

6.5.6 HISPANICS

Biculturalism and Acculturation among Latinos
28 min., color VHS, 1991.

Examines efforts to retain Latino culture in the process of assimilation.
FILMS FOR THE HUMANITIES
AND SOCIAL SCIENCES

Chicanos in Transition
30 min., 1/2" VHS, color, ca. 1983.

Examination of the lifestyle of Chicanos in a small Ohio city provides focus for discussing issues of assimilation and traditional cultural values. Includes a brief historical survey of Chicano presence in the United States.
UNIVERSITY FILM & VIDEO

Cubans in America *
15 min., color filmstrip, audiocassette/ discussion guide.

The film explores how the new immigrants of the 1960s influenced life in the nation's Cuban communities which date from the 1830s.
ANTI-DEFAMATION LEAGUE OF B'NAI B'RITH

Hispanic America
13 min., 16mm color video, 1980.

CBS-TV correspondent Ed Rabel surveys one of the nation's fastest-growing minorities, fourteen to sixteen million Hispanic residents, including Cubans in Florida, Puerto Ricans in New York, and Mexicans in the Southwest.
ANTI-DEFAMATION LEAGUE OF B'NAI B'RITH

Home Is Struggle
37 min., color video, 1991, Spanish with subtitles.

Creates a picture of the "Latina" identity and the immigrant experience through an exploration of the lives of women who have come to the United States from different Latin American countries.
WOMEN MAKE MOVIES

An Island in America
28 min., 16mm, color video, 1972, with discussion guide.

Explores the lives of Puerto Ricans on the mainland, within context of the history of Puerto Rico. Compares today's migration with that of years past.
ANTI-DEFAMATION LEAGUE OF B'NAI B'RITH

Living in America: A Hundred Years of Ybor City
53 min., VHS, ca. 1988; version with English subtitles available.

Describes a multicultural Florida community founded in the 1880s by Cuban, Spanish, and Italian immigrants who worked together in cigar-making factories.
FILMAKERS LIBRARY

Mexican Americans: An Historic Profile
29 min., 16mm & video, B&W, 1970.

Maclovio Barraza, Chairman of the Board of the Southwest Council of La Raza, relates the history of Mexican Americans, including present-day grassroots organizations attempting to improve economic conditions.
ANTI-DEFAMATION LEAGUE OF B'NAI B'RITH

Miguel: Up from Puerto Rico
"Many Americans" series
15 min., 16mm, color, ca. 1970.

Portrays an American boy, born in Puerto Rico, who learns the advantages of biculturalism. Filmed on location in New York City and Puerto Rico.
UNIVERSITY FILM & VIDEO

One World, Many Worlds: Hispanic

Diversity in the U.S.
22 min., color video and guide, 1993.

Topics include historical background, how and why Hispanics came to the United States, and contributions to U.S. culture.
KNOWLEDGE UNLIMITED

The Piñata Makers
17 min., video, 1988.

A Mexican family makes pinatas and talks about how they have adapted to life in the United States.
BARR MEDIA GROUP

The Status of Latina Women
26 min., color VHS.

Looks at Latina women in their countries of origin and after immigration to the United States.
FILMS FOR THE HUMANITIES AND SOCIAL SCIENCES

6.5.7 IRISH

Five Points
20 min., 1/2" video, 1987.

New York City of the 1850s appears through the conflicting perspectives of a native-born Protestant reformer and an immigrant Irish-Catholic family. Many immigrants lived in the Five Points slum of lower Manhattan.
AMERICAN SOCIAL HISTORY PROJECT FILM LIBRARY

Golden Door
"Ireland Rediscovered" series
28 min., 16mm, B&W, ca. 1963.

First in a series of thirteen programs describing the Irish contribution to world culture, this film studies the impact of Irish settlers and immigrants on the Americas.
UNIVERSITY FILM & VIDEO

The Irish
30 min., 16mm & video, color, 1974.

Edmund O'Brien narrates the story of a people's journey from poverty and prejudice to acceptance in their new land.
FILMS, INC.

Land of Heart's Desire
29 min., 16mm & videotape. 1978.

An elderly Irish American couple from New York returns to visit the land of their birth, the west coast of Ireland.
CENTRE PRODUCTIONS

On a Clear Day You Could See Boston
"Destination America" series
52 min., video, 1975.

Describes the Irish immigration to Boston and the creation of a political base.
MEDIA GUILD

Out of Ireland
110 min., video, color, 1995.

Focuses on the Irish in Ireland and America and the causes and consequences of their migration. Based on the letters and lives of seven or eight immigrants.
SHANACHIE ENTERTAINMENT (for home video)
PBS VIDEO (for schools, libraries, institutions)

6.5.8 ITALIANS

A Place in the Sun
"Destination America" series
52 min., color video, 1975.

Reminiscences of Italian immigrants who settled in San Francisco.
MEDIA GUILD

Heaven Will Protect the Working Girl
"Who Built America?" series
28 min., 1/2" VHS video, 1993.

Framed by the story of the 1909 shirtwaist strike, this film presents the world of immigrant working women in New York through the experiences of Italian and Jewish immigrant protagonists.
AMERICAN SOCIAL HISTORY PRODUCTIONS

Italian Americans
26 min., 16mm & video, color, 1975.

Directed by Martin Scorsese, the film offers insights about ethnicity and assimilation through a brief interview with Scorsese's parents.
FILMS, INC.

Italians in America*
Two color filmstrips, 1973, with discussion guide.

Frank Langella narrates the dramatic text, written by Emmy® Award-winning playwright Millard Lampell.
> *Part 1.* **The Untold Story**
> see **6.5** above.
> *Part 2.* **Children of Columbus**
> 20 min., color filmstrip.
> Immigrants fleeing poverty and oppression for a better life establish

communities in the New World amid bigotry and injustice, and become citizens who fight gallantly in two world wars.

ANTI-DEFAMATION LEAGUE OF B'NAI B'RITH

My Town — Mio Paese
26 min., 1/2" VHS, color, ca. 1986.

Describes a flourishing Italian American community in Massachusetts settled by immigrants from the southern Italian town of Palermiti.

UNIVERSITY FILM & VIDEO

The Stone Carvers
29 min., 1/2" VHS, color.

An Oscar® winning documentary. Amidst the gargoyles of Washington Cathedral, some of the last remaining stone carvers in America demonstrate their traditional skills and exchange lively stories about their customs and work experiences. The Stone Carvers captures the great pride and creative spirit
of these remarkable Italian master craftsmen.

UNIVERSITY FILM & VIDEO

6.5.9 CARIBBEAN

Curried Goat Jamaican Style
55 min., 1/2" video, color, 1985.

In a conversational style, the film describes the life of a Jamaican apple picker—one of many illegal Caribbean immigrants working U.S. farms and orchards—in New York's Hudson River valley.

C. KHOSRAVI

Rice & Peas
12 min., 16mm or video, color, 1990.

As a New York City restaurant owner prepares rice and peas, she talks about keeping her West Indian cultural heritage intact.

FIRST RUN/ICARUS

6.5.10 JEWS

The Biggest Jewish City in the World
"Destination America" series
52 min., color video, 1975.

Sam Levinson narrates the story of how New York became the largest Jewish city in the world.

MEDIA GUILD

Chicken Soup
14 min., B&W, 1971; in Yiddish and English.

Tale of a wife who prepares kosher chicken soup for her husband and herself.

CAROUSEL FILMS

The Forward: From Immigrants to Americans
58 min., 16mm, color, 1988.

Documentary about the *Jewish Daily Forward*, the major Yiddish-language newspaper, founded in 1870. Includes a visit to the paper's New York City editorial office and readings from its "Bintel Brief" (a Dear Abby-style column) and "Gallery of Missing Husbands."

DIRECT CINEMA

Free Voice of Labor — The Jewish Anarchists
60 min., 16mm, color, 1980.

Blends still photos, newsreel footage, and interviews to describe Jewish anarchism, and its relationship with the U.S. labor movement, and the development of American Yiddish culture.

CINEMA GUILD

The Golden Age of Second Avenue
56 min., 16mm, color, 1968.

Documents the American Yiddish theater with footage of early Second Avenue in New York City and scenes from some of the best-known plays and movies.

ARTHUR CANTOR, INC.

The Golden Land (1654-1932)
60 min., 1/2" video, color, 1984.

Episode 7 of the series "Heritage: Civilization and the Jews" traces Jewish migration and settlement in the United States.

FILMS, INC.

Isaac in America: A Journey with Isaac Bashevis Singer
58 min., 16mm, color, 1986.

Documents the life of a famous Yiddish author as he reminisces about his youth in Warsaw, migration to the United States in 1935, and his years at the *Jewish Daily Forward* in New York City.

DIRECT CINEMA

Jewish American

26 min., 16mm & video, B&W, 1970.

Personal narrative of the Jewish experience in the United States. Herschel Bernardi explains how the Jewish East Side of New York City abolished itself through work, union organizing, and the desire to assimilate.
FILMS INC.

Jews in America *

Two color filmstrips, 19 min. and 20 min., with discussion guide.

Music, readings, and narration on a cassette accompany the filmstrips.

Part 1: The Ingathering
Contributions of Jews to settlement of the United States; rise of anti-Semitism in wake of late nineteenth century immigration from eastern Europe.

Part 2: Inside the Golden Door
Contribution of Jewish immigration to the growth of the U.S. economy. The Holocaust and its aftermath, including creation of state of Israel. Efforts to curb anti-Semitism in the United States and worldwide.
ANTI-DEFAMATION LEAGUE OF B'NAI B'RITH

The Land Was Theirs

55 min., VHS, color; B&W, 1993.

Looks at Jewish farmers and their communities in New Jersey as they adapt to new lifestyles and conventions while maintaining their cultural heritage.
NATIONAL CENTER FOR JEWISH FILM

Rendezvous with Freedom

37 min., 16mm, color, 1974.

Traces causes of Jewish migration to the New World from 1654 until the twentieth century.
ANTI-DEFAMATION LEAGUE OF B'NAI B'RITH

Roads from the Ghetto (1789–1914)

Episode six of the series "Heritage: Civilization and the Jews" describes the European context of Jewish life and culture.
FILMS INC.

Shoah

9 hours, 30 min., color, 1985.

Monumental epic about the Holocaust that contains none of the horrific images often found in films on this subject but raises important ethical and historical questions. Available at video stores.
FILMIC ARCHIVES

We Were so Beloved

145 min., 16mm, color and B&W, 1985.

Documentary about German and Austrian Jews who fled Nazi persecution during the 1930s and built a new life in the United States, many settling in the Washington Heights section of New York City.
ICARUS FILMS

6.5.11 NATIVE AMERICANS

The Dakota Conflict

60 min., VHS, color and B&W, 1992.

Describes the Sioux uprising that began the thirty-year conflict over the Great Plains, which ended at Wounded Knee.
FILMIC ARCHIVES

The Faith Keeper

58 min., VHS, color, 1991.

The chief of the Turtle Clan of the Onondaga Indians, speaking with Bill Moyers, talks about the past and future of Native Americans.
FILMIC ARCHIVES

Indians of North America

10 cassettes, 30 min. each; also available separately.

Based on a book series of the same name, the programs feature leading scholars discussing the history and culture of ten peoples: Apache, Aztec, Cherokee, Cheyenne, Comanche, Iroquois, Maya, Navajo, Seminole, and Yankton Sioux.
FILMIC ARCHIVES

Sacred Ground: The North American Indians' Relation to the Land

60 min., VHS, color, 1990.

Examines origins, culture, and society.
FILMIC ARCHIVES

Surviving Columbus

60 min., VHS, color, 1992.

History of Pueblo civilization before the arrival of Europeans.
KNOWLEDGE UNLIMITED

Winds of Change: A Matter of Choice

60 min., VHS, color, 1990.

Documentary about the Hopi, the oldest continually inhabited community in North America.
FILMIC ARCHIVES

6.5.12 POLES

After Solidarity: Three Polish Families in America
"Destination America" series
58 min., 1/2" video, 1989; in Polish with English subtitles.

A personal chronicle of three Solidarity activists and their families, working-class men and women forced to leave Poland. Relates the migration experience as it happens, beginning with initial euphoria through the experience of joblessness and culture shock.
UNIVERSITY FILM & VIDEO

City of Big Shoulders
"Destination America" series
52 min., color video, 1975.

Interviews with stockyards and steel mill workers capture the Polish experience in Chicago, which holds more people of Polish descent than any other city in the world.
MEDIA GUILD

6.5.13 SCANDINAVIANS

Go West, Young Man
"Destination America" series
52 min., color, 1982.

Describes large Norwegian immigration to the upper Midwest.
MEDIA GUILD

Prairie Cabin — A Norwegian Pioneer Woman's Story
17 min., video color, 1992.

Personal narratives portray a woman's life after immigrating to the Midwestern prairie. Resource guide available separately.
HER OWN WORDS

6.5.14 UKRAINIANS

Teach Me to Dance
28 min., 16mm & video, 1978.

Dramatic account of the experiences of Ukrainian immigrants to Canada's Alberta province early in the twentieth century.
FILMS INC.

6.6 DISTRIBUTORS

AMERICAN SOCIAL HISTORY PRODUCTIONS
Purchasing Department
99 Hudson Street, Third Floor
New York, NY 10013
(212) 966-4248 ext. 201
fax: (212) 966-4589

ANTI-DEFAMATION LEAGUE
OF B'NAI B'RITH
823 United Nations Plaza
New York, NY 10017
(212) 490-2525
1-800-343-5540
fax: (212) 867-0779

The titles listed above appear in the catalogue "Human Relations Materials for the School" and may be rented or purchased from the New York City office or from all regional offices.

ART INSTITUTE OF CHICAGO
111 S. Michigan Ave
Chicago, IL 60603
(312) 443-3793

ARTHUR CANTOR, INC.
510 Broadway, Suite 403
New York, NY 10036
(212) 496-5710
(800) 237-3801
fax: (212) 496-5718

BARR MEDIA GROUP
12801 Schabarum Avenue
Irwindale, CA 91706-7878
(800) 234-7878
(818) 814-2672

CALIFORNIA NEWSREEL RESOLUTION INC.
149 9th St., Suite 420
San Francisco, CA 94103
(415) 621-6196
fax: (415) 621-6522

CAROUSEL FILMS, INC.
260 Fifth Ave., Rm. 405
New York, NY 10001
(212) 683-1660
(800) 683-1660
fax: (212) 683-1662

CENTRE PRODUCTIONS
1800 30th St., Suite 207
Boulder, CO 80301
(800) 886-116
(303) 444-1166

CHINATOWN HISTORY MUSEUM
70 Mulberry St.
New York, NY 10013
(212) 619-4785

CINEMA GUILD
Div. of Document Assoc.
1697 Broadway, Suite 207
New York, NY 10019
(212) 246-5522
(800) 723-5522
fax: (212) 246-5525

CORONET INSTRUCTIONAL FILMS
Dist. by Simon & Schuster Film
4350 Equity Drive
Columbus, OH 43228
(800) 321-3106

CROSSCURRENT MEDIA
346 Ninth Street, 2nd Floor
San Francisco, CA, 94103
(415) 552-9550
fax: (415) 863-7428

DALLAS COMMUNITY COLLEGE DISTRICT
9596 Walnut Street
Dallas, TX 75243
(214) 952-0330
fax: (214) 952-0329

DIRECT CINEMA, LTD.
P.O. Box 10003
Santa Monica, CA 90410
(310) 396-4774
(800) 525-0000
fax: (310) 396-3233

DOWNTOWN COMMUNITY
TELEVISION CENTER
Att: Quang Nguyen
87 Lafayette St.
New York, NY 10013
(212) 966-4510
(800) VIDEO NY
fax: (212) 219-0248

FILMAKERS LIBRARY, INC.
124 E. 40th St.
New York, NY 10016
(212) 808-4980
(800) 555-9815
fax: (212) 808-4983

FILMIC ARCHIVES
The Cinema Center
Botsford, CT 06404
(800) 366-1920
fax: (203) 268-1796
Purchase only.

FILMS, INC.
(Northeast U.S.)
35 South West St.
Mount Vernon, NY 10550
(800) 323-4222, x-323

FILMS, INC.
(Central, South, and West U.S.)
5547 N. Ravenswood Ave.
Chicago, IL 60640-1199
(800) 323-4222, x-42
(312) 878-2600, x-42
fax: (312) 878-0416

FILMS FOR THE HUMANITIES AND SCIENCES
P.O. Box 2053
Princeton, NJ 08543-2053
(609) 275-1400
(800) 257-5126
fax (609) 275-3767

GUIDANCE ASSOCIATES
100 S. Bedford
Communications Park
Box 1000
Mt. Kisco, NY 10549-9989
(914) 666-4100
1-800-431-1242
fax: (914) 666-5319

HANDEL FILM CORP.
8787 Shoreham Drive, Suite 609
West Hollywood, CA 90069
(310) 657-8990
(800) 395-8990
fax: (310) 657-2746

HER OWN WORDS
P.O. Box 5264
Madison, WI 53705
(608) 271-7083

THE HISTORY CHANNEL
235 E. 45th St.
New York, NY 10017

ICARUS FILMS INC./ FIRST RUN
153 Waverly Place
New York, NY 10012
(212) 727-1711
(800) 876-1710
fax: (212) 989-7649

INSTRUCTIONAL VIDEO
P.O. Box 21
Maumee, OH 43537
(419) 865-7670
fax: (419) 867-3813

C. KHOSRAVI
P.O. Box 735
Woodstock, NY 12498

KNOWLEDGE UNLIMITED
P.O. Box 52
Madison, WI 53701-0052
608/836-6660
(800) 356-2303
fax: (608) 831-1570

LOWER EAST SIDE TENEMENT MUSEUM
66 Allen Street
New York, NY 10002
(212) 431-0233
fax: (212) 431-0402

MEDIA GUILD
11722 Sorrento Valley Rd., Suite E
San Diego, CA 92121-1021
(619) 755-9191
(800) 886-9191
fax: (619) 755-4931

MODERN CURRICULUM PRESS
PO Box 70935
Chicago, IL 60673-0933
(800) 621-2131 or 940-3600

MUSEUM OF MODERN ART FILM LIBRARY
11 W. 53d St.
New York, NY 10019
(212) 708-9530
fax: (212) 708-9531

NATIONAL CENTER FOR JEWISH FILM
Brandeis University
Waltham, MA 02254-9110
(617) 899-7044
fax: (617) 736-2070

NATIONAL GEOGRAPHIC SOCIETY
Educational Services
P.O. Box 98019
Washington, DC 20090
(301) 921-1330
(800) 368-2728
fax: 301-921-1575

NATIONAL TECHNICAL
INFORMATION SERVICE
(formerly National Video Archives)
5285 Port Royal Road
Springfield, VA 22161
(703) 487-4726
fax: (703) 321-8547

NEW DIMENSION MEDIA
85803 Lorane Highway
Eugene, OR 97405
(503) 484-7125
(800) 288-4456
fax: (503) 484-5267

PANORAMA PRODUCTIONS
P. O. Box 11218
Burbank, CA

PBS VIDEO
1320 Braddock Place
Alexandria, VA 22314-1698
(800) 344-3337

RAINBOW EDUCATIONAL VIDEO
170 Keyland Court
Bohemia, NY 11716
(516) 589-6643
(800) 331-4047

SHANACHIE ENTERTAINMENT
37 East Clinton
Newton, NJ 07860
(800) 497-1043
fax: (201) 579-7083

STERLING EDUCATIONAL FILMS
141 W. 54th St.
New York, NY 10019
(212) 262-9433

TAPESTRY PRODUCTIONS
920 Broadway, 16th Floor
New York, NY 10010
(212) 677-6007
fax: (212) 473-8164

THIRD WORLD NEWS REEL
335 W. 38th St., 5th Floor
New York, NY 10018
(212) 947-9277
fax: (212) 594-6417

UNIVERSITY FILM & VIDEO
University of Minnesota
Continuing Education and Extension
1313 Fifth St., S.E., Suite 108
Minneapolis, MN 55414
(612) 627-0013 local
(800) 542-0013 Minnesota toll free
(800) 847-8251 out of state toll free
fax (612) 627-4280
(Comprehensive catalogue available
upon request.)

UNIVERSITY OF CALIFORNIA EXTENSION
Center for Media and Independent Learning
200 Center Street, 4th Floor
Berkeley, CA 94704
(510) 642-0460
fax: (510) 643-9271

U.S. NATIONAL AUDIOVISUAL CENTER
(USNAC)
8700 Edgeworth Dr.
Capitol Heights, MD 20743-3701
(301) 763-1896

WEST GLENN COMMUNICATIONS
1430 Broadway
New York, NY 10018-3396
(212) 921-2800

WOMEN MAKE MOVIES
462 Broadway, Suite 50
New York, NY 10013
(212) 925-0606
(212) 925-2052

YOUTH FILMS, INC./GOSPEL FILMS
P.O. Box 455
Muskegon, MI 49443
(616) 773-3361
fax: (616) 777-7598

About the Statue of Liberty-Ellis Island Foundation, Inc.

The Statue of Liberty-Ellis Island Foundation, Inc., a non-profit organization, was founded in 1982 to raise funds for the restoration and preservation of the Statue of Liberty and Ellis Island. Under the leadership of Lee Iacocca and working in conjunction with the National Park Service, the sole administrator of the sites, the Foundation has restored the Statue and the Main Building at Ellis Island and created the Ellis Island Immigration Museum which opened in September 1990, restored additional buildings on Ellis Island's north side, and established a $20 million endowment to sustain both monuments throughout the years. The largest restoration and preservation project in American history, it was funded entirely by the American people. Over twenty million private citizens contributed to the effort.

The Foundation's current efforts include The American Immigrant Wall of Honor® and the creation of The American Family Immigration History Center ™, both at Ellis Island.

The interpretive plan for the Ellis Island Museum documented the historic function of the island as an immigrant-processing center, but a major exhibit on the Museum's first floor "The Peopling of America" exhibit, contextualizes that story by documenting immigration to the United States from all the world's continents including Africa, Asia and South America over the course of American history. The American Immigrant Wall of Honor, the largest wall of names in the world, dramatically outlines the island shore and testifies to the emotional significance which Americans ascribe to the intersection between their family histories and national history. Almost every nationality is represented here. Those who endured forced migration from Africa are included as are Native Americans and the earliest European colonists. George Washington's great grandfather, John F. Kennedy's grandparents, the families of Cicely Tyson and Barbra Streisand stand along side the ancestors of thousands of other American family ancestors. These interpretive and fund-raising activities represent an effort to make Ellis Island a truly inclusive national symbol.

About the Ellis Island Immigration Museum

The following information is taken from official publications of the National Park services. All phone numbers, hours, and fees are subject to change.

Site

Ellis Island, located in New York Harbor near the Statue of Liberty, was designated as part of the Statue of Liberty National Monument on May 11, 1965. The National Park Service manages it along with all other national parks. Through the years, Ellis Island was enlarged from its original 3.3 acres to 27.5 acres mostly by landfill obtained from ship ballast and possibly excess earth from the construction of the New York City subway system.

Before being designated as the site of one of the first Federal immigration stations by President Benjamin Harrison in 1890, Ellis Island had a varied history. The local Indian tribes had called it "Kioshk" or Gull Island. It served various functions for European settlers: a hanging site for pirates, a harbor fort, ammunition and ordinance depot named Fort Gibson, and finally an immigration station. Between 1892 and 1954, approximately 12 million steerage and third-class steamship passengers who entered the United States through the port of New York were legally and medically inspected at Ellis Island. Reopened on September 10, 1990, after a massive restoration, the Main Building on Ellis Island is now a museum dedicated to the history of immigration and the important role this island played in the history of immigration.

Telephone/Fax/Websites

(212) 363-3200 (recorded message),
(212) 363-7620 (school group reservations),
(212) 363-6307 (library)
Website: for Ellis Island Home Page, www.Ellisisland.org; for all National Park Service sites including Ellis Island and the Statue of Liberty National Monument www.NPS.gov

Operating Hours

Both the Statue and Ellis Island are open daily except on December 25. Operating hours for the Ellis Island Museum are 9:30 AM-5 PM daily; the Statue opens at 9:45 AM and closes at 5pm. From July 4 to Labor Day, Ellis Island closes at 6 PM.

Visitation

Highest in July and August; lowest in January and February. Average annual visitation to both Liberty and Ellis Islands is approximately 4.2 million people. Plan to spend a minimum of half a day visiting both monuments. Because the sites are so popular, especially during the summer months, it is best to arrive early. It can take 45 minutes to purchase ferry tickets and board the ferry. If you are interested in spending a full day at Ellis and Liberty Islands, plan to take one of the first ferries of the day. It is advisable to arrive at Liberty Island early, especially if you plan a climb to the Statue's crown. By 11:30 on a typical summer day, waiting times for the climb can exceed three hours.

Directions and Transportation

Liberty and Ellis Islands are accessible by Statue of Liberty/Ellis Island Ferry, Inc. Ferries only. One round-trip ferry ticket includes visits to both islands. Ferries depart from Battery Park in New York and Liberty State Park in New Jersey. Private vessels are not permitted to dock at the islands.

Ferry Service from New York. Purchase round-trip ferry tickets at Castle Clinton National Monument in Lower Manhattan. Ferries from New York operate on a loop, stopping first at Liberty Island and then at Ellis Island before returning to Battery Park, New York.

To get to Battery Park in Lower Manhattan by *subway*, take the 1 or 9 train to the South Ferry station, 4 or 5 train to the Bowling Green station, or the N or R train to the Whitehall Street station.

To get to Battery Park and Lower Manhattan by bus, take the M15 (East Side) marked "South Ferry," or the M6 (West Side) from 57th Street.

To get to Battery Park and Lower Manhattan by auto, take the East Side Drive (FDR Drive) south to Battery Park and State St. Or the West Side Highway/West Street/ Route 9A south to Battery Place. Designated parking is not available. Privately operated parking lots located along West Street and South Street (beneath the FDR Drive) have limited capacity, so it is best to arrive early or to rely on public transportation.

Ferry Service to New Jersey. Purchase round-trip ferry tickets at the Railroad Terminal Building and Museum in Liberty State Park in New Jersey. Ferries from Liberty State Park operate on a loop, stopping first at Ellis Island and then at Liberty Island before returning to Liberty State Park, New Jersey.

To get to Liberty State Park and Jersey City by bus, take the Central Avenue bus from platform A3 at the Journal Square Terminal in Jersey City to Liberty State Park.

To get to Liberty State Park and Jersey City by auto, take the New Jersey Turnpike (Interstate 95) to exit 14B. There is ample parking available in Liberty State Park for a fee.

Fees

Admission to the Statue of Liberty and Ellis Island is free and all programs run by the National Park Service are free. Donations are appreciated and used for maintaining the resources on both islands. Round-trip ferry tickets cost $7.00 for adults, $3.00 for children and $5.00 for senior citizens. Call the ferry operator directly at (212) 269-5755 or (201) 435-9499 for additional information.

Programs and Activities

The Ellis Island Immigration Museum offers a variety of exhibits and programs about the history of Ellis Island and the immigration process. The three floors of the Ellis Island Immigration Museum were designed as a self-guided museum. The Ellis Island brochure available at the museum guides visitors through the museum at their own pace. For a plan of the museum, see page 76 and 77 of this guide. Audio tours and ranger tours are described below. School group tours and activities are described in the Resources section of this guide.

Permanent Exhibits

The permanent exhibits occupy over 40,000 square feet on three floors of the Main Building; they include museum objects, photographs, prints, videos, interactive displays and oral histories. The largest exhibit is the building itself; the imposing French Renaissance Revival structure designed by Boring and Tilton, built in 1900 and restored to its 1918-1924 appearance.

The Baggage Room
(first floor, restored to 1918-1924):
Thousands of immigrants crowded into this room on a daily basis where they could check their baggage before climbing the steps to the Registry Room.

The Peopling of America
(first floor, restored to 1918-24):
Originally the Railroad Ticket Office, where immigrants could make travel arrangements to their final destinations in the United States. It now contains exhibits covering 400 years of immigration history. The exhibits situate the Ellis Island era in a broad historical context and allow visitors, whatever their ancestors' place of origin, to identify the immigration flows in which their own families participated.

Registry Room
(second floor, restored to 1918-1924):
The historic Great Hall, once filled with new arrivals waiting to be inspected and registered by Immigration officers, now contains historic benches and reproduction inspection desks.

Through America's Gate
(second floor, restored to 1911):
Exhibits illustrate the processing of immigrants at Ellis Island, including the Special Inquiry Room, refurbished to 1911.

Peak Immigration Years (second floor):
The history of immigration to the United States between 1880-1924.

Dormitory Room
(third floor, restored and refurbished to 1908), contains examples of the crowded bunks on which detained immigrants slept; provides a notion of what the detained individual's experience was like.

Ellis Island Chronicles (third floor):
Overview of the island's growth and development from prehistory to the closing of all island facilities in 1954.

Treasures from Home (third floor): Cherished objects, photographs, and papers brought from the homeland are on display. Portrays immigration in intimate, personal terms.

Silent Voices
The immigrant station closed and abandoned after 1954. Restoring a Landmark. Transforming the ruins into a national museum of immigration, 1985-1990.

American Immigrant Wall of Honor
A popular exhibit at the Museum located outdoors, just outside the *Peopling of America Exhibit*. The Wall honors America's immigrants regardless of when they immigrated or through which port they entered. The Wall is currently inscribed with over 500,000 names. Those who would like to add a name to the Wall of Honor, and are interested in making a donation to the Statue of Liberty-Ellis Island Foundation, please contact the Foundation at (212) 883-1986.

Temporary Exhibits
From time to time, the museum offers temporary exhibits with themes relating to immigration.

Ranger-Guided Tours
The National Park Service provides ranger-guided walking tours of the museum. The tours last approximately 45 minutes and are accessible for handicapped visitors. Tours include museum highlights and are offered on a first come-first served basis, staff levels permitting. Check at the information desk for details.

Audio Tours
An audio tour of the museum may be rented through the Ellis Island concessionaire for a fee of $3.50 for adults, $3.00 for seniors, $2.50 for children. Group rates are available. Narrated by news anchor Tom Brokaw, the audio tour guides visitors through the museum exhibits and takes approximately one hour and 15 minutes to complete. Audio tours are available in English, French, German, Spanish, and Italian. For more information, call Aramark at (212) 344-0996

Documentary Film
The 30-minute award-winning documentary film *Island of Hope, Island of Tears* is shown in two theaters at regularly scheduled hours. Theater 1 offers the film alone. Theater 2 offers the film accompanied by a 15-minute park ranger introductory talk. Each theater seats 140 people. Tickets are required and available for free at the Ellis Island information desk. Visitors who wish to see the film must plan to include it in a schedule for the day. A shorter continuously running video is planned to accommodate those who are not able to fit the scheduled film into their agendas.

School Group Programs
Programs for school groups are conducted by reservation only. Please call the reservations coordinator for more information at (212) 363-7620, and consult the **Resources** section of this guide for more detailed information on educational programs.

Living History Programs
Throughout the spring, summer, and fall, a 30-minute play entitled "Ellis Island Stories" is offered. The play is derived from the oral histories of actual immigrants that are contained in the museum's oral history collection. Professional actors portray immigrants going through an inspection process at Ellis Island and the experience of immigrating to a strange new place. The play is shown at regularly scheduled times. Free tickets are available at the information desk.

Board of Special Inquiry Program
This living-history program presents the accounts of actual immigrant hearings conducted during the time of peak immigration at Ellis Island. This program is conducted in the "Hearing Room", which has been carefully restored to the period 1908-1911. Audience participation decides the fate of the immigrant standing before them. Visitors learn the importance of immigration policy at the turn of the century and current-day immigration law. This program if offered at a regularly schedule time. For details, check at the information desk.

Genealogy Workshop
The National Park Service, with the collaboration of The National Archives, presents a workshop for visitors who wish to research their family immigration history. This workshop is offered on a monthly basis and provides instruction about how to gather, interpret, and use historical data to trace family histories. The workshop is free to all visitors of the museum. Call (212) 363-7620 for additional information.

Volunteers in Parks (VIP) Program
The National Park Service is officially entrusted with preserving more than 360

National Parks in the United States. Thousands of citizens help ensure that the best of America will be protected by assisting the National Park Service when they volunteer their time and talents. Volunteers at the Ellis Island Immigration Museum assist park staff and visitors by providing many types of services, both in public view (helping visitors at the information desk, leading guided tours) and behind the scenes (assisting in cataloging museum objects and assembling temporary exhibits). If you are interested in volunteering at the Statue of Liberty and Ellis Island please contact the "Volunteers in the Parks" coordinator at (212) 363-6307.

Library, Archives and Oral History Collection

The museum includes a research library that contains materials related to the Statue of Liberty, Ellis Island, and immigration history. The Library collection, like the museum collections, operate under a basic curatorial planning document required by NPS Management Policies for all parks. It serves to guide the Park in the acquisition and preservation of museum objects that contribute directly to the museum collection as a whole, the understanding and interpretation of the Park's themes and additional objects that the NPS is legally mandated to preserve.

The Ellis Island Oral History Project
at the Museum is the oldest and largest oral history project dedicated to preserving the first-hand recollections of immigrants coming to America during the years Ellis Island was in operation, 1892-1954. Begun in 1973, the collection includes over 1,500 taped and transcribed interviews of actual Ellis Island immigrants and staff, all of which are accessible to the public for research. Interviews contain information concerning everyday life in the country of origin, family history, reasons for immigrating, the journey to the port, experiences on the ship, arrival and processing at the Ellis Island facility, and an in-depth look at the adjustment to living in the United States. People from dozens of countries, former Ellis Island and Statue of Liberty employees, people stationed in the military on both islands are included. Most interviewees are in their late eighties, the oldest to date being 106 and the youngest being 46. Interviews are conducted either in the Project's recording studio on Ellis Island or in the individual's home with portable equipment. If you believe you are a good candidate for an interview, or know someone else who would be, write to: Oral History Project, Ellis Island Immigration Museum, New York, New York 10004 or call (212) 363-5807 or fax (212) 363-6302. Interviews are now added to a computer database that can be accessed in the Library at the Ellis Island Immigration Museum.

Library

The library of the Statue of Liberty National Monument and Ellis Island, on the third floor of the Immigration Museum, is a research library with special emphasis on the Statue, Ellis Island, immigration and ethnic research. No immigration or genealogical records are located here, but the staff can provide information concerning other institutions that contain this kind of information.

Special Collections

Historic photographs of the Statue of Liberty and Ellis Island, including unique photograph collections by August F. Sherman and Colonel John B. Weber; the Foxlee Papers, the Maud Mosher Papers, and a sixteen-volume collection of periodicals and newspaper articles by Gino Speranza on immigration and related subjects between 1900 and 1927.

Library Services

Photographs and photocopies, duplication, and general reference services. The reference services includes assisting researchers and answering correspondence regarding the Statue of Liberty and Ellis Island, including historical inquiries about immigration. The researchers who use the library are teachers, students, writers, publishers, journalists, and filmmakers. All researchers are required to sign a research agreement.

Library materials include books, manuscripts, films, photographs, and general reference files which may be used by researchers on site only. The library is open to the public on a walk-in basis; researchers are advised to call ahead for appointments. All services which are described here are available through the library staff. Call (212) 363-6307 or fax (212) 363-6302 for further information. Both the Library and Oral History Collection are open to the public during regular operating hours of the museum.

Accessibility Information

Seeing-eye and other assist animals are welcome. Emergency medical services are available on both Liberty and Ellis Islands. There a limited number of wheelchairs available at both islands on a first come-first served basis. Contact any National Park Service employee for assistance. There are level walkways to the ferry boarding areas. There are handicapped accessible rest rooms at Liberty State Park and at Castle Clinton National Mounument; ferry ticket counters in New York are handicapped accessible. In New York ferry personnel provide assistance on the ferry gangways. Aboard the ferries, enclosed areas are available. Rest rooms aboard ferries are not handicapped accessible.

All outdoor areas on both islands are level and paved.

Ellis Island is completely wheelchair accessible with elevator access to all museum areas. Closed captioning for the film *Island of Hope, Island of Tears* is available upon request. The museum contains tactile models of the island layout and a floor plan with Braille legend. Theaters and ranger-guided tours can accommodate all visitors. An audio tour is available for a fee, but was not specifically designed for the visually impaired. All exhibit areas and the library are wheelchair accessible.

The highest level of the Statue of Liberty accessible by elevator is the observation level at the top of the pedestal. The museum exhibits within the Statue's pedestal are completely accessible by elevator and there are tactile exhibits for the visually impaired. All buildings are handicapped accessible. The observation level at the top of the pedestal can be reached by using the main elevator along with a 24-step climb. Inside the Statue's lobby, there is a five-minute video describing the ascent to the Statue's crown for those visitors unable to climb the 354 steps. Tactile models of the

island, armature bars and full-scale replicas of the Statue's foot and face are located in the museum exhibits. All videos are closed-captioned. Rest rooms inside the Statue are handicapped accessible. For safety precautions, all visitors must pass through a metal detector and an x-ray machine.

Food Service areas on Liberty and Ellis Islands can accommodate all visitors. Seating is available in both areas. The condiment counter at Ellis Island is not accessible, but assistance is available.

Basic Health and Safety Recommendations for a Trip to Ellis Island and the Statue of Liberty

Arrive early, drink plenty of fluids, remember to bring any medication and dress warmly in the wintertime. Visitors with any health problems should not attempt to climb up the Statue of Liberty's crown, which is a 22-story climb. The interior of the Statue's crown can exceed the outside temperature by as much as 20 degrees. Both islands have emergency medical staff available who respond to unexpected injuries and illnesses. Transportation to the mainland for hospitalization in the event of a medical emergency can be provided.

Dining, Gift Shops, and Conferences

There are restaurants at Ellis Island and the Statue with indoor and outdoor seating and fabulous views of the New York and New Jersey skylines. The Ellis Island Cafe is operated by the Aramark Corporation. The Cafe is open daily and offers an appetizing array of both international and American foods and beverages. For groups, Aramark can pre-arrange lunches and/or video vouchers to facilitate your visit. The Ellis

Island Gift Shop provides a wide range of souvenirs and international gifts, including books, videotapes and posters. Genealogy publications are offered, and all gift shop items are available through mail order. Call (212) 344-0996 for more details. The Statue of Liberty Cafeteria is operated by the Evelyn Hill Corporation. The Cafeteria is open daily and the menu offers a variety of foods and beverages. The Gift Shop is located nearby. Gifts, books, videotapes, and souvenirs relate to the Statue and her history. There is also a small book shop located inside the Statue's pedestal on the third level. Call (212) 363 3180 for details.

Permits

Information and permits for public assembly, commercial photography/filming, and the distribution of printed matter can be obtained by calling (212) 363-3260.

Conferences and Evening Events

In association with the National Park Service, Aramark offers groups the exclusive use of the Ellis Island Immigration Museum for private evening events. The magnificent Great Hall is magically transformed into a historic, unique, and spectacular venue for sit-down dinners of 750 or more people. The Baggage Room and Great Lawn can each accommodate 1,000 or more people for cocktails. Special features include breathtaking views of Manhattan and the private use of the entire museum and its facilities during your event. Conference room facilities are also available for day meetings and functions for up to 125 people. For more information, write to Aramark, Ellis Island, New York, N.Y. 10004 or call (212) 344-0996, fax (212) 344-0219.

About the Authors

Virginia Yans-McLaughlin, Professor of History at Rutgers, the State University of New Jersey, served for seven years as an advisor to the National Park Service and the Statue of Liberty-Ellis Island Foudation on the historical reconstruction of both mounuments and on their museum exhibits. She is the author of *Family and Community: Italian Immigrants in Buffalo, 1880-1930* and editor of *Immigration Reconsidered: History, Sociology, Politics.*

Marjorie Lightman is acting executive director of the International League for Human Rights and former director of the Institute for Research in History in New York City

Hall Smyth is the director of the design studio BAD and the founder of The Research Center for Validity Testing. RCVT/BAD recently collaborated in the exhibition, *Making History: Fifteen Minutes of Fame Fortune and Fax Machines*, at the Storefront for Art and Architecture.

Books of Related Interest
from The New Press

Malaika Adero

Up South: Stories, Studies, and Letters of This Century's African American Migrations

PB, $12.95, 1-56584-168-9, 238 PP.

Primary sources from the greatest migration in American history.

American Social History Project

Freedom's Unfinished Revolution: An Inquiry into the Civil War and Reconstruction

PB, $17.95, 1-56584-198-0, 320 PP.

From the award-winning authors of Who Built America?, *a groundbreaking high school level presentation of the Civil War and Reconstruction.*

William Ayers and Patricia Ford, editors

City Kids, City Teachers: Reports from the Front Row

HC, $25.00, 1-56584-328-3;
PB, $16.00, 1-56584-051-8; 368 PP.

Classic writings on urban education from America's leading experts.

Ira Berlin and Leslie S. Rowland, editors

Families and Freedom: A Documentary History of African-American Kinship in the Civil War Era

HC, $25.00, 1-56584-026-9, 304 PP.

A sequel to the award-winning Free at Last, *moving letters from freed slaves to their families.*

Ira Berlin and Barbara J. Fields, et al.

Free at Last: A Documentary History of Slavery, Freedom, and the Civil War

HC, $27.50, 1-56584-015-1;
PB, $15.95, 1-56584-120-4, 608 PP.

A winner of the 1994 Lincoln Prize , some of the most remarkable and moving letters ever written by Americans, depicting the drama of Emancipation in the midst of the nation's bloodiest conflict.

Ira Berlin

Slaves without Masters: The Free Negro in the Antebellum South

PB, $14.95, 1-56584-028-3, 448 PP.

A vivid and moving history of the quarter of a million free blacks who lived in the South before the Civil War.

The Brooklyn Museum

The Native American Look Book: Art and Activities for Kids from The Brooklyn Museum

HC, $15.95, 1-56584-022-4, 48 PP.

A children's book of stories, art, and activities based on objects from three Native American cultures.

Lisa D. Delpit

Other People's Children: Cultural Conflict in the Classroom

HC, $21.00, 1-56584-179-4;
PB, $11.95, 1-56584-180-8; 224 PP.

A MacArthur Fellow's revolutionary analysis of the role of race in the classroom. Winner of Choice *magazine's Outstanding Academic Book Award, the American Education Studies Association Critic's Choice Award, and one of* Teacher *magazine's Great Books of 1995.*

Michele Foster
Black Teachers on Teaching
HC, $23.00, 1-56584-320-7, 240 PP.
The first wave of black teachers in desegregated schools speak out on the politics of educating black children.

Mary Frosch
Coming of Age in America:
A Multicultural Anthology
HC, $22.95, 1-56584-146-8;
PB, $11.95, 1-56584-147-6; 288 PP.
The acne and ecstasy of adolescence— a muliticultural collection of short stories and fiction excerpts that Library Journal *calls "wonderfully diverse from the standard fare."*

Elaine H. Kim and Yu Eui Young, editors
East to America:
Korean American Life Stories
HC, $25.00, 1-56584-297-0;
PB, $14.95, 1-56584-399-1; 408 PP.
The highly praised first oral history of the Korean American community—a Kiriwama Book Prize finalist.

Herbert Kohl
"I Won't Learn from You"
and Other Thoughts on Creative
Maladjustment
PB, $10.00, 1-56584-096-8, 176 PP.
"One of the most important books on teaching published in many years."—Jonathan Kozol

Herbert Kohl
Should We Burn Babar?: Essays on
Children's Literature and the Power
of Stories
HC, $18.95, 1-56584-258-8;
PB, $11.00, 1-56584-259-6; 192 PP.
The prize-winning educator's thoughts on the politics of children's literature.

Joann Faung Jean Lee
Asian Americans: Oral Histories
of First Generation Americans from
China, the Philippines, Japan,
India, the Pacific Islands, Vietnam
and Cambodia
PB, $11.95, 1-56584-023-2, 256 PP.
A fascinating firsthand account of the diverse Asian American community.

David Levine, Robert Lowe,
Robert Peterson, and Rita Tenorio, editors
Rethinking Schools:
An Agenda for Change
PB, $16.00, 1-56584-215-4, 304 PP.
The country's leading education reformers propose ways to change our schools.

James W. Loewen
Lies My Teacher Told Me:
Everything Your American History
Textbook Got Wrong
HC, $24.95, 1-56584-100-X, 384 PP.
The best-selling, award-winning, iconoclastic look at the errors, misrepresentations, and omissions in the leading American history textbooks.

James W. Loewen
The Truth about Columbus:
A Subversively True Poster Book
for a Dubiously Celebratory Occasion
PB WITH POSTER, $12.95, 1-56584-008-9, 48 PP.
A provocative educational poster and booklet that draws on recent scholarship to debunk the myths and discover the man.

Daphne Muse, editor
The New Press Guide to Multicultural
Resources for Young Readers
HC, $60.00, 1-56584-339-8, 700 PP.
A comprehensive guide to multicultural children's literature, featuring over 1,000 critical book reviews, essays, indexes cross-referenced by theme and ethnicity, and extensive resource listings.

Laurie Olsen
Made in America: Immigrant
Students in Our Public Schools
HC, $25.00, 1-56584-400-9, 244 PP.
An up-to-the minute look at immigrant students in American public schools, through a portrait of one prototypical high school.

Georges Perec and Robert Bober
Ellis Island
PB, $16.95, 1-56584-318-5, 160 PP.
An exploration of Ellis Island from acclaimed French novelist Georges Perec and filmmaker Robert Bober.

Judith Rényi

Going Public: Schooling for a Diverse Democracy

HC, $25.00, 1-56584-083-6, 304 PP.

An historically informed overview of the multicultural education debate from a leading advocate.

Stephen J. Rose

Social Stratification in the United States: The American Profile Poster Revised and Expanded

PB, $14.95, 1-56584-021-6, 48 PP.

A graphic presentation of the distibution of wealth in America.

Lore Segal

Her First American

PB, $11.95, 1-56584-145-X, 304 PP.

A classic novel of the immigrant experience. "Segal may have come closer than anyone to writing the Great American Novel."
—New York Times Book Review

Anne E. Wheelock

Crossing the Tracks: How "Untracking" Can Save America's Schools

HC, $22.95, 1-56584-013-5;
PB, $12.95, 1-56584-038-0; 336 PP.

A highly praised study of ways in which schools have successfully experimented with heterogeneous grouping in the classroom.

Howard Zinn

A People's History of the United States: Teaching Edition

HC, $25.00, 1-56584-366-5;
PB, $13.00, 1-56584-379-7; 496 PP.

An abridged edition of Howard Zinn's best-selling—over 425,000 copies—history of the United States.

Howard Zinn and George Kirschner

A People's History of the United States: The Wall Charts

PORTFOLIO, $25.00, 1-56584-171-9,
48-PAGE BOOKLET WITH TWO POSTERS

Two oversized posters based on Zinn's best-selling social history.